SOFT fURNISHINGS
for your home

SOFT fURNISHINGS
for your home

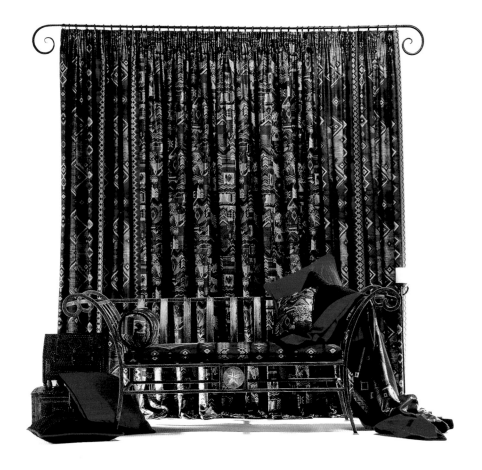

Written and compiled by
Sharyn Skrabanich

Dealerfield

EDITORIAL
Managing Editor: Judy Poulos
Editorial Assistant: Ella Martin
Editorial Coordinator: Margaret Kelly

PHOTOGRAPHY
Andrew Payne
Additional photography by Andrew Elton

ILLUSTRATIONS
Carol Dunn

DESIGN AND PRODUCTION
Manager: Sheridan Carter
Cover design and book design concept:
Michelle Withers
Cover Art Direction: Christine Davis
Layout: Margie Mulray, Lulu Dougherty

Formatted by J.B. Fairfax Press Pty Limited
Printed by Toppan Printing Co, Singapore

JBFP 228 UK/D

SOFT FURNISHINGS FOR YOUR HOME
Includes Index
ISBN 1 85927 034 4

DEDICATION
*This book is dedicated to my husband, Phillip;
my parents, Robert and Shelagh Dounan; and
Ivy Skrabanich. Without their love and support,
this book would not have been possible. I would
also like to thank Graeme Dann, Tim Starkey,
Joanne Potts, Frank Kerklaan and my colleagues
at Maurice Kain Textiles.*

Introduction

Fabric designers must create a master artwork that combines the elements of colour, scale, pattern and proportion, uniting them with harmony and balance to create a finished design that is interesting and pleasing to the eye. In approaching this task, fabric designers take into account the proposed function of the fabric.

The designer will experiment with different forms of colour, pattern, scale and proportion in order to compose their final artwork. This design process is quite lengthy and complex, passing through planned steps – and unplanned hiccups. When all the elements are working in unison, the artwork is finally completed.

The home decorator must also make decisions about mood or style and faces a similar challenge. Like the designer, the home decorator must consider all the design elements and how they will affect the final result. The elements then take shape in the form of fabric choices and colour schemes, which in turn are converted into individual projects, such as those in this book.

As you see your planning taking shape, then comes the feeling of satisfaction in being able to say 'I did it myself'. **Soft Furnishings for Your Home** not only shows you how to achieve seven enticing and wonderful room settings, it also encourages you to combine elements from the various chapters to create a unique look for your home.

The first section of the book 'Creating Your Style', covers the planning process involved in combining all the design elements to create a master plan. Before you cut your first metre of fabric or sew your first stitch, you are made fully aware of the many things to consider when you design and make your own soft furnishings: the effects of colour and texture, the choice of an appropriate fabric, the selection of trims and accessories to adorn and define your projects and the essential equipment are all highlighted and illustrated in this section. Individual chapters, based on soft furnishing groupings – such as curtains, cushions or table linen – will give you more specific instructions for making those particular items. Each project has step-by-step instructions and the details in 'Creating Your Style' can be used for a quick and easy reference to help you achieve a professional result.

Soft Furnishings for Your Home presents many different design styles, each project so inviting and so easy that you will want to attempt them all. There are no hidden secrets or tricks used in this book. As long as you are able to sew a straight line and have the basic equipment to achieve a professional finish, you will be able to conjure up new and unique creations in a matter of hours!

Contents

Creating Your Style

Making major changes to home decor can perplex the most enthusiastic home decorator. Make a couple of wrong choices and you could end up with something that is not how you intended it to be. What's more, the time and effort involved in making major changes can be very disruptive to the entire family.

Style

Planning to change your entire decor can be an expensive exercise. Sentiment also plays a major part in deciding what to change and what to keep. Imagine having to part with your favourite comfortable chair because the colour won't work with your new scheme or because the arms and seat are too worn and you have been told it is beyond salvation! This is where the decorator in you must take control and overcome sentiment.

How to begin

Making the decision to do something may leave you asking, 'So where do I begin?'. In fact, you have already begun! You have been influenced by things you have seen that you like and you know what you want to change about your rooms. A good way to prepare yourself is to collect pictures from magazines showing colour schemes, ideas and projects that you like. Keep them in a folder or scrapbook for easy reference. Make a list of the positive and negative elements of your home and make a mental note of the things you like and dislike about other homes you visit. Soon you will see that there is a pattern forming in your selection process. You may be drawn to a certain colour scheme, to the grandeur of high ceilings or the plushness of rich vibrant fabrics. It may be the simplicity of a room that pleases your eye, where the texture of the fabrics and furniture pieces are more important than the use of colour.

Once you have made a selection of the features you like about an interior, try to analyse the decorating style. Is it the richness of pattern commonly used in the Victorian style? Is it the modern clean lines of the minimalist approach? Is it the simplicity

of materials and objects more commonly associated with French provincial decorating? It is imperative that once you have decided on what you like about a room you make a commitment that this is what you want to create.

Do not slavishly follow the current trends in decorating. If you do not like the currently fashionable look, don't feel obliged to incorporate it into your new scheme. If clean minimalistic decorating lines are in, but you feel that gathering your personal treasures around you makes you feel relaxed and happy, then follow your heart.

Once you have set your goals in the direction of the style you want to achieve, it is time to consider all the other elements that will help bring your plans to fruition.

*Left: The sample board
Below: The uncluttered simplicity of this living room is enhanced by the choice of fabrics*

Colour

Colour is the basis to any room setting. Your colour selections will invoke a certain atmosphere within a room, so it is important to work with colours that reflect the mood you are trying to create. Ruby red, for example, creates a feeling of warmth and passion, whilst subtle, refreshing blue creates a sense of calm and coolness.

Working with colour

Decorating with soft furnishings often means that a colour scheme is already in place for the walls and floor of your room. The fabrics you select for your soft furnishings will either transform your room into something totally new and unique, work with your existing furnishings and ornaments to create a fresh look, or blend and harmonise with your general colour scheme to ensure that other focal points, such as paintings or objets d'art, take pride of place in your room setting.

Not only will fabric colour create a mood, but the pattern and texture of the fabric will also play a very important role in the overall style of the room. The tactile qualities of fabric absorb and reflect light to create varying degrees of warmth.

The effect of one colour in relation to another can also have a major bearing on your final colour scheme. In some instances, heavily patterned and dyed fabrics absorb surrounding colours into them, totally washing them out. This phenomenon is further emphasised by the variation in the light. Light and shadow will have a major bearing on the final effect of colour in a

Above: Create a romantic bedroom setting
Top: The sample board

room: a light colour in a sunlit room will be washed out even further by strong light and give your walls or fabrics a lighter tint; dark colours in rooms with little natural light will often appear darker and in some places, such as corners, will often appear as black.

To decide what kind of effect you want to create, you must consider the features of your room. The positive features should be highlighted and brought to the forefront through the use of suitably coloured or textured fabrics. A beautifully shaped bay window or an elegant chaise longue would be ideal focal points, highlighted in patterned fabric or vibrant colours.

It may be that the only positive features of a room are structural, such as the height of the ceiling or decorative architraves, and all the other parts need to be changed. This is where the principles of colour should be applied in order to emphasise the ceiling height and enhance the decorative mouldings without the room becoming too austere and overpowering.

Colour can also be used to play clever tricks and remedy faults that would otherwise require major alterations. A long hallway will seem shorter painted in a warm colour with the far back wall of the hallway painted in a stronger or lighter tone of the wall colour.

The colour wheel

❖

The colour wheel allows you to experiment with colours without losing control of your decorative objectives or having to deal with the cost of expensive failures.

Warm and cool tonings

When a greater portion of one primary colour is combined with its partner, a warm or cool toning of a secondary colour is formed. For example, seventy per cent blue and thirty per cent yellow make blue/green, a cool colour, but if the proportions were altered to seventy per cent yellow and thirty per cent blue, the resultant yellow/green would be a warm colour.

Warm and cool colours play very important roles in the visual effect we can create in a room. Blues and greens, found on the right-hand side of the colour wheel, are cool, calming colours, creating the illusion of space and distance. For this reason, they are ideal for giving a feeling of spaciousness to a small or awkwardly shaped room.

Red, orange and violet, with the inclusion of yellow, are warm colours. Yellow and violet are in interesting positions at the top and bottom of the wheel. Their effect can be varied depending on whether they tend to the cool or warm side of the wheel.

Neutral colours

Black and white, described as neutral colours, are often used as tints to vary the strength of a primary or secondary colour. Neutral colours can also be warm or cool. Browns and greys are also neutral colours

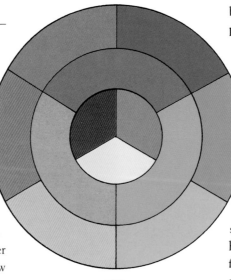

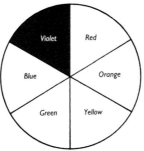

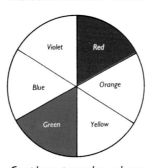

Monochromatic colour scheme

Complementary colour scheme

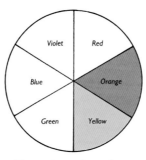

Harmonious colour scheme

and they too can be tinted with black or white to give the impression of coolness or warmth.

Monochromatic colour schemes

In a monochromatic colour scheme, various tones of a single base colour are used to produce a very subtle colour scheme. Quite often, monochromatic schemes are based on neutral shades, such as cream or ivory. In such a scheme, you might find cushions in cream raw silk, curtains in creamy-white, hand-loomed cotton, and embossed furnishing fabrics in a creamy-beige; all serve to create very exciting textured effects, even though there is only a slight variation in the overall colour scheme.

Harmonious or analogous colour schemes

These colours are grouped together on the colour wheel and, when used together, are the easiest and safest colour choices for decorating.

Complementary colour schemes

Complementary colours are found directly opposite one another on the colour wheel, for example red and green, or blue and yellow. Whilst most of us could not live in a room decorated in red and green, the softer tonings on the outer ring of the colour wheel can provide interesting decorative effects.

Accent colours

Accent colours are just that – a way of providing an accent or highlight in an overall colour scheme; such as a light colour against a dark one or a cool colour against a warm one.

Fabrics & fabric selection

Today, home decorators have a vast selection of fabric styles from which to select soft furnishing treatments. This endless variety of fabric is very exciting and even awe-inspiring when it comes to making choices.

Remember when purchasing fabric, do not skimp on the amount. A full-bodied curtain which flows on to the floor below, makes a statement of grandeur. If you feel the cost of making such a statement could be out of your price range, shop around! Fabric suppliers are usually happy to help you compare prices and quality and you will be surprised at the amount of variation. Visiting showrooms will enable you to see a range of the latest fabrics so you can select the best one in your price range. This is also an opportunity to be creative – lashings of unbleached calico or cotton, used extravagantly, will often create as much ambience as a more expensive fabric.

The beauty of decorating with fabric is that it can, for example, adorn a window for a few years and then be cut down to make a flurry of cushion covers. It can then be used with other fabrics to create a patchwork masterpiece for your bed.

Pattern and texture
When people think of fabrics they immediately think of patterns. Pattern, although the most noticeable feature of some fabrics, is by no means the only one. The texture and hand or 'feel' of a fabric are elements which should not be overlooked. Many natural fabrics such as silk or wool are natural fibres spun into uneven yarns which are woven together to form a cloth, creating an uneven slub-like texture to the finished fabric. Crisp linens and polished chintzed cottons also have pleasing textural qualities, while hand-loomed cottons provide a rough uneven texture due to the unevenness of the natural fibres.

Know your fabric
Today, manufacturers often have helpful information printed on the sample cards, telling you about a fabric's 'washability'. Fabrics are only guaranteed by the manufacturer if they are used and cleaned as recommended.

Golden rules for choosing fabrics
1 Be certain that the fabric you choose is suitable for its intended use. For example, don't expect a shiny chintz to be long-lasting in a child's bedroom or lace curtains to block out the light.

2 Be sure you are making an economically sound purchase. Don't spend loads of money on areas that don't warrant the expense, but do invest in a good quality fabric for high-traffic areas or for pieces of classic design.

3 If you are going to sew soft furnishings, be sure that your machine can sew your chosen fabric.

4 Look into how you plan to care for the fabric and make sure the one you have chosen is suitable for this regime. For example, if you are going to wash your curtains at home rather than have them professionally cleaned, be sure that your fabric is washable and will not shrink or distort.

Below: The sample board
Bottom: Rich fabrics and trims enhance this formal dining room

Fabric types & qualities

Today, you still have the choice of all the natural fibres, but you also have access to a very wide range of man-made or synthetic fibres. This variety can sometimes be confusing so it is useful to know a little about the properties of various fibres and the resultant fabrics.

The four natural fibres (cotton, wool, silk and linen) are all commonly used to make home furnishings.

Natural fibres

• *Cotton* has long been the leader for sheets, towels and most curtains. It is mass-produced, making it relatively inexpensive to manufacture into fabrics of many weights and textures.

• *Wool* is commonly the basis of traditional and modern floor coverings. It is the best fabric insulator, while being hard-wearing, flame-retardant, light and fairly waterproof. It is long-lasting, but needs care with laundering.

• *Silk* is the glamour fabric, providing traditional materials for upholstery, tassels and braids, cushions and luxury rugs. Silk is a very fine and soft fibre and is a good insulator, but it is quite expensive compared to other natural fibres. It is the most lustrous fibre of all.

Linen is the world's oldest domestic fibre. There have always been sheets and household napery made from linen, with its main appeal being its sheer endurance – it never seems to wear out!

The natural fibres and fabrics are very easy to clean but, on the negative side, due to their often loose or uneven weave they are prone to shrink, crease or distort if laundered incorrectly. This unevenness can only be rectified if the natural fibre is woven with a man-made fibre.

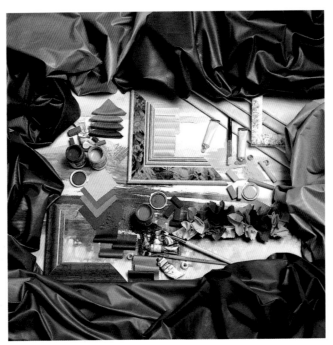

Decorating with fabric is like painting a picture

Synthetic fibres

Synthetic or man-made fibres are becoming increasingly popular and are often blended with natural fibres in fabrics. This serves two purposes: the cost is reduced and very often the synthetic fibres give added strength. Synthetic fabrics usually wash very well, the fibres do not absorb dirt and moisture, and they are long-wearing. They also provide insulation and effective light control where required.

The most commonly used man-made fibres are acetate, polyester, acrylic and viscose – all produced by chemical processes and all with valuable qualities.

• *Acetates* are created by treating cotton linters or cotton fibres. It is often used as a substitute for silk in moires or brocades and feels soft to the touch with good draping qualities. An acetate works best in a tightly woven fabric because it tends to sag in looser weaves.

• *Acrylics* are bulky pile fabrics which also feel soft to the touch. They have excellent draping qualities and are crease-resistant. Acrylic fibres are often blended with polyester, cotton or wool for lasting strength and easy maintenance.

• *Nylon* is a by-product of coal. Whilst not as soft as polyester, it is still drapable and is often found mixed with other fibres to form synthetic laces, net or satin. Washing is easy and the fabric can be drip-dried, requiring little ironing.

• *Polyester* is the hardest wearing of the man-made fabrics. It combines well with many natural fibres, such as cotton, to provide an easy-care, wrinkle-free fabric which has excellent draping qualities.

Pattern

Patterns have been used throughout the centuries to adorn the walls of caves, naive shelters, houses and stately castles. Ancient civilisations were inspired by the patterns found in nature and often copied the markings on insects and reptiles when painting their bodies.

The printing of patterns on fabric by screen printing or stencils are techniques still commonly used today for both hand-crafted and mass-produced items. During the eighteenth century, copper rollers were engraved with patterns that were rolled over a fabric to form a repetitive pattern (known as a repeat), giving birth to the printed patterns that are still used, such as for many of the motifs on highly polished chintzed fabrics.

The effects of pattern

Pattern can be used in different ways to achieve different effects. In a small room, a bold chintzed floral drape can be used as a focal point;

Top left: The sample board
Above: Combine different prints with a common colour for an interesting visual effect

in a larger room, the pattern of one fabric can be used with other patterned fabrics as part of the overall decorative rhythm or theme.

Coordination of patterns is now a breeze for home decorators with many top fabric manufacturers providing totally coordinated ranges to choose from.

Whilst there are no set rules for coordinating fabrics there are some general guidelines for you to refer to. For example, larger scale prints work best when used over larger pieces such as lounge suites or for drapes in larger rooms; vertical stripes will emphasise the height of a wall or window area; smaller florals are ideal for cushions and accents; and plain fabrics in complementary colours make ideal trims.

Scale and proportion

The next element to consider when selecting patterned fabrics is the size and scale of the pattern. Wall coverings are usually best suited to smaller scale prints, whilst larger scale elaborate designs work better when draped into folds for curtains (fig. 1).

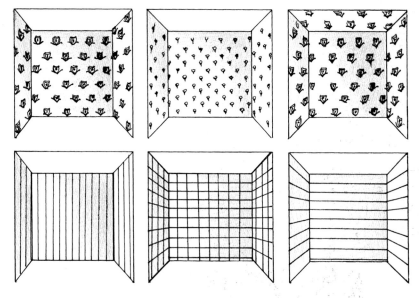

Fig. 1: Patterns create different visual effects

If you are working with a fabric manufacturer's coordinated range, always purchase good-sized samples showing a full repeat. It is important to see how a fabric will drape as a curtain, as opposed to just being stretched over a chair or cushion.

Mixing patterns

Usually people prefer to use just one pattern and mix it with plains or tonings of that print in a room. With a little more daring, you can select a similar pattern to the first one, in either a larger or smaller scale or in reversed colorations.

However, very different patterns can also be used right next to each other, in balance, and will produce very interesting effects.

To mix patterns confidently, there should be some common element, such as colour.

Sample boards

A sample board is the ideal way to consider whether colour, scale, pattern and proportion are working harmoniously. Most importantly, a sample board provides a working space which can be altered – much less expensive than scrapping the new curtains and starting again.

You must ensure that the elements of your sample board are in proportion to one another and to the scale of the room. The sample of your sofa fabric must be much larger than the sofa piping or trim that you are using as a contrasting touch. Paint swatches showing wall colours, or a piece of board painted in your wall colours, allows for better matching to curtain fabrics. Present your fabrics as they will appear in the room. For example, try to fold or drape your curtain sample as it will appear on your window.

We made up sample boards for each of our room settings before we began the design process. You can see from the sample boards shown with each picture how the final effects have evolved from the design stage to the final presentation in the room.

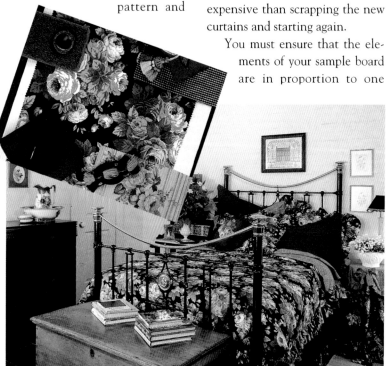

Left: The sample board
Below: Combinations of pattern and texture work in a two-colour scheme

Top left: The sample board
Left: Rich colours and strong patterns are a feature of this stylish bedroom

Pattern matching

When you are using patterned fabric where lengths are joined across the width, you must take care that the patterns match. To do this, you must determine the pattern repeat. A pattern repeat is the length of the pattern from beginning to end, running down the length of a fabric. If your fabric has a strong motif running across it, it is a good idea to place a complete motif at the top and, if possible, another one at the bottom. If there is a strong motif running vertically through the fabric, this should be centred, as far as possible, in the finished project.

Obviously, you will not always be able to have a complete pattern repeat at the top and at the bottom. The broken repeat should be where it is least visible – at the top in a shorter curtain and at the bottom in a floor length one (fig. 1).

Joining panels

Ideally, fabric panels should be joined in such a way that the stitching is as unobtrusive as possible.

1 Place the two panels together with right sides facing. Stitch them together with a 1.5 cm seam and press the seam flat (fig. 2).

2 Trim the seam allowance on one side back to 3 mm and turn in 3 mm on the raw edge of the other seam allowance (figs 3 and 4).

3 Press the folded edge over to the seam line on the other fabric piece, enclosing the raw edges. Slipstitch the folded edge over the previous stitching (fig. 5).

Each print poses a different challenge when it comes to pattern matching

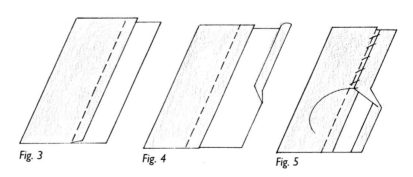

Fig. 1

Fig. 2

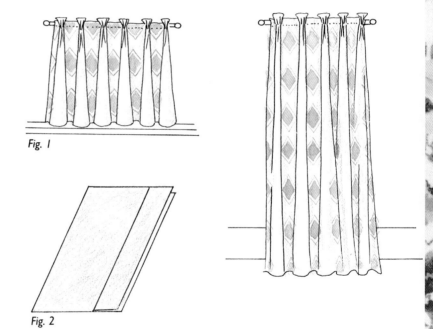

Fig. 3

Fig. 4

Fig. 5

Trims

Decorative trims provide the finishing touch to many of your soft furnishing projects. Interior designers have always valued the 'extra something' given to a piece of furniture or accessory by the addition of well-chosen trims. In this book, we feature a variety of trims and show how the same trim can be applied to different projects to achieve a totally different look.

It may be the colour or texture of the trim selected or the extravagance of rich bullion trims, feminine ruffles and lace, or the defined lines of bias and piping details that provide the stylish finishes.

Today's furnishings are increasingly ornate and generous in proportion. This trend is exemplified in the softness and fullness of a well-padded sofa

with feather-filled cushions, or in generous metres of fabric draped across curtains to form swagged pelmets or gathered into festoon blinds. These generous lines are often accentuated by the choice of trims. Equally, if you prefer the look of straight sharp edges, the well-defined lines of a bonded blind or the crispness of starched bed linen, the selection of the perfect trim or braid will underline the effect you are trying to create.

Most stockists of furnishing fabrics have a good range of trims for you to choose from, and many are surprisingly inexpensive. While cost is a most important consideration, if only because it is possible to overembellish an inexpensive fabric, there are several other considerations to bear in mind when selecting your borders and trims.

While creativity frequently challenges rules of colour and suitability, your eye will tell you if a trim suits a fabric. Fabrics that are generally dull rather than lustrous tend to look casual, while shimmery fabrics will always

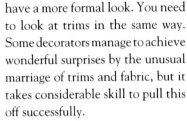

have a more formal look. You need to look at trims in the same way. Some decorators manage to achieve wonderful surprises by the unusual marriage of trims and fabric, but it takes considerable skill to pull this off successfully.

Too much of a contrasting trim will become the focal point of a design. This is not generally a problem if the trim is the same colour as the fabric, as the trim will not compete with the fabric; rather it will add interesting textured effects.

Wearability

For the best results when selecting trims, ensure that the trims and the fabric are similar or compatible in weight; delicate lace will not work with a heavy velvet. This is particularly important when it comes to the care and cleaning of your soft furnishing item. If you are making cushion covers that you plan to wash, make sure that the trim you use is washable. Is the braid washable? Will the colour run in water? If you are planning to wash the trimmed item, you should wash the trim and the fabric separately before you begin. This also applies if you are trimming an existing item. It may seem like a lot of extra work, but checking shrinkage and colour fastness now will save you heartache later. Sometimes a handful of cooking salt thrown into cold rinsing water will help to set the dyes in trims, but it is better to be sure.

Will the braid be as long-wearing as the fabric? This may not be a major consideration, but if your fabric is expensive you will

The choice of trims available to the home sewer is rich and wide

have to consider the life expectancy of your trims. Be mindful of where you use the trim – arm rests and head rests are more prone to wearing than the back of a sofa. If your cushion cover will be used on the family-room sofa, much loved by the kids and the family dog, do not choose a delicate lace ruffle.

It is sometimes a good idea to purchase right at the beginning more braid, ribbon or lace than you need, to allow for replacement of worn areas later on.

Applying trims

When applying trims to fabric, pins may pucker, stretch or distort the fabric or trim. To avoid this problem, use a fabric or craft glue to temporarily secure the trim to the fabric while you stitch. (Make sure the glue is dry before you begin sewing.) There are also a number of 'glues' available that bond both fabric and trim, without sewing. Many of these glues can also be laundered regularly, whilst remaining quite secure.

Always try to work with a continuous length of trim, but if cutting is required allow enough excess for joins and corners. When working the trim or braid around a corner, baste the trim at the corner before sewing. When applying a ruffle to a corner, such as that on a cushion cover, allow extra fullness at the corner to prevent pulling. (See how to sew corners on page 22.)

Binding

❖

How to make continuous bias binding

1 Cut a piece of bias fabric (fig. 1). Decide on the width of your bias strip, including seam allowances, and mark the bias strips as shown.
2 Fold the fabric with the right sides together, so that both points A and both points B are matching. Note that one strip width extends on each side. Join AA to BB with a 6 mm seam. Press the seam open. Cut along the marked line for the bias strip, giving you one continuous strip of bias fabric (fig. 2).

Making and joining strips of bias binding

1 To find the bias on a piece of fabric, fold in one corner so that the top edge is parallel to the selvage. Press the fold. This pressed line is the bias. Draw in lines parallel to the pressed line, the desired width of the bias strip apart. Cut along these lines to produce your bias strips.
2 Join two strips by placing one length of bias right side up and the second length of fabric wrong side up across each other at an angle of 45 degrees, with the raw edges matching at the end (fig. 3).
3 Stitch the ends together as shown. Press the seam open (fig. 4).

Attaching the binding

By machine
Fold the bias strip in half length-ways with the wrong sides facing and place it over both raw edges of the seam. If you are using bias binding you have made yourself, you will need to fold the raw edges under before you pin it in position.

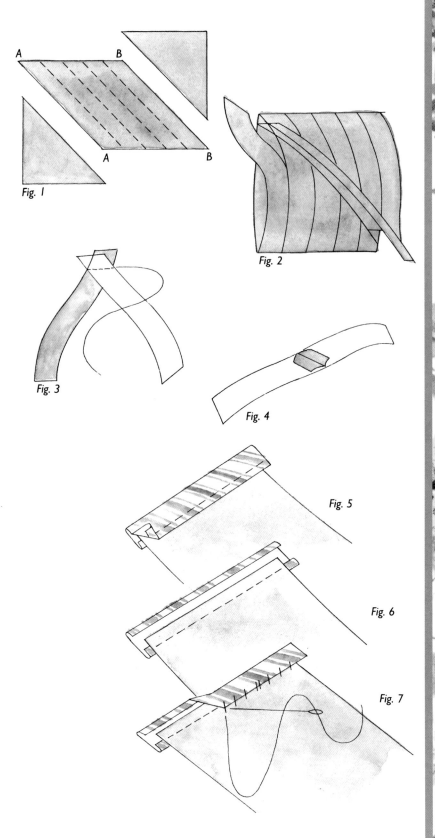

Fig. 1

Fig. 2

Fig. 3

Fig. 4

Fig. 5

Fig. 6

Fig. 7

Pin and stitch the bias strip into place inside the seam allowance, catching both sides of the bias in the seam (fig. 5).

By hand
Open out the bias binding. With the right sides facing, match one of the raw edges of the fabric with one raw edge of the bias binding. Pin and stitch them together, stitching close to the fold line of the bias binding (fig. 6). Fold the binding in half on to the wrong side of the fabric, enclosing all the raw edges. Slipstitch the binding into place, covering the first line of stitching (fig. 7).

Piping

Piping differs from binding in that the cut lengths of bias fabric cover a purchased length of cording, which is in turn sewn into a flat seam so that the covered cord or piping is sandwiched between the layers of fabric. Piping cords can be purchased in various thicknesses so that a number of different styles can be achieved for different end uses, such as for upholstery, cushion covers or napery.

The method for cutting and joining lengths of bias fabric is the same as for making the continuous bias on page 20. Remember, the bias strip must be wide enough to wrap around the piping cord, leaving sufficient seam allowances on both sides for the stitching.

To make piping
1 Measure the length of piping you will require for your project. Cords can be joined, if necessary, by butting two ends together and binding

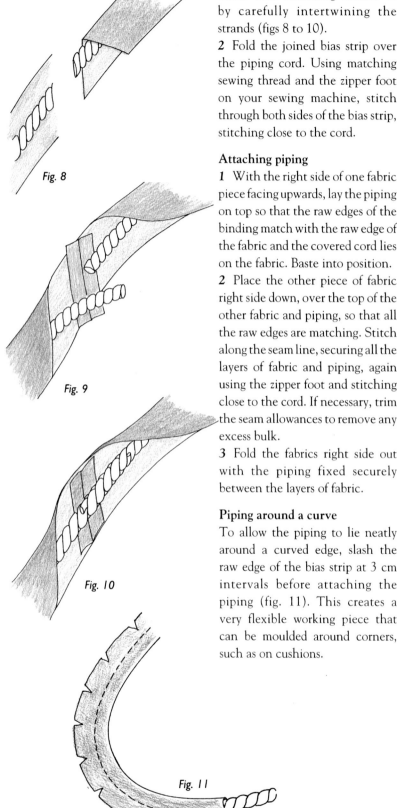

Fig. 8

Fig. 9

Fig. 10

Fig. 11

them with matching thread or by carefully intertwining the strands (figs 8 to 10).
2 Fold the joined bias strip over the piping cord. Using matching sewing thread and the zipper foot on your sewing machine, stitch through both sides of the bias strip, stitching close to the cord.

Attaching piping
1 With the right side of one fabric piece facing upwards, lay the piping on top so that the raw edges of the binding match with the raw edge of the fabric and the covered cord lies on the fabric. Baste into position.
2 Place the other piece of fabric right side down, over the top of the other fabric and piping, so that all the raw edges are matching. Stitch along the seam line, securing all the layers of fabric and piping, again using the zipper foot and stitching close to the cord. If necessary, trim the seam allowances to remove any excess bulk.
3 Fold the fabrics right side out with the piping fixed securely between the layers of fabric.

Piping around a curve
To allow the piping to lie neatly around a curved edge, slash the raw edge of the bias strip at 3 cm intervals before attaching the piping (fig. 11). This creates a very flexible working piece that can be moulded around corners, such as on cushions.

Corners

Corners can be a little tricky to sew neatly, so it's worthwhile taking a moment to learn a trick or two.

Sewing a right-angled corner
1 Stitch until the needle is 1.5 cm from the fabric edge (or the distance of your set seam allowance, if that is not 1.5 cm). Lift the machine foot and turn the fabric through an angle of 90 degrees. Lower the machine foot so that it is parallel to the raw edge of the fabric and continue sewing.
2 To allow the corner to be turned out neatly, cut diagonally across the seam allowance at the corner. You can also trim the seams to remove any excess bulk of fabric (fig. 1).

Sewing a sharp corner
Work in the same way as for the right-angled corner, but add one or two stitches across the corner for extra strength. Trim the corner across the diagonal as for the right-angled corner (fig. 2).

Sewing a mitred corner
Mitred corners give a particularly neat square finish to your corners, particularly on table linen and where piping is a feature.
1 To sew a mitred corner, such as on a tablecloth, press in 3 mm on both raw edges to neaten them, then press in the seam allowances (fig. 3).
2 Open out the corner and press it in towards the centre so that the pressed lines are matching. Press the diagonal; this will be your stitching line (fig. 4).
3 Open out the corner again and refold it diagonally through the corner. Stitch along the diagonal

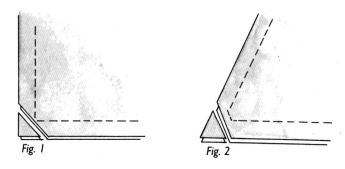

Fig. 1

Fig. 2

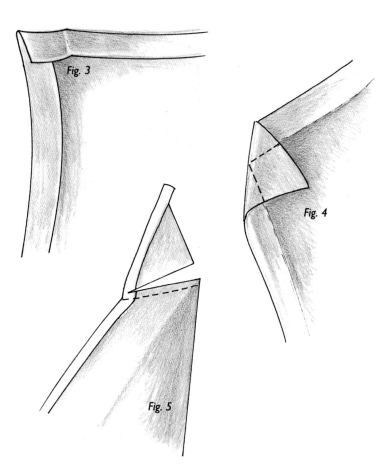

Fig. 3

Fig. 4

Fig. 5

line. Trim the corner, cutting off the excess fabric (fig. 5). Turn the corner right side out and press carefully.

Sewing a mitred corner on a trim
1 Fold the trim over double with the wrong sides together so the raw edges are matching. Pick up the top piece and fold it to one side, so that its edges are now at right angles to the edges of the lower piece and you have formed a diagonal fold. Finger-press the fold (fig. 6).
2 On the wrong side, pin and stitch diagonally from the corner to the edge along the fold, then cut away the excess fabric, so that the corner lies flat Press the seam open (figs 7 and 8).

To mitre a corner with piping,

pin and baste the piping into place up to the corner. At the corner, snip into the seam allowance of the piping so that the snip forms an L-shape. Bend the piping. To mitre a corner on a border where there is a raw edge on both sides remember, before you stitch the corner, to turn under the seam allowance on the raw edge which will remain visible.

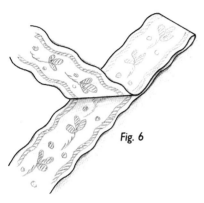
Fig. 6

Ruffles can really dress up a collection of cushions

Frills & ruffles

Frills and ruffles are one of the easiest decorating finishes for a variety of soft furnishing projects, including cushions, curtains, blinds and bed linen. Whether used singly or in layers of frills, they are pretty and feminine and bound to please. How full you make the ruffle will depend on your fabric and where it is to be applied. Generally, the lighter the fabric, the fuller the ruffle. As a general rule, allow about twice the finished length when cutting the strip for the ruffle.

A single plain ruffle (fig. 9)
1 Cut out a strip for the ruffle, adding 3 cm for the bottom hem. If you need to join strips to achieve the full length, add 1.5 cm for each joining seam allowance.

2 Double hem the bottom edge of the ruffle. To gather the ruffle, handsew or machine-sew two parallel rows of gathering stitches across the raw edge in the seam allowance (figs 10 and 11).

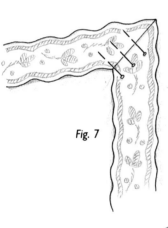
Fig. 7

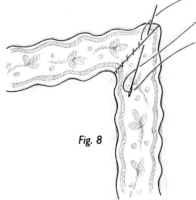
Fig. 8

Fig. 9

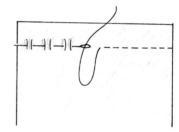
Fig. 10

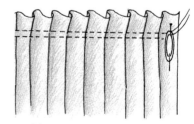
Fig. 11

*Add a ruffle to the bottom of
an Austrian blind*

3 Pin the gathered edge of the ruffle to the raw edge of the other fabric piece, adjusting the gathering for evenness and a good fit. Machine-sew the ruffle in place, stitching very close to the gathering stitches.

Sewing a ruffle with a heading (figs 1 and 2)

Generally, this attractive ruffle is used to finish the bottom edge of a curtain, where the upper ruffle is narrower than the lower one.

1 Cut the ruffle strip with the same seam allowances as for the single ruffle but add the additional width required for the upper ruffle or heading. Join strips as necessary to achieve the correct length.

2 Double hem both the upper and lower raw edges. Mark where the heading is to be attached to the curtain and handsew or machine-sew two parallel rows of gathering stitches just below that line.

3 Pin the ruffle into position along the gathering line, adjusting the gathers so they are even. Stitch between the two rows of gathering. Remove the gathering threads when the stitching is complete.

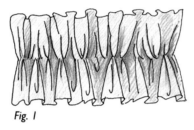

Fig. 1

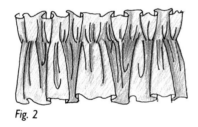

Fig. 2

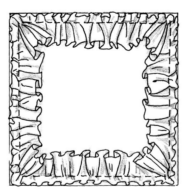

Fig. 3

Sewing a double ruffle

Giving a look with more body than a single ruffle, this variation eliminates the need for a bottom hem.

1 Cut the ruffle to double the required width and add 1.5 cm for each seam allowance.

2 Fold the ruffle in half with wrong sides together and iron it flat. Gather up the ruffle with two rows of gathering stitches inside the 1.5 cm seam allowance.

3 Attach the ruffle in the same way as the ruffle with the heading.

Applying a ruffle

1 There is a technique to ensure that the ruffling looks even on your finished project. Marking with pins, divide the length of the ruffle into equal parts and then divide the edge to which it will be applied into the same number of equal parts. For smaller projects, four divisions are usual, but for larger projects and circles, six equal parts may be required. If you are attaching the ruffle to a cushion, use the four corners as your marks.

2 Pin the ruffle on, matching the pin marks and adjusting the gathering evenly between them. Pin and baste, then stitch the ruffle into place (fig. 3).

Fastenings

Today, we are able to choose from a number of alternatives to close projects such as quilt covers and cushions. Take into account not only the appearance of your fastenings but their practicality, particularly on pieces which will be laundered.

Press studs (either singly or on a tape), Velcro, zippers, hooks and eyes are all excellent methods of securing openings. Knowing how to apply these products will save you time with little effort.

Hook and eyes

Where the edges overlap, stitch the hook on the underside of the overlapping edge and the eye on the outside of the other edge (fig. 4). Where the fabrics meet edge to edge, stitch the eye on the wrong side, slightly over the edge, and stitch the hook so that the end is flush with the fabric's edge (fig. 5).

Fastening tapes

Hook and loop fastenings, such as Velcro, come in various shapes and sizes but the most common is in the form of long continuous strips, purchased by the metre (fig. 6). Circles can be used for closures, such as on a quilt cover. These fastenings are quite simple to attach by stitching down close to the outside edges.

Another type of fastening tape utilises press studs (fig. 7). It is best to attach this tape using the zipper foot on your sewing machine, enabling you to stitch quite close to the press studs but not over them.

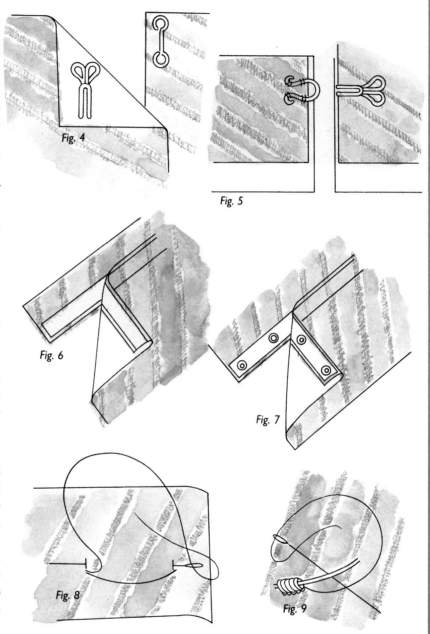

Fig. 4

Fig. 5

Fig. 6

Fig. 7

Fig. 8

Fig. 9

Making a thread eye

Because a thread eye is less obvious than a metal one, there may be times when you prefer it. Mark the required length for the eye and sew slack, continuous long stitches along that length, securing both ends (fig. 8). Sew a line of blanket stitches over the loose stitches for extra strength and a neat finish (fig. 9). Remember a thread eye is not as strong as a metal one.

Buttons

Buttons can be both functional and decorative. On continental quilt covers, pillowcases and cushion covers, they provide a very decorative fastening method. Select buttons in shell or wood to provide interesting texture and scale.

Creating a button shank

Sometimes, such as when attaching a button to thick fabric, it is useful to create a shank for the button.

1 Secure the thread in the fabric where the button is to be attached and bring the needle to the right side of the fabric. Pass the needle and thread through the first hole in the button.

2 Place a matchstick on top of the holes in the button and work several stitches over the matchstick, through the holes in the button and through the fabric (fig. 1).

3 Remove the matchstick and pull up the button. Wind the thread around the shank at least six or eight times, then secure it.

If the button has a shank, work fifteen stitches through the fabric and shank before fastening off.

Zippers

Zippers are most commonly used for loose covers. A concealed zipper usually means that the cushion can be used on both sides.

Choose a good quality zipper to ensure the long life of your project. How frustrating to make a beautiful frilled and piped cushion only to have the zipper fail not long after.

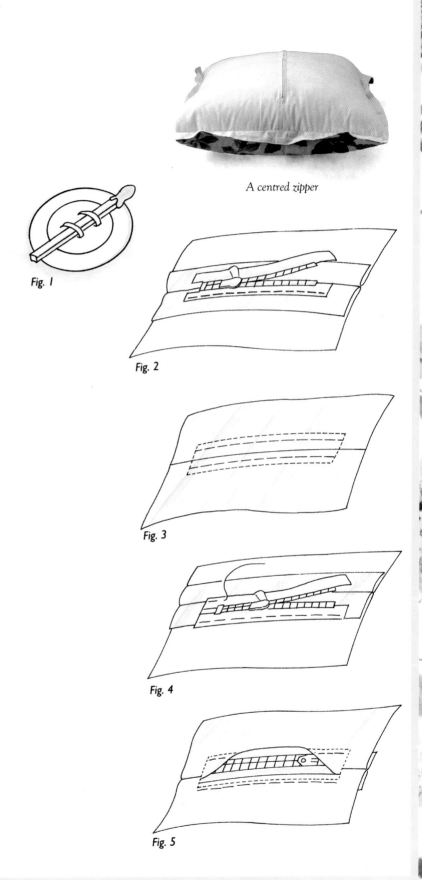

A centred zipper

Fig. 1

Fig. 2

Fig. 3

Fig. 4

Fig. 5

Inserting a centred zipper

1 Mark the length of the zipper opening, adding 5 cm. Stitch the two ends of the seam and baste the zipper opening closed. Press the seam open.

2 Open the zipper and position it face down on the seam allowance so that the zipper teeth are along the seam line. Pin and baste the length of one side of the zipper tape to the fabric, stitching through all thicknesses approximately 3 mm from the zipper teeth (fig. 2).

3 Close the zipper and position the zipper tape on the other seam allowance. Pin and baste the other side into place as before.

4 Turn the fabric right side up with the zipper underneath. Commencing at the top of the zipper and using the zipper foot on your sewing machine, topstitch down one side, approximately 5 mm away from the zipper teeth. Continue to stitch across the bottom of the zipper, close to the end, then back up to the top of the zipper on the other side. Remove the basting stitches and press carefully (fig. 3).

To insert an offset zipper

If you do not wish the zipper to be seen, you can insert it, offset, by the following method.

1 Mark the zipper opening as for the centred zipper. Sew the ends of the zipper opening seam and baste closed the zipper opening.

2 With the zipper open and face down, position it over the seam so that the teeth are centred over the right-hand seam allowance. Baste the right-hand side of the zipper tape into position close to the zipper teeth (fig. 4).

3 Close the zipper and baste the other zipper tape in place, closer

An offset zipper

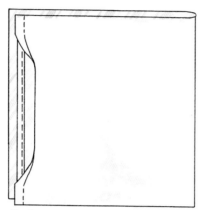

Fig. 6

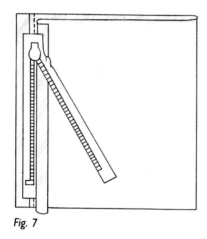

Fig. 7

A zipper in the side seam

to the edge of the zipper tape.

4 On the right side and using the zipper foot of your sewing machine, topstitch through all the layers of fabric down both sides of the zipper and across the bottom. Remove the basting (fig. 5).

Lapped zipper in a piped seam

Occasionally, you will need to insert a zipper into a seam which already has piping in it, such as on one of the sides of a cushion cover, and this can be quite bulky and difficult to manage.

1 On the side without the piping, press under the seam allowance of the zipper opening along the seam line.

2 Pull back the top seam allowance to view the piping seam allowance (fig. 6). Open the zipper and lay it face down over the extended seam allowance with the zipper teeth resting on the top of the piping. Baste into position (fig. 7). Check that the zipper will open and close easily before stitching. Using the zipper foot on your sewing machine, stitch on the zipper tape close to the zipper teeth, then remove the basting stitches.

3 Stitch the other side of the zipper tape to the seam allowance on the other side.

If you want to avoid the problem, cut the fabric for the back of the cushion in two halves, remembering to add 1.5 cm at the centre back for the seam allowances. Insert the zipper into this centre back seam, using the method for applying a centred zipper, then make up the cushion cover in the usual way.

Equipment

One of the nicest things about decorating with soft furnishings is that you do not need to invest immense amounts of money in hardware to complete your projects. When creating soft furnishings, the majority of home sewers have already made the investment in the number one timesaver: a sewing machine.

Cutting table

A clean working surface is also necessary to achieve a professional finish in your sewing. If you do not have a table large enough, invest in a cutting board which has a grid marked in 2.5 cm squares. A cutting board such as this will be very valuable when you are working with large pieces of fabric where straight even cutting is essential. In a project such as a bonded blind, having a cutting table could make the difference between an average job and a truly professional one.

Needles and pins

Just as you need a variety of machine needles, it is helpful to have a variety of handsewing needles.

Medium sharps are useful for everyday sewing projects. A curved upholstery needle should be used for heavy projects and can also be useful for sewing buttons on to cushions. In addition to these, choose needles that are appropriate to specific jobs, such as quilting, embroidery and tapestry.

There is also a variety of pins available. Stainless steel dressmaking pins are the most common; some have coloured plastic rounded ends which make them very easy to see. Quilters pins are longer than most other pins and can be useful for pinning a fabric to a padded surface.

Glues, adhesives and bonding webs

There are a large number of glues, spray adhesives and bonding webs available in most craft and fabric suppliers. Their use in appliqué, fixing hems and bonding fabric and trims to a variety of surfaces means that many decorative applications can now be applied quickly and easily to complete projects that, in the past, you might have thought too difficult or too fiddly to attempt.

Iron

A good steam iron is an essential piece of equipment if you are going to achieve a truly professional finish. All seams should be pressed with a warm steam iron. A pressing cloth is another worthwhile investment, especially for use with delicate fabrics.

Turning hook

A long wire-like object with a hook at the end makes turning fabrics for loops and rouleaux so much easier than the old-fashioned methods.

Scissors

Make sure your scissors are sharp. Fabrics can be snagged or damaged by blunt scissors. Dressmakers shears are the most commonly used and are ideal for everyday projects. Embroidery scissors are ideal for appliqué and cutting out intricate shapes. Pinking shears are a useful timesaving device for neatening seam allowances.

Sewing machine

You do not necessarily need a top-of-the-line machine for sewing soft furnishings. It is important that your sewing machine is able to give a good depth of tension variations for sewing different weights of fabric, and that it can sew a basic straight stitch, a zigzag stitch, insert a zipper and make a buttonhole. The latest electronic machines feature many embroidery stitch variations which are wonderful for adding decorative interest to your project.

Regular oiling of machine parts and cleaning with a fine brush may be all that is required to keep your sewing machine in top working order for many years.

Various machine feet are available which allow specific tasks to be performed, such as attaching a zipper, sewing a buttonhole, ruffling and darning. A zipper foot is a great asset for inserting piping as well as zippers. Rufflers are a great timesaver for making up long lengths of ruffles while hemming, and blind stitch feet make hems a breeze. A quilting foot, which has marked guidelines for your stitching, is very handy for sewing quilting patterns on table napkins, quilts and cushion covers.

A variety of machine needle sizes are also essential, including a size 9 (65) for the finest fabrics, size 11 (75) or size 14 (90) for medium-weight cottons, and a size 18 (110) for heavy brocades or velvets.

A stitch guide is a magnetic

device that can be attached to the machine bed or plate and will help you to measure even seam widths.

Tape measure

A tape measure, made from flexible synthetic or fibreglass material, is essential so that measurements can't be distorted by tearing or stretching of the tape. Make sure your tape measure is in good condition and with ends that are not damaged or frayed. A metal tape or ruler is also necessary for measuring up your window dimensions and for drawing the straight long edges required when making bonded blinds. A T-square is also very useful for ruling straight lines as is a set of French curves for curved lines.

Tailors chalk

Chalk should be used to mark fabric; after sewing, the chalk can easily be removed with a stiff brush.

Most of the equipment is already in your home

Stitch Guide

Basting (fig. 1)

This is a row of larger-than-usual running stitches which are used to join fabrics together, usually temporarily. Start with a knot, then take even stitches along the seam line. This is also called tacking.

Gathering (figs 2 and 3)

This running stitch is used to pull up excess width. Knot the thread end securely or take a small back stitch to begin. It is best to have two rows of gathering, 3 to 5 mm apart, either side of the seam line. Using two rows gives a more even gather and gives you a little insurance in case one thread should break while you are pulling up the gathering. Pull up the threads carefully until you achieve the desired width. Secure the gathering by knotting the two threads together or with a couple of back stitches.

Oversewing (fig. 4)

This is a way of neatening a raw edge or loosely joining two pieces of fabric. Make small diagonal stitches, keeping the tension loose.

Blanket stitch (fig. 5)

This is another stitch commonly used to neaten raw edges. As its name implies, it was the common way of finishing the edges of blankets. These days it is more commonly used for embroidery. Take a stitch from the front to the back, about 6 mm from the edge. Keeping the thread close to the fabric under the point of the needle, pull the stitch through, forming a loop on the fabric edge.

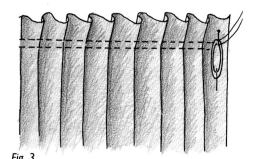

Fig. 1

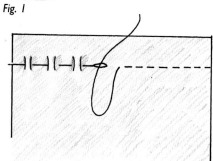

Fig. 2

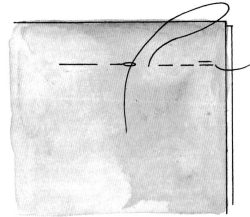

Fig. 3

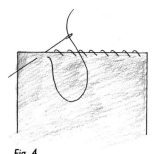

Fig. 4

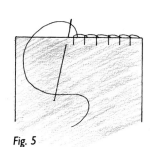

Fig. 5

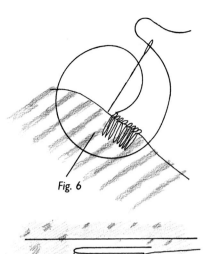

Fig. 6

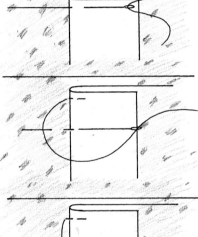

Fig. 7

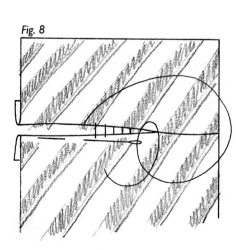

Fig. 8

Buttonhole stitch (fig. 6)

This stitch is similar to blanket stitch but is worked from the back to the front with the stitches lying very close together. Pass the thread under the needle before pulling the stitch through.

Lock stitch (fig. 7)

This stitch is often used to secure a lining to an outer fabric where the stitching should not be visible, such as on the sides of curtains. Pin the two fabrics together with the lining on top, right side up. Fold back the lining and work loose blanket-type stitches, joining the folded edge to the fabric beneath. Make sure the stitches are big and loose so that the fabric falls without puckers.

Slipstitch (fig. 8)

This is a most useful stitch for all types of handsewing, particularly when openings in seams need to be closed or for finishing corners. Working on the outside (right side) of your work, take a small stitch in the fold on one edge of the fabric and then through the fold on the other edge. Pull up the stitches to bring the edges together. Do not pull the thread too tightly.

Hemming (fig. 9)

In hemming, small diagonal stitches catch the fabric to the hem. Pick up only a few threads at a time so they are not too visible on the outside. Try to keep the stitching even, without pulling the fabric.

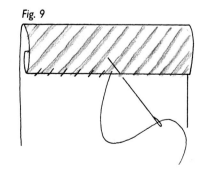

Fig. 9

Ladder stitch (figs 1 and 2)

This stitch is most useful for joining two patterned fabrics when the pattern must be matched perfectly on both sides. Fold and press the seam allowance under on one side. Place this folded edge over the raw edge of the other piece of fabric until the patterns match exactly, then pin the top piece in place. Take small stitches, passing the needle along inside the fold and placing the stitches on the lower fabric, close to the fold.

Seams

❖

Flat seam (figs 3 and 4)

Place the fabrics with right sides together. Stitch the seam with the required seam allowance. Trim the seam if necessary, then press it open.

Flat fell seam (figs 3 to 5)

Place the fabrics with right sides together. Stitch the seam with a 12 mm seam allowance. Trim the seam on one side back to 6 mm, then press the seam open. Fold over the raw edge on the longer side then fold it again, covering the shorter side and enclosing the seam allowances. Stitch down close to the folded edge.

French seam (figs 6 to 9)

Place the fabrics together with the wrong sides facing. Stitch the seam with a 1 cm seam allowance. Trim the seam allowance back to about 5 mm. Fold the fabrics along the seam line so that the right sides are facing. Stitch the seam, 1 cm from the folded edge, enclosing the raw edges of the first seam as you sew. Press the seam to one side.

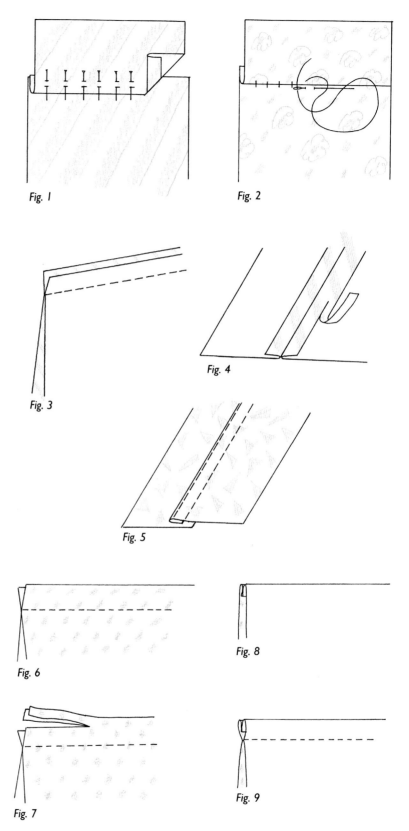

Fig. 1

Fig. 2

Fig. 3

Fig. 4

Fig. 5

Fig. 6

Fig. 7

Fig. 8

Fig. 9

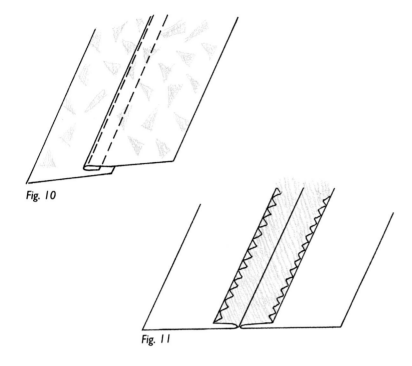

Fig. 10

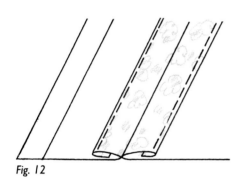

Fig. 11

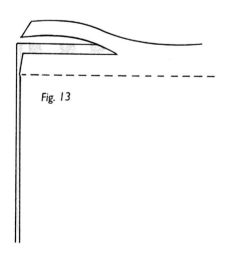

Fig. 12

Fig. 13

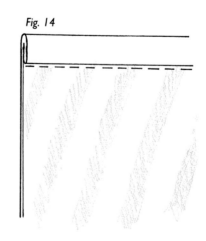

Fig. 14

Lapped seam (fig. 10)

Press under 1.5 cm on one edge of one fabric. Pin it on to the right side of the second piece of fabric, 1 cm from the raw edge. On the right side, machine-stitch along the fold. Pin and stitch again as shown.

Zigzag (fig. 11)

This stitch is most commonly used to neaten raw edges on seams. Select the stitch width and length that best suits your fabric.

Edgestitched seams (fig. 12)

Stitch the seam in the ordinary way (see flat seam) and press open the seam allowances. Turn under 3 mm on both raw edges and stitch close to the folded edge keeping the main fabric free.

Self-bound seams (figs 13 to 14)

This seam is similar to the flat fell seam except that it is not stitched down flat. With the right sides of the fabric facing, stitch the seam as for a flat seam. Trim the seam allowance on one side, back to half its original width. Fold the other seam allowance over it, fold under the raw edge and slipstitch it along the seam line.

Curtains

Curtains

BY CHOOSING THE CORRECT WINDOW COVERING, YOU CAN CONTROL THE
LEVEL OF LIGHT ADMITTED, CREATE VARYING LEVELS OF PRIVACY, REDUCE
NOISE AND, TO A CERTAIN EXTENT, BLOCK OUT HEAT AND COLD.

Over the years, architectural styles have been the major factor in determining the types of windows found in a home. Additions and alterations to a home at different architectural periods will usually result in there being a variety of windows that are rarely uniform in size or shape. This allows plenty of scope for variation in window treatments.

The basic functions of a window are to allow light and air to flow through the house and to keep cold and rain out.

Whilst it is often costly or too difficult to alter the shape or position of a window, the choice and style of your window coverings can transform the look and feel of a room.

Window shapes

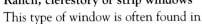

When looking at how to dress a window, it is a good idea to understand the basic window types and how their shape affects the choice of window dressing.

Double-hung window
In this type of window, two sashes move up and down to open and close the window. It is usually the easiest style to decorate and is the one most commonly found in modern homes; more elaborate versions are found in many Georgian period homes. Many different window treatments can be used to complement the double-hung window, including Austrian and Roman blinds.

Picture windows
This style of window is also found in many modern homes where an extensive window is used to frame an outside

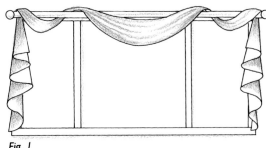

Fig. 1

view, hence the term 'picture window'. Often it is a combination of a large fixed centre window with double-hung windows at the sides for ventilation (fig. 1). Due to the size of picture windows, there are many opportunities for window decoration. Larger scale prints and patterns become much easier to work with on a window of this size. Linings are an important feature when decorating picture windows and remember they can be seen quite clearly from the outside.

Ranch, clerestory or strip windows
This type of window is often found in

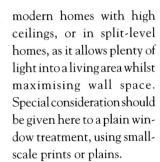

modern homes with high ceilings, or in split-level homes, as it allows plenty of light into a living area whilst maximising wall space. Special consideration should be given here to a plain window treatment, using small-scale prints or plains.

Corner window
To maximise light, two windows may meet in a corner, leaving only a small amount of space in between. Even though you may feel limited in your choices when it comes to dressing these windows, you may be surprised to find there are a number of practical and decorative options available (fig. 2).

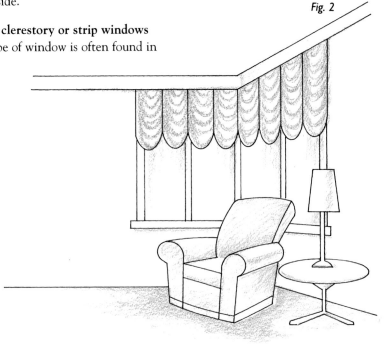

Fig. 2

Bay window

A bay window has three or more windows set at an angle to each other to form an alcove inside. This style of window can be dressed up, using individual decorative treatments for each window, or played down by adopting a uniform style for all the windows (fig. 3).

Dormer window

A dormer window is deeply recessed, often giving the use of a window seat. These windows are a feature of attics and, these days, of upper floor extensions to existing homes. Dormer windows usually require special window treatments, and decorative pelmets can often be used to define the area of a dormer window.

French doors

This elegant window style can take several forms, the most common consisting of a pair of inward or outward opening doors, often flanked by vertical windows. This style is often best treated as an individual window, allowing for a number of options (fig. 4).

Sliding doors

Many modern homes have sliding doors, allowing maximum light filtration and easy access into a garden or courtyard. They require special attention when it comes to choosing coverings that maintain their use as doors but also provide night-time privacy and warmth (fig. 5).

A creative curtain treatment for an unusual window

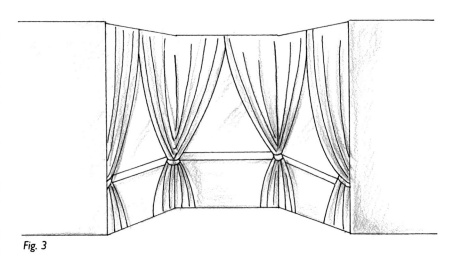

Fig. 3

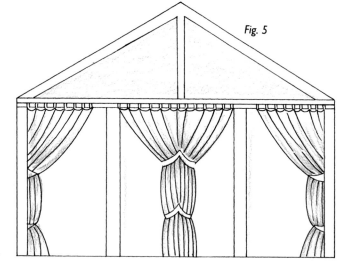

Fig. 5

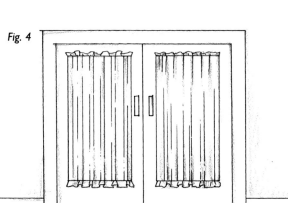

Fig. 4

Tracks & poles

More than ever, the variety of hardware on which to hang, drape and support window treatments is extensive and interesting. From the simple conduit or rod we now have ornate and decorative poles, fashioned from wood, cast iron and brass which add a decorator's touch to your windows.

Choosing the right track or pole is crucial. Never underestimate the importance of the hardware that you use to mount your curtains. There is nothing worse than investing time and money in making a wonderfully sumptuous curtain from expensive fabrics and trims only to find that the flimsy pole you have purchased will not support the weight.

The quality of the hardware you purchase will ultimately determine how your curtain will hang, just as your selection of heading tape will define how it drapes. Remember to match hooks, gliders and finials (those pretty end pieces at the ends of the pole that stop the curtains from sliding off) to the style of the curtain heading tape you have chosen.

Beautiful curtains must sit squarely on accurately positioned fittings. Arm yourself with a retractable fibreglass or metal tape measure and carefully measure the window dimensions, frame size and the distance from the top of the window frame to the ceiling, from the bottom of the window frame to the floor and from the sides of the window frame to the corners of adjacent walls. These measurements are essential when planning special effects; for example, if you wish to create an impression of height on a shallow window, you can do this by hanging long curtains from poles or on tracks raised well above the natural top of the window or even suspended from the ceiling. More on these clever tricks later.

Your choice of curtain poles or tracks will be based on the shape and function of your window, the effect you want to create, and your budget. If a pelmet is to be fitted, select a simple track and a simple heading style for your curtain because both will be covered by the pelmet.

If you live in rented accommodation, you should opt for poles, which are usually less expensive, easier to install and are highly portable. Special extendable poles allow you to change the length of the pole to suit different windows – another plus for rent payers!

Unless curtains are frequently drawn, poles are the answer for heavy drapes which frame a window, or for lightweight privacy curtains. More sophisticated poles may be fitted with drawcords and decorative finials. Prices will vary according to the style you choose.

Tracks range from simple, straight or curved styles to pricier, composite products which can support both curtains and a pelmet. These may have extension brackets to vary the distance between the curtains, the walls and the pelmet. Tracking systems are usually used when two or more window treatments are combined over a single window frame. A combination of a sheer blind, a curtain and a pelmet is an example of a window treatment requiring multiple-tracking systems.

Always anchor poles or tracks firmly with strong brackets screwed to wooden battens, or attached with wall plugs.

If possible, avoid hanging new curtains on old tracks or poles. Choose fittings appropriate to the shape and style of your curtains. Heavy curtains may require special reinforcement, especially if they will be frequently opened and closed.

Purchased kits should contain everything you will need, including extra supporting brackets that are spaced at intervals between the usual end and centre brackets.

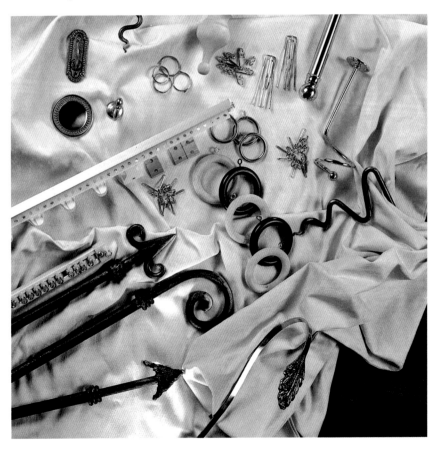

A selection of curtain tracks, rods and hardware

Choose fittings that frame your windows beautifully and do their job reliably. Make sure the track you choose allows heavy curtains to completely retract to maximise light. For recessed windows, select flexible or curved metal tracks which fit the shape of modern bay windows hung with one continuous curtain or three separate ones. Traditional bay windows in three sections separated by wide corner frames can use a single track or three separate curtain poles. Instead of finials (end-stops), fit the last hook to a wall-mounted ring-fitting to hide the ends of the track and to avoid ugly gaps between curtains and walls. Never hang curtains straight across the face of a recessed window; this will darken the room and detract from the charm of a traditional bay or dormer window.

Curtain headings

The finished style of a curtain or blind will depend on your choice of heading tape. Different heading tapes cause the curtain to fall or drape in various ways. You can choose neat pleats for a formal look, soft gathers for a romantic style or a curtain shirred into a flurry of folds for volume and definition.

The choice of tape will also determine how the curtain is to be connected to the rod and what hardware, such as hooks, will be needed. Here we show you how finished heading styles are achieved with certain types of tape as well as which poles and hardware will combine to produce the look you are aiming for. Embellishments such as covered buttons, tabs and bows can then be added to create your own style.

Gathered heading

Simple gathered headings can be achieved with the aid of a standard tape, which gathers in the fabric and is generally used where a pelmet is included in the window-dressing plan. Allow at least one and a half times the length of the track in fabric width. The actual width will depend on the type of fabric and the effect you want to create. Experiment with a piece of fabric before you buy the entire amount. A simple hook is required to connect the curtain tape to the track or ring.

Rod pocket

This provides another way of achieving a simple gathered curtain but without tape or hooks. Although the method of construction is simple, the inclusion of bindings and trims can make the final result quite sophisticated. Allow twice the final length of the rod for the width of your fabric.

A rod pocket curtain

Pencil-pleated

This very popular heading style forms a continuous line of even pencil pleats. The advantage of this style of curtain is that it can be adjusted – either stretched or condensed – if your measurements are not one hundred per cent accurate. Pencil-pleating tape is suitable for most fabric weights and for either tracks or poles. For best coverage, you will need fabric from two to two and a half times the width of the track (figs 1 and 2).

Triple-pleated

A formal style of heading, most commonly used on plain fabrics or where a tailored look is desired. Allow twice the length of the track in fabric width to achieve this style (figs 3 and 4).

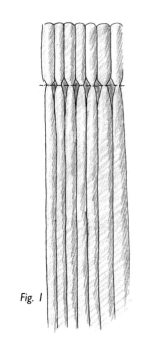

Fig. 1

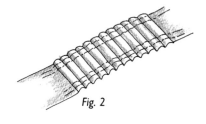

Fig. 2

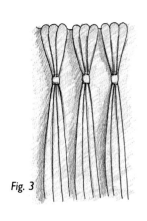

Fig. 3

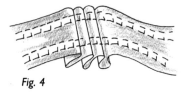

Fig. 4

Cartridge-pleated

Ideal for heavier weight fabrics such as velvets or brocades, cartridge-pleating tape pulls up the curtains into evenly spaced ruched cartridge pleats. To ensure that the two curtains match in the centre of the track, it is important to check the spacing of the pleats. You will need from two to two and a half times the track length in fabric width (figs 1 and 2).

Box-pleated

When this tape is pulled up, the fabric pulls into evenly spaced box pleats, again ideal for heavier fabrics and, like cartridge-pleating, it is necessary to ensure that the pleats are matched across both curtains. To be successful, box-pleating tape requires two and a half times the track length in fabric width (figs 3 and 4).

How much tape?

To determine the amount of heading tape required for your curtains, use the same method as for calculating fabric widths for the style of tape you are using, and allow an additional 10 cm for the turnings at the ends.

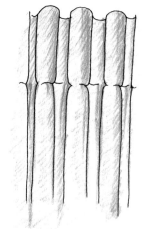

Fig. I

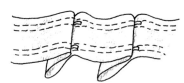

Fig. 2

Fig. 3

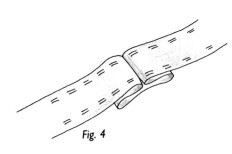

Fig. 4

Measuring up

❖

Measuring up your windows for curtains is a simple process. To accurately complete the job, all you will need is a metal ruler, and notepaper and a pen to take down the measurements. To ensure that accurate figures are recorded, it is better if there are two people to measure for curtains.

If you are installing new tracks or poles, do not measure for your curtains before the tracks or poles are in place. The track should extend up to 30 cm beyond the sides of the window to allow for the curtains to be drawn back during the day.

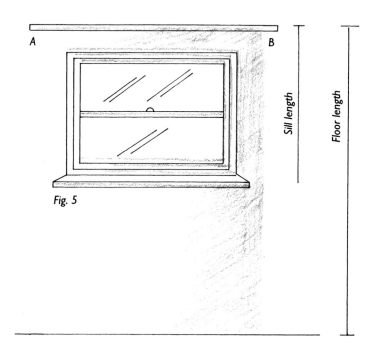

Fig. 5

The width

Measure the exact length of the track or pole between the two points between which the curtain will drape (A and B) – do not measure the window (fig. 5).

If the track or pole has overlaps or returns, measure from the edge of the returns to the end of the overlap on both the right- and left-hand sides.

The drop

The drop or length of your curtains is a matter of personal preference. However, in the majority of cases there are three obvious lengths to choose from: sill length; below sill length; or floor length (fig. 5).

Curtains should finish approximately 1 cm above the sill or 2.5 cm from the floor. The drop should be measured from the top of the curtain track or, if using a pole with rings, from the underside of the ring (fig. 6).

A plain fabric needs no pattern matching

Fig. 6

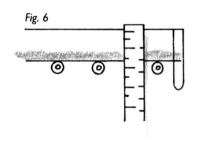

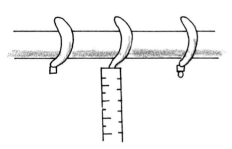

Fabric yield

How much fabric do you need to purchase? Having made a decision as to which rod or track type to use and the style of your curtains, it is now time to work out how much fabric you will require to complete the project.

First determine the pattern repeat (see page 17). The supplier's tag should be attached to the roll of fabric and should state the size of the repeat. If not, the assistant in the soft furnishings department should be able to assist you.

Always check your calculations twice and feel free to show them to a soft furnishings expert where you originally purchased your fabric. They will be only too happy to give you their professional advice. Remember to give them the length and style of your pole or track, as well as the curtain drop required, to ensure they have all the necessary information.

If you are still unsure about your measurements, it is always best to buy an extra half metre of fabric, which could get you out of a jam. If the fabric is not required for the curtain, it can always be made into a cushion or a trim, or even used for coordinating tiebacks.

Plain (unpatterned) fabric

Where you have a plain fabric, you have no pattern to match, so calculations are easy to make, following the steps below.

To calculate the total length of fabric required when there is no pattern match, use the following measurements:

1 Total width = finished width + side hem allowance + any joining seam allowance + allowance for fullness

2 Number of fabric widths required = total width/fabric width (always round this figure up to the next whole number; for example, six and a half = seven)

3 Fabric cut length = finished length + hem allowance + top heading allowance + 2.5 cm for squaring or ravelling ends

4 Total fabric required = cut length x the number of fabric widths

Patterned fabric

Correct pattern match will ensure that the finished design running across your window is uniform.

The calculation method is the same for steps 1 and 2 as for unpatterned fabrics; however, in step 3, determining the cut length is a bit different. To do this, look at how many times the pattern is repeated down a width so that each width can be cut and matched accurately. Again, always purchase that extra half metre of fabric to get you out of trouble if required.

To calculate the total fabric required for a patterned fabric, use the following measurements:

1 Total width = finished width + side hem allowances + any joining seam allowances + allowance for fullness

2 Number of fabric widths required = total width/fabric width (always round this figure up to the next whole number; for example, six and a half = seven)

3 Number of repeats required for each cut length = cut length/pattern repeat length (round this figure up if the answer is a fraction)

4 Adjusted cut length = the pattern repeat x number of repeats required for each cut length + allowances for hem and heading

5 Total fabric required = adjusted cut length x number of widths required

Linings

❖

Linings add substantially to the luxurious appearance necessary for good window treatments and also provide a fuller look for maintaining a soft drapable hand.

When you are selecting a fabric, consider the function it will perform. If your home fronts on to a major thoroughfare, you will want to ensure that noise is eliminated or blocked somewhat. A heavy, close-knitted or woven fabric will act as an insulator and, given the extra volume of lining,

noise will be even further reduced.

As with fabrics, there are a number of lining options to be considered:

• Does your fabric need to be lined?
• Does your window face early morning or afternoon sun?
• Is the curtain purely decorative?

Unlined pattern fabrics or sheers can provide interesting illusionary effects when light is filtered through them, providing a dappled warm feeling to a room. However, linings add many benefits to a finished curtain. Firstly, linings provide a luxurious look to a good window treatment and

Linings can be attached at the curtain heading

help to provide better draping qualities and maintain a fuller pleated look. A lined curtain provides uniformity to the exterior appearance of a home whilst allowing a variety of decorative choices such as patterns, weaves and colour variation to be used inside. Whilst sunlight and air pollution have varying effects on the colour of a fabric, a lining will help to combat these elements, thereby helping to keep the inside of your home warmer during the cooler months, cooler during the summer and your fabric looking fresher for much longer. The extra fabric will absorb some of the noise of your teenager's stereo; no doubt an added bonus for your neighbours.

There are two major types of linings:

tightly woven one hundred per cent cotton lining, which comes in a variety of neutral tonings and in the same widths as your fabric; and a lining with a coating made from particles of aluminium, which may be flocked to give it good draping properties. In addition there are block-out linings which consist of layers of coatings with a layer of grey aluminium particles sandwiched in between for light diffusion. These linings are excellent for bedrooms, especially for shiftworkers needing to sleep at odd hours; for windows that face the afternoon sun; in nurseries; or in commercial applications, such as hotels, where complete sun block-out may be required throughout the day.

As well as loose linings, it has become an increasing trend for fabrics to come with their own coating, flocked directly on to the back of the fabric. The bonus is that you only need to handle one layer of fabric while sewing, but the curtain will still have the drape, handling and insulating qualities of one with a lining.

Linings can be attached in a number of ways. One way to attach a loose lining to a curtain is with a lining tape known as pocket tape. The tape splits in half, with one half being sewn to the lining and the other half, which contains small pockets, sewn to the curtain fabric. Hooks are passed through both tapes, fastening the lining to the curtain. This arrangement also means that drapes and linings can be easily separated for cleaning.

Bagging out the curtain fabric with a lining is another popular method of attaching linings. Here heading and side hems are sewn together as for a bag, and the bottom hems are treated separately. This is an ideal method to add weights into lining and hems for the ultimate professional look.

Pattern matching & joining panels

❖

To match patterns

1 Cut the first fabric piece from the length of the fabric, placing the beginning of a pattern repeat at the top edge, and lay it flat on a table (fig. 1). Mark the pattern repeat with two pins or tailors chalk and fold under the selvages.

2 Before cutting the second length of fabric, find the beginning of the next pattern repeat and measure your required length from this point, allowing for any necessary seam allowance above this point.

3 Fold in the selvages and baste the two pieces together so that the repeats are matching. Continue, adding as many lengths as you require in this way.

4 Trim the top and bottom edges to be even at the correct length when all the lengths are joined.

Joining panels

Ideally, fabric panels should be joined in such a way that the stitching is as unobtrusive as possible.

1 Place the two panels together with right sides facing. Stitch them together with a 1.5 cm seam and press the seam flat (fig. 2).

2 Trim the seam allowance on one side back to 3 mm and turn in 3 mm on the raw edge of the other seam allowance (figs 3 and 4).

3 Press the folded edge over to the seam line on the other fabric piece, enclosing the raw edges. Slipstitch the folded edge over the previous stitching (fig. 5).

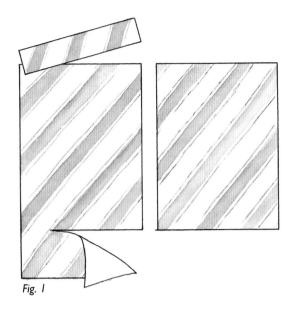

Fig. 1

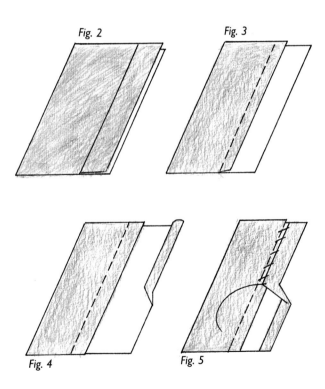

Fig. 2

Fig. 3

Fig. 4

Fig. 5

Scale & proportion

Less-than-ideal room or window proportions can be improved through the use of visual effects. While this particularly applies to paints and wallpaper, you can also contribute greatly to the effect by choosing the right fabric and style for your curtains.

A narrow window can be made to look wider by extending the curtain track or pole for 30 to 60 cm on each side (fig. 1). To diminish the size of a too-large window, pull the curtains back to the sides of the sill in a graceful drape and secure them with interesting tiebacks or bows (fig. 2). To avoid covering a wall-mounted heater or air conditioner, either stop the curtains at the lower sill length or permanently fix drapes to either side of the window, using a pull-down blind for privacy (fig. 3).

Window heights can appear to be increased or decreased with the aid of a pelmet. To add height to a too-short window, mount the pelmet 15 cm above the top window frame, making sure the depth of the pelmet covers the frame and the heading tape on the curtains. Deep pelmet boxes will also diminish the height of a too-tall window when fixed snugly on to the window frame (fig. 4).

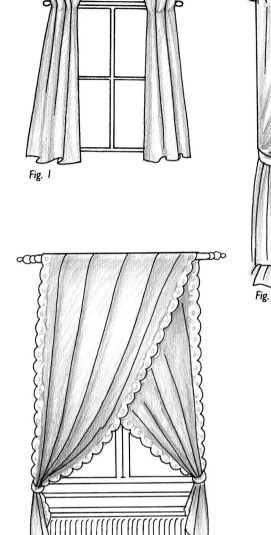

Fig. 1

Fig. 2

Fig. 3

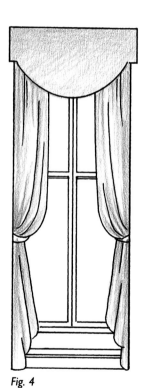

Fig. 4

The pelmet has been fixed at a greater height than usual to give the appearance of a taller window

Unlined Curtains

THE SIMPLEST OF ALL CURTAINS ARE THE ROD POCKET AND
GATHER TAPE UNLINED CURTAINS.

Rod pocket curtain

Before you begin Back-coated fabrics are not suited to this style of curtain, because over time the coating can stick to the metal rod due to the effects of heat and moisture, sometimes causing the backing to peel away.

Measuring
To calculate the total width of fabric, double the length of your rod and add 1.5 cm for each joining seam and 2.5 cm for each side hem. If your curtain is to consist of two panels opening at the centre, divide the total width by two. Determine the length of the curtain by measuring from 2.5 cm above the top of the rod (or the point you

wish your heading to commence) to the point where your curtain will finish. Add an additional 12 cm for the bottom hem and 10 cm for the heading and casing. Calculate the amount of fabric you will require, following the guide on page 41 and taking into account any additional fabric required for pattern matching (see page 42).

MATERIALS
sufficient fabric
matching sewing machine thread
sufficient 12 cm wide contrasting bias-cut fabric to bind the edges of your curtain
pins
scissors
tape measure
sewing machine

Method

1 Cut the number of drops required to achieve the total width. Cut off the selvages. Pin, then stitch the drops together with a flat fell seam. Press.
2 Turn in and press 1 cm on one long edge of each curtain panel (the edge that will be the outer edge of the curtain), then turn in and press another 1.5 cm. Pin and stitch the side hem. Press.
3 Press in 1 cm on both sides of the bias-cut fabric. Fold the bias strip over double with the wrong sides together and pressed edges even. Press.
4 Pin the folded bias strip over the remaining raw side edge of each curtain panel (the one that will be the inner edge of the curtain). Turn in the raw

A rod pocket curtain is quick and easy to make

edges at each end of the binding. Pin, then stitch, catching both sides of the bias in the seam.

5 Measure the diameter of your rod. Turn in and press 1 cm at the top edge of your curtain, then turn in and press another 9 cm. Stitch along the folded edge. This line of stitching will fall underneath the rod.

6 Stitch a second line of stitching the diameter of the rod plus 1 cm above the row just stitched to form the casing. Slip the rod into the casing and adjust the gathering before you hang the curtain. Hang the curtain and leave it for a day or two before you hem it.

7 Once your curtain is in position, determine how long you want it to be. Remember, if the curtain is to be pulled or tied back on each side, allow a few extra centimetres. Mark the hem while the curtain is hanging. You can machine the hem or slipstitch it in place by hand. Either way, it is a good idea to take the curtain down, turn in and press the hem first, then sew it by your preferred method.

Distribute the gathering evenly

Gather tape curtain

Before you begin Laces, voiles and sheers are ideal fabrics for use with gather tape. Gather tape is not recommended for heavier fabrics where the more durable pencil-pleating tape would be a better choice and will achieve the same look.

Gather tape is suitable for unlined curtains or small windows where there is not much fabric to add bulk and weight to the curtain. However, a loose cotton lining can be added and coated fabrics can also be used.

Measuring

To determine the total width of fabric you require, measure the length of your rod. Multiply that figure by two or, for greater fullness, by two and a half, to give you the total width, then add 1.5 cm for each joining seam and 2.5 cm for each side seam. If your curtain is to consist of two panels opening at the centre, divide the total width by two. To determine the length of the curtain, measure from the top of the rod to the point where you wish your curtain to finish, then add 12 cm for the bottom hem and an additional 6 cm for the curtain heading.

Calculate the amount of fabric you will require following the guide on page 41 and taking into account any additional fabric required for pattern matching (see page 42).

You will need the same length of tape as the total fabric width plus 10 cm for turnings.

MATERIALS
sufficient fabric
matching sewing machine thread
sufficient gather tape and appropriate hooks
pins
scissors
tape measure
sewing machine

Fig. 1

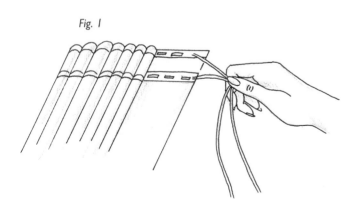

Fig. 2

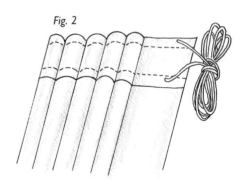

Method

1 Cut the number of drops required to achieve the total width of your curtain. Cut off the selvages. Pin, then stitch the drops together with a flat fell seam. Press.

2 Turn in and press 1 cm, then turn in and press another 1.5 cm on the outside edges of the curtain. Pin and stitch the side hems. Press.

3 Turn in and press 2 cm at the top edge. Position the gather tape on the wrong side of the fabric, 2.5 cm from the folded edge. Pin the tape in place, folding in the raw edges of the tape at each end. Stitch the tape into place. Knot the cords together at one end of the tape. Pull up the tape from the other end, forming folds (fig. 1).

4 Hang the curtains in place. Once you are happy with the width and the amount of gathering, tie off the cords (fig. 2). You can also cut off any excess cord to avoid bulk.

5 If the curtain has a loose weave, such as Indian cotton, allow it to hang for a day or two before hemming, then mark the hem at your desired length. Take the curtain down. Turn in and press 2 cm, then turn in and press another 10 cm at the bottom edge. Stitch the hem in place and press.

Above right: The lace Austrian blind is made in exactly the same way as the Austrian blind on page 84

Far right: A close-up of the gather tape

Right: Detail of the gather tape curtain heading

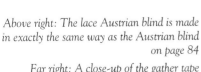
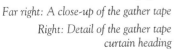

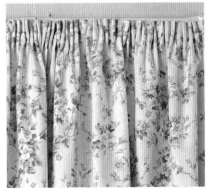

Tie-on Curtains

TIE-ON CURTAINS ARE IDEAL IF YOU HAVE DECORATIVE POLES WHICH YOU WANT
TO FEATURE AS PART OF THE OVERALL EFFECT OF YOUR WINDOW SETTING.

Before you begin In the method set out below, the curtain is bound on the sides and the top edge with a co-ordinating fabric. Again, the combination of colour, print and texture will determine the final effect. The ties were made from a second coordinating fabric.

Measuring

To calculate the total width of fabric you will require, measure the length of your rod. Multiply that figure by two and a half and add 1.5 cm for each joining seam and 2.5 cm for each side seam. If your curtain is to consist of two panels opening at the centre, divide the total width by two. Determine the length of the curtain by measuring from 2.5 cm above the top of the rod (or the point where you wish your heading to start) to the point where you wish the curtain to finish. Add 12 cm for the bottom hem and another 10 cm for the curtain heading.

MATERIALS
sufficient fabric
two contrasting fabrics for the borders and the ties
matching sewing machine thread
sufficient gather tape
split rings, plastic or metal, one for every 10 cm of tape used
tailors chalk
pins
tape measure
scissors
sewing machine

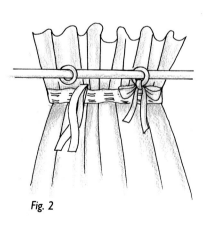

Make the ties from matching or contrasting fabric

Method

1 Cut the number of drops required to achieve the total width of the curtain. Cut off the selvages. Pin, then stitch the drops together with a flat fell seam. Press.

2 Cut two 23 cm wide strips, each the same length as the panel. Turn in and press 1 cm on both the raw edges of the strips. Press the binding over double with the wrong sides together. Pin the binding over the raw edges of the curtains, sandwiching the curtain between the folded edges of the binding. Stitch through all thicknesses.

3 Cut a strip 10 cm wide and bind the top edge of the curtain in the same way as the sides, turning in the raw edges at each end.

4 Pin the gather tape to the top of the wrong side of the curtain, 8 cm from the top. Stitch into place with two rows of machine-stitching.

5 Cut bias fabric, 10 cm x 22 cm, for the ties. Fold each length over double with the right sides together and the raw edges matching. Stitch the long side and one end closed in a 1 cm seam. Turn to the right side and press. Slipstitch the remaining end closed.

6 Fold the ties in half then pin them, evenly spaced, across the back of the curtain, approximately 1 cm from the top of the heading tape (fig. 1).

7 Pull up the heading tape to the desired width. Tie the cords, then cut off any excess tape and cords. Attach the

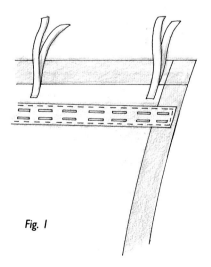

Fig. 1

Fig. 2

curtain to the rings with the ties tied into bows (fig. 2).

8 Once the curtain is in place over the window, determine the final length. If the curtain is to be pulled back to the sides, add a few extra centimetres to allow for this. Mark the hemline with the tailors chalk or pins, then take down the curtain. Turn in and press 2 cm on the raw edge, then turn in and press another 10 cm. Stitch along the first fold by hand or by machine. Slipstitch the ends closed. Press again.

Tie-on curtains have a delightfully informal look

Lined Curtains

CURTAINS CAN EITHER HAVE A LOOSE LINING, ATTACHED AT THE
HEADING, OR A DETACHABLE LINING.

Pinch-pleated curtain with loose lining

Before you begin Usually, no pelmet is required with this heading as it is an attractive finish in its own right. Often found in lounge or formal dining rooms, pinch-pleated curtains can be used wherever you are looking for a neat, tailored finish. Loose linings are the perfect partner.

The method for loose linings is somewhat different to detachable linings in that the lining is fixed, before the heading tape is applied. Back-coated fabrics provide an alternative to loose linings and create less bulk. They also halve your sewing time.

To make the fabric-covered rod, glue matching fabric around a wooden pole with craft glue. Add a pair of colour-matched finials to complete the picture. With a little imagination, a piece of dowel can be converted into this delightful feature.

There are two types of pinch-pleating tapes: one has cords which when pulled up form neat pinch pleats, the other has a series of slots to hold pronged hooks which form the pleat.

Measuring

To determine the total width of fabric you require, measure the length of your rod. Multiply that figure by two and a half to give you the final width, then add 1.5 cm for each joining seam and 2.5 cm for each side seam. If your curtain is to consist of two or more panels, divide the total width by two or the appropriate number. To determine the length of the curtain, measure from the top of the rod to the point where you wish your curtain to finish. Add an additional 12 cm for the bottom hem and an additional 6 cm for the heading. Calculate the amount of fabric you will require, following the guide on page 41, and taking into account any additional fabric required for pattern matching (see page 42).

The same amount of fabric will be required for the lining, except that you will not need to allow any extra fabric for pattern matching.

You will need the same length of tape as the total fabric width plus 10 cm for turnings.

Lined, pinch-pleated curtains have a generous appearance

Top: Hang the curtain with colour-matched rings

Above: Pinch-pleating tape draws up the lining and the fabric together

MATERIALS
sufficient fabric and lining
matching sewing machine thread
pinch-pleating tape and appropriate hooks
tape measure
pins
scissors
sewing machine

Method

1 Cut the number of drops required to achieve the total width of your curtain. Remember to cut an even number of drops for both panels. Cut off the selvages. Pin, then stitch the drops together with a flat fell seam. Press. Cut and join the lining pieces in the same way.

2 Turn in and press a double hem on the bottom of the lining so that the lining is 10 cm shorter than the planned finished length of the curtain.

3 Centre the lining on the wrong side of the curtain fabric. Pin the two layers together and from now on treat them as a single layer. Turn in and press 1 cm, then turn in and press another 1.5 cm on the sides of the curtain and of the lining. Pin and stitch the side hems. Hem the top edge in the same way.

4 Do not stitch the bottom hem of the curtain until the final hem adjustment is made.

5 Pin the tape to the top edge of the fabric, on top of the lining, folding under the raw ends of the tape. Stitch down the top and bottom edges of the tape.

6 If the tape is the one that pleats, knot the cords together at one end of the tape and pull the cords up, forming the pleats. If the tape is the slotted type, insert the pronged hooks. Both styles of tape will result in the same effect.

7 Hang the curtains in position. If the curtain is a loose-weave fabric, such as Indian cotton, allow it to hang for a day or two before hemming, then mark the correct length. Take down the curtain. Turn in and press 2 cm at the bottom edge, then turn in and press another 10 cm. Stitch the hem by hand or machine. Press.

Pencil-pleated curtain with detachable lining

Before you begin Quite often, where pencil-pleating tape is used the heading will ultimately be covered by a pelmet.

Pencil-pleating tape has three positional placings where hooks can be inserted to adjust the length of drop, if necessary.

Detachable linings provide the body and protection your curtain needs and, most importantly, detachable linings are quick and easy to remove for cleaning. They can be incorporated quite simply in most curtain treatments.

Measuring

To determine the amount of fabric required, measure the length of your track or rod. Multiply that figure by two or, for greater fullness, by two and a half, to give you the total width, then add 1.5 cm for each joining seam and 2.5 cm for each side seam. If your curtain has two panels opening at the centre, divide the total width by two. To determine the length of the curtain, measure from the top of the rod to the point where you wish your curtain to finish. Add an additional 12 cm for the bottom hem and an additional 6 cm for the heading. Calculate the amount of fabric you will require, following the guide on page 41 and taking into account any additional fabric required for pattern matching (see page 42).

The same amount of fabric will be required for the lining except that you will not need the allowance for pattern matching.

You will need the same length of tape as the total fabric width plus 10 cm for turnings.

MATERIALS
sufficient fabric and lining
matching sewing machine thread
pencil-pleating tape and appropriate hooks
small hooks for attaching the lining
pins
scissors
tape measure
sewing machine

Method

Curtain

1 Cut the number of drops required to achieve the total width of your curtain. Remember to cut an even number of panels for both sides if your curtains open in the centre. Cut off the selvages. Pin, then stitch the drops together with a flat fell seam. Press.

2 Turn in and press 1 cm, then turn in and press another 1.5 cm at the sides of the curtain. Pin and stitch the side hems. Press.

3 Turn in and press 2.5 cm on the top edge. Pin the tape into place along the top edge of the fabric, covering the raw edge, folding in the raw edges of the tape at each end. Stitch the tape into place. Knot the cords together at one end of the tape. Do not pull up the tape if you are adding a detachable lining.

Detachable lining

1 Cut and join the lining drops to be the same width and length as the cut size of the curtain. Make the side hems in the same way as for the side of the curtain.

2 Turn in the raw edge on the top of the lining and attach the lining heading tape to the top of the lining in the same way as for the curtain. Pull up the tapes on both the curtain and the lining. Tie off the ends but do not cut them.

3 Attach the lining to the bottom row of the pencil-pleating tape with the small hooks. Make any adjustment to the length of the tape on the curtain or lining.

4 Hang the curtain and lining on your track or rod. Allow the curtain to hang for a day or two before hemming. Mark the curtain hem. Take down the curtain and pin up both hems, having the lining hem 2.5 cm shorter than the outer fabric. Turn in and press 2 cm then turn in and press another 10 cm at the bottom edge of both the curtain and the lining. Cut off any excess length on the curtain or the lining tape. Stitch both hems. Press.

Above and left: This pencil-pleated curtain has a detachable lining

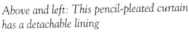

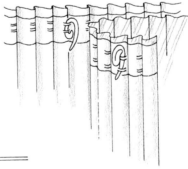

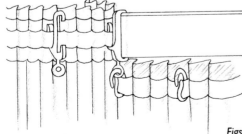

Figs 1 and 2: Two main types of tape for detachable linings

Café Curtains

THIS SIMPLE METHOD OF WINDOW DRESSING WILL AFFORD PRIVACY AND AT THE SAME
TIME ALLOW PLENTY OF LIGHT TO ENTER THE ROOM.

Before you begin Café curtains can be casual or formal, soft and feminine or dramatically contemporary, depending on the fabric you choose. Plain fabrics can be stencilled, appliquéd or braid-trimmed.

The method for making a café curtain has remained the same over the years, but with the increasing sophistication of decorative fabrics – such as chintzes, fine laces and linens – and the creative use of embellishment the café curtain has come of age.

Placement of rods

Before you begin making your café curtains, consider your window frame and then decide on how best to place your rods. Do you need total privacy or would you like to allow light to shine through and to be able to see out? Consider whether you want your curtains to overlap each other, giving an undulating effect down the window. You can create space between your curtains and highlight your rods by finishing the upper curtain 1 cm above the lower rod. This is particularly successful when working with special headings, such as a scalloped heading.

Windows with café curtains look better if the window is divided equally into halves, thirds or quarters.

If you have more than one vertical tier of curtains and privacy is paramount, overlap the bottom of the upper curtain over the lower curtain by about 8 cm. In this case, install the top rod then measure from the top of the rod (or from the bottom of the rings, if rings are to be used) to the finished length of the bottom curtain. Divide this length by the number of tiers of curtains you are planning. If you plan a double tier, divide that length by two and mark this position on the window frame. Measure upwards from this mark for 8 cm. This point is the position for the second rod. If you are planning three tiers, divide the length into thirds. Mark the point for each rod 8 cm up from the two lower markings.

If privacy is important, but you want to highlight the decorative details, such as scallops, follow this method for mounting the rods to give you a perfect fit. Mount the top rod with a ring on it.

Rings are essential for scalloped curtains so measure the distance from the bottom of the rings to the finished length of the bottom tier. Divide this length by two or three, depending on the number of tiers. These are the positions of the bottom of your second and third rows of rings. Place the second rod at a suitable height above the second point (depending on the size of the rings) and position the third rod (if there is one) in the same way.

When a certain amount of privacy is desired, but you would still like to be able to look out over the bottom curtain, install spaced or graduated café curtains. Mount the top rod to the top of the window frame. Measure how long you would like the decorative pelmet curtain to be by measuring from this rod. Measure from the bottom point of the decorative pelmet curtain to the point where you wish the bottom curtain to finish. Divide this measurement in half and fix the second rod at that point for the best proportioned effect.

Hardware for café curtains

Hardware for café curtains need not be expensive. Covered wire casings with small hooks at either end can be used to mount café curtains on to your window frames. They remain hidden under the fabric folds of the finished curtain.

As with regular straight-drop curtains, it is best to install the rods or wires before hanging the curtains.

Above left: This café curtain makes clever use of the fabric pattern

Left: The rod pocket heading is perfect for café curtains

Basic café curtains

Before you begin

To calculate the total width of fabric, measure the length of your rod or wire. Double that length and add 1.5 cm for each joining seam and 5 cm for each side hem. For a two panel curtain, opening at the centre, divide the total width by two. Determine the length by measuring from the bottom of the rings to the point where you wish the curtain to finish. (See page 53 for more on rod placement.) To this measurement add 15 cm for the bottom hem and 5 cm for the top hem.

This café curtain is hung on rings on café curtain wire

MATERIALS
sufficient fabric
café curtain wire and hooks or a rod
round split rings or hooks (you will need one for every 10 cm width of fabric)
matching sewing machine thread
tailors chalk
pins
scissors
tape measure
sewing machine

Method

1 Cut the number of drops required to achieve the correct width. Cut off the selvages. Make sure you cut an even number of drops for each side of the curtain, if it is to open in the middle. Pin and stitch the drops together with a flat fell seam. Press.

2 Turn in and press 7.5 cm at the bottom edge, then turn in and press another 7.5 cm. Pin and stitch the bottom hem in place by hand or machine (fig. 1).

3 Turn in and press 2.5 cm on the sides, then turn in and press another 2.5 cm. Stitch the side hems (fig. 2).

4 Measure the finished length of the curtain from the bottom hemline up to the top. With the tailors chalk, mark a dotted line along the right side of the fabric at this top point. Mark another dotted line 5 cm above the first line. Trim any excess fabric above this second line (fig. 3).

5 Turn in and press 2.5 cm on the top, then fold again so that the curtain will finish on the top dotted line. Stitch the hem in place and press.

6 Mark 10 cm intervals along the top of the curtain. Handsew a ring to each marking.

Scalloped café curtains

Before you begin

Scalloped café curtains are a stylish way to dress a window. Unlike other curtain styles they require less fullness – only one and a half times the rod length instead of the usual twice.

For a feminine feel, add decorative bows for attaching the curtain, rather than the traditional rings, or try sewing a number of shells or buttons to the top of your curtain for a fresh summer look. Sew eyelets into your tab headings and then twine a length of coloured cord through the eyelets and over the rod for a country look that's sure to please.

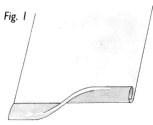
Fig. 1

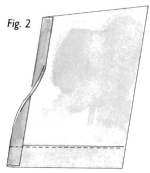
Fig. 2

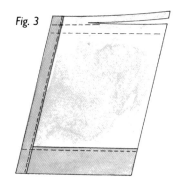
Fig. 3

Measuring

To work out how much fabric you will need, follow the instructions for the basic café curtains, adding 10 cm for the heading and another 15 cm for the bottom hem. Allow 2.5 cm for each side hem. If you need to join panels to achieve the desired width, don't forget to allow 1.5 cm for both sides of the joining seams. If your curtain is to consist of two panels opening at the centre, divide the total width by two.

MATERIALS
sufficient fabric
one hoop ring for every 10 cm of curtain length and one for each end
glass or cup
firm plastic or cardboard for a template
pencil
tailors chalk or dressmakers tracing wheel
matching sewing machine thread
pins
tape measure
scissors
sewing machine

Method

1 Cut the number of drops required to achieve the total width of your curtain. If your curtain is to open in the middle, make sure you have an even number of drops in both panels. Cut off the selvages. Pin and stitch the drops together with a flat fell seam. Press.

2 Turn in and press 5 mm on the sides, then turn in and press another 1 cm. Stitch the side hems.

3 Turn in and press 7.5 cm at the bottom edge, then turn in and press another 7.5 cm. Pin and stitch the bottom hem in place by hand or machine.

4 Make a template or pattern for the scalloped edge, using the glass or cup. Our glass had a 10 cm diameter and we allowed 2 cm between each scallop. It is easier if you make a paper pattern with five or six scallops, rather than trying to use the cup for each scallop

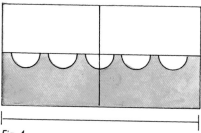
Fig. 4

individually. You may need to make a slight adjustment if you do not have room for a complete scallop at each end (fig. 4).

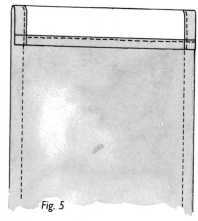
Fig. 5

5 Turn in and press 5 mm at the top edge and then turn in and press another 5 mm. Stitch into place.

6 With the right sides together, fold the top of the curtain over for 9 cm and press. Pin the fold in place or slipstitch the sides together for extra stability (fig. 5).

7 Pin the template on the fold line of the fabric with the flat edge of the scallops lying along the fold. Trace around the scallops with the tailors chalk or the tracing wheel. Remove the template (fig. 6).

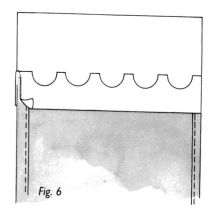
Fig. 6

Graceful scallops decorate this café curtain. Team it with a ruffled valance gathered on a pole for a more formal look

8 Stitch along the marked lines. Cut out the scallops, cutting 5 mm outside the stitching. Trim and clip the seam allowance to just above the stitching (fig. 1).

9 Turn the curtain right sides out and press carefully. Slipstitch the side and bottom edges of the scalloped panel to the curtain.

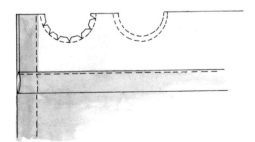

Fig. 1

10 Attach rings to the top edge at each peak. Sew a ring to each end. If you prefer a prettier look, make ties or cut ribbons and sew them to the top of the curtain in pairs (fig. 2). If using ribbons, allow 30 cm for each ribbon tie.

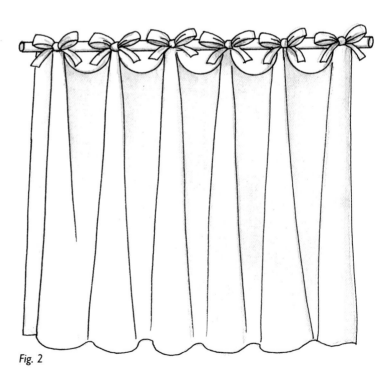

Fig. 2

Sash Curtain

Before you begin

Sash curtains are stretched between two rods or curtain wires. In such an arrangement, the lower rod or wire keeps the fabric from catching when the window is opened and closed. Sash curtains such as these are ideal for French doors and casement windows. The headings can be varied, but the simplest of all styles is the rod pocket style shown here.

Measuring

To calculate the total width of fabric you will require, measure the length of the rod or wire. Double that length to allow for gathering and add 1.5 cm for each joining seam and 2.5 cm for each side seam. If your curtain is to consist of two panels opening at the centre, divide the width by two and then add the hem allowances. The only additional measurement you will need is for the depth of the curtain. Don't forget to allow for the circumference of the rod plus 12 cm for top and bottom hems.

MATERIALS
sufficient fabric

two café curtain wires or rods, and attachments

matching sewing machine threads

tailors chalk

pins

scissors

tape measure

sewing machine

Method

1 Cut the number of drops required to achieve the total width of the curtain. Cut off the selvages. If your curtains are to open in the middle, make sure you have an even number of drops in each panel. Join the drops together with a

Left: Sash curtains, like these, are also ideal for French doors

flat fell seam. Press.

2 Turn in and press 5 mm on the raw side edges. Turn in and press another 2 cm. Stitch the side hems.

3 Working on the wrong side of the fabric, turn in and press 3 cm on the lower raw edge. Turn in and press another 3 cm. Stitch close to the first fold. Check for an accurate fit by measuring from the top of the bottom pocket to where the bottom of the top pocket is to be. Mark this point across the curtain width with the tailors chalk. Cut the fabric 6 cm above this line. Make a double hem as for the bottom pocket, turning in and pressing 3 cm each time. Stitch along the marked line.

4 Insert a rod or wire into each pocket (fig. 3). Adjust the gathers evenly.

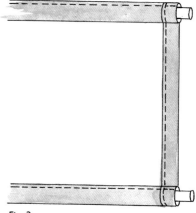

Fig. 3

Right: This rod pocket café curtain and valance is made in exactly the same way as the one above, omitting the bottom rod pocket

Decorator Scarf

A DECORATOR SCARF IS MADE FROM TWO LENGTHS OF COORDINATING FABRICS THAT CAN BE DRAPED ACROSS A CURTAIN ROD TO GIVE A VERY ELEGANT LOOK.

Before you begin

Simple to make, the scarf can be trimmed with tassels, braid or piping to add a little formality. If the contrast of the fabrics is dramatic enough, no embellishment is necessary. We used two coordinating fabrics with a decorative fringe trim.

Measuring

To calculate how much fabric you will need, use the following formula: The width of the window plus twice the desired side length plus 1 m draping allowance for every 2 m of pole length. You will need fabric this length and about 60 cm wide. For this reason, 120 cm or 150 cm wide fabric is ideal because you can cut down the length of the fabric to double your fabric yield.

MATERIALS
sufficient main fabric and the same amount of coordinating fabric
sufficient decorative fringing
matching sewing machine thread
pins
scissors
tape measure
sewing machine

A decorator scarf gives a very elegant look to a formal dining room

Method

1 Cut the fabric down the centre, lengthways, to give you two pieces. Join them with a flat fell seam to achieve the correct length. Repeat this step for the coordinating fabric.

2 Place the main fabric and the coordinating fabric together with the right sides facing. Cut both ends to form diagonals, taking care to cut the diagonals in opposite directions.

3 Remove the coordinating fabric. Pin the fringing down one long side of the scarf, leaving a 2 cm overhang at both ends. Work on the right side of the main fabric and have the straight edge of the fringing matching the raw edge of the fabric. Baste. Repeat for the short ends.

4 Place the coordinating fabric on top of the main fabric with the right sides together and all the raw edges matching. Using the zipper foot on your sewing machine and starting halfway down the untrimmed side, stitch all around the scarf through all thicknesses and leaving a 30 cm opening for turning. Keep your stitching as close to the fringing as you can. Snip into the corners so that you will have sharp points at the corners of the scarf. Trim the excess fringing. Turn the scarf through to the right side, taking care to turn the corners out neatly. Press. Slipstitch the opening closed.

5 Drape the scarf over the pole and around the finials, leaving even amounts of fabric to fall from both ends of the pole.

Curtain Trims

UP TO NOW WE HAVE BEEN LOOKING AT BASIC CURTAIN STYLES, BUT THEY
CAN ALL BE EMBELLISHED TO GIVE A PERSONAL TOUCH.

The inside edge of a curtain can often be made a feature of a straight-drop curtain. With just a little imagination, you can give a very professional finish to your curtains using ruffles, piping and braids. These are just a few of the ways you can individualise your curtains.

Ruffles Attach a self-fabric ruffle or a contrast ruffle, using a plain chintz or a smaller print fabric, to the inner edges of your curtains. (See the section on ruffles on pages 23 and 24.)

Double ruffles Usually the outer ruffle is a self-fabric one with the inner one being plain or contrasting with the main fabric (fig. 1).

Piping and ruffles In this case, the piping is usually made in a colour which appears in the pattern and that you

wish to highlight. The ruffle could be in a self-fabric or in another, more dramatic, plain colour. (See the section on ruffles on pages 23 and 24 and the one on piping on page 21.)

Flat trim This kind of trimming is usually made from a contrasting fabric, but you can achieve a very interesting effect by cutting a bias strip of the main curtain fabric and using that as the trim. The trim width can be varied according to your personal preference (fig. 2). (See the section on making and attaching bias strips on pages 20 to 21.)

Inset trim An elegant row of braiding can be stitched directly on to the curtain, 3 to 5 cm in from the edge of the curtain (fig. 3).

Other decorative embellishments, such as fancy braids and cords, can also

be added to the inner edge of your curtain. Check the display at your local soft furnishings speciality store. You will be amazed at the variety of colours, styles and finishes to choose from. Some of these trims can be very costly but often only a small amount can give a special lift to a plain curtain in an inexpensive fabric. Well worth the cost!

When you are planning to add these extra touches to your curtains or drapes, purchase a sample piece of the braid or make a short length of ruffle and pin it into position to see if you are happy with the effect before you purchase the whole amount. As well as these relatively simple solutions, you can give a touch of drama to your curtains with a row of tassels, such as the decorator scarf on page 58.

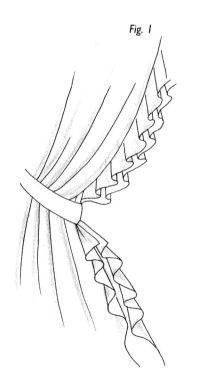

Fig. 1

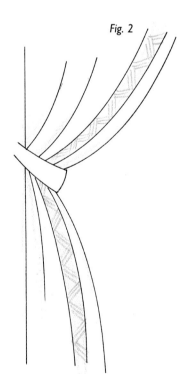

Fig. 2

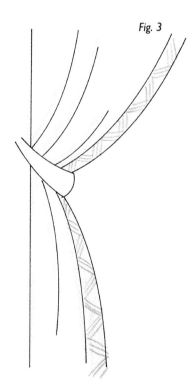

Fig. 3

Swags and Tails

THIS WINDOW TREATMENT IS STYLISH YET SIMPLE.

Before you begin

Two shaped curtains are caught back to reveal the contrasting fabric beneath and a swag is draped across the top of a pole or board and stapled into position.

This type of arrangement is commonly known as a dress curtain because when hung it is not adjustable; the curtains cannot be opened or closed. However, with the addition of a second pole underneath the swag, the curtains could be drawn back and forth. Alternatively, you can hang a sheer curtain or blind, if you want more privacy.

Measuring

To calculate the total width of fabric and lining required, measure the length of your pole. This style of curtain looks best when two panels are drawn back to each side, so if you use the length of the pole for the width of each panel this will give you a generous allowance for gathering. If you need to join drops to achieve the required width, add 1.5 cm for each joining seam allowance.

To determine the length required for your curtain, measure from the top of the pole to where you want the curtain to finish, allowing for the drape to each side and adding 12 cm for the bottom hem and 10 cm for the heading.

MATERIALS
two contrasting fabrics (main fabric and lining) plus fabric for the swag

contrasting bias binding tape or self-fabric bias

matching sewing machine thread

paper to make a paper pattern

pencil

steel ruler

tape measure

staple gun and staples

mounting board

pins

scissors

sewing machine

Method

Swag

1 Measure the width of the window to be covered and add half this length again. Measure the depth of the swag by holding a fabric tape measure at one end of the top of the mounting board, draping it to the desired length and bringing the tape back up to the other end of the top of the pole. Allow an extra 5 cm for stapling along the top edge. This measurement is the depth.

2 Cut a rectangle twice the depth of the final depth required plus 6 cm. Fold the rectangle in half, widthways, placing the fold at the bottom, and draw the shorter edges up on each side, forming soft folds as you go.

3 Sew a line of basting stitches along the top edge to hold the folds in position (fig. 1). Pull up the basting until the swag fits the mounting board. Secure the stitches.

4 Turn in and press the raw edges at the top and staple the swag to the mounting board.

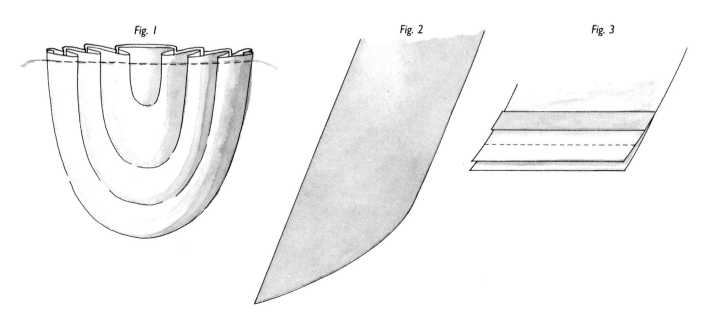

Fig. 1   Fig. 2   Fig. 3

NOTE: Several swags may be used across the width of a window, overlapping the edges of each swag as you work along the board. Hanging curtains from a rod or track mounted under the board will allow the curtains to be opened and closed.

Curtain tails

1 To make a paper pattern for your curtain tails, draw in the shape, marking in a gentle curved line on the inner edge (for the right-hand side) starting just above windowsill height down to the left-hand side of your pattern to the point where you wish the tail to end on the left-hand side (fig. 2).

2 Using the pattern, cut out two pieces of the main fabric so that the longest side of the pattern is always running up and down the frame of the window, making sure you cut a right- and a left-hand side tail. Repeat the process for the lining fabric.

3 With the wrong sides facing and using a 1.5 cm seam allowance, stitch one main fabric and one lining piece together along the straight and curved long edges.

4 At the top edge, turn in and press 1 cm on the raw edge.

5 Bind the curved edge and then the straight edges around the curtain tails with purchased or self-fabric bias binding that you have made yourself (fig. 3). If you wish to make a dramatic statement with this binding, make it quite wide, but if you wish it to be more unobtrusive, make the binding narrower. (See pages 20 to 21 for how to make and apply bias binding.)

6 Staple the top edge of the tails to the top of the mounting board over the ends of the swag.

Above: A pretty floral is the perfect choice for this swag and tails arrangement

Left: For a more dramatic effect, choose a strongly contrasting colour and fabric

Tiebacks

TIEBACKS ARE BOTH PRACTICAL AND DECORATIVE, GIVING A DECORATOR'S TOUCH TO YOUR WINDOW TREATMENT. THE RIGHT TIEBACK CAN ADD LIFE AND COLOUR TO A PLAIN WINDOW TREATMENT.

Tiebacks offer a great opportunity for creative use of braids, ribbons and tassels. Plain fabric tiebacks can be painted with stencilled motifs which are echoed on the walls. Tiebacks can be imaginative and even a touch outrageous. In the right setting, a tieback trimmed with a collection of coloured glass beads or appliquéd with felt motifs will add a touch of fun. For a festive effect, wind some fine wire around holly or silk flowers, then attach the garland to a standard tieback.

Braid and tassel tiebacks are very expensive, but with a little imagination you can make your own from the selection of braids and trims at your haberdashery shop. The flow of the line of a loose-knotted tieback will be a very pleasing complement to a swag.

The size of the tieback should also be considered; the larger the tieback, the greater the impact it will have. It is also important to keep in mind the weight which the tieback will be holding back. If your curtain is a heavy fabric, line your fabric tiebacks with stiffening or interfacing for extra support.

Remember to allow enough fabric in the body of your tieback to hold the drape in place without bunching up the drape fabric or creasing it too much.

A tieback is generally attached to a hook at windowsill height on each side of the window. The length of the loop which attaches it will vary according to the size of the hook. When the hook is small, the loop need only be about 10 cm long. If the loop has to fit over a tieback with an ornate heading, the loop will need to be somewhat longer.

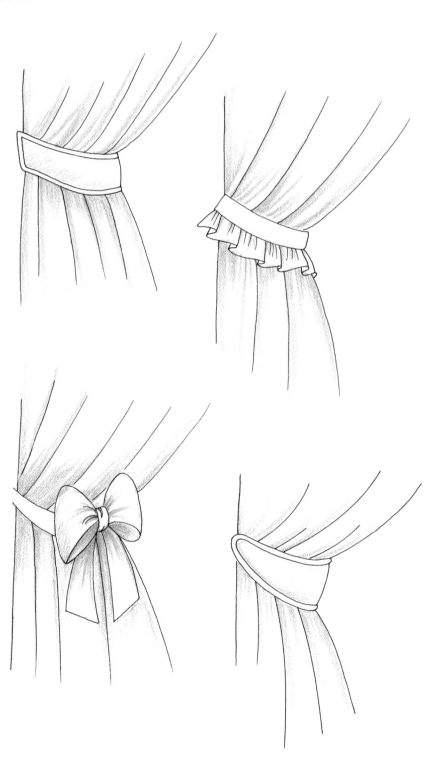

Shaped piped tieback

Before you begin

This is the basic method for making a lined tieback. Braids, piping and other accessories can be added.

Fusible interfacing is used to give the tieback stability and support, especially for larger tiebacks or where there is a lot of fabric weight to be supported.

The finished size of this tieback is 11 cm x 59 cm. Make appropriate adjustments to the length or width to suit your own drape and window.

MATERIALS
25 cm fabric
25 cm fusible interfacing
sufficient contrasting piping to bind all the edges of the tieback
sufficient 6 cm wide bias strip for two loops with a finished size of 4 cm x 15 cm plus 1.5 cm on each loop for turnings
matching sewing machine thread
pins
cardboard for the template
felt tip marker pen
tailors chalk
scissors
turning hook or knitting needle

Method

1 Draw the shape of the tieback at the size you need on to the cardboard with the marker pen, following the illustration given here (fig. 1).

2 Using the template, cut out two fabric pieces and one interfacing piece for each tieback. Cut two bias strips for the loops.

3 With a warm iron, fuse the interfacing to the wrong side of one of the fabric pieces.

4 Pin the piping around the fabric piece without interfacing, with the right sides facing and the raw edges matching. Clip the seam allowance of the piping to allow it to bend smoothly around the curve (fig. 2). Baste the piping in place.

5 Place the interfaced fabric on the piped fabric with the right sides facing and the raw edges matching. Pin, then baste. Clip the seam allowances at the curves for ease.

6 Stitch through all thicknesses with the zipper foot on your sewing machine, stitching as close as possible to the piping and leaving a 5 cm opening for turning. Trim the seam allowance. Turn the tieback through to the right side. Slipstitch the opening closed.

7 Fold the bias strips for the loops over double with wrong sides together. Stitch the long sides. Turn through to the right side. Fold each strip into a loop and slipstitch one to each end of the tieback on the wrong side and 2 cm in from the end.

The simplest of all lined tiebacks, this one is still very effective

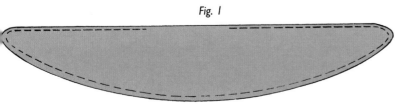

Fig. 1

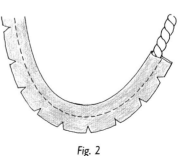

Fig. 2

Ruffled tieback

Before you begin To calculate how much fabric you will need for the ruffle, see the section on ruffles on pages 23 and 24. The finished size of this tieback is 11 cm x 59 cm. Make adjustments to the length or width to suit your own drape and window.

MATERIALS
25 cm main fabric
25 cm fusible interfacing
sufficient ruffle fabric for all the edges of the tieback, approximately 15 cm x 120 cm
four metal rings, 2 cm diameter
matching sewing machine thread
pins
cardboard for the template
felt tip marker pen
tailors chalk
scissors
sewing machine
turning hook or knitting needle

Method

1 Draw the shape of the tieback at the size you need on to the cardboard with the marker pen, following the diagram given here (fig. 1).

2 Using the template, cut out two fabric pieces and one interfacing piece for each tieback.

3 With a warm iron, fuse the interfacing to the wrong side of one of the fabric pieces.

4 Cut a strip for the ruffle to the desired size; it should be at least twice the total measurement around the outside edge of the tieback. If you need to join pieces to achieve this length, don't forget to add 1.5 cm for each seam allowance. Fold the ruffle strip over double, lengthways, with the right sides facing. Press. With the right sides facing, stitch the ends of the strip together to form a

The ruffling on this tieback adds a charming detail

circle. Turn the ruffle to the right side.

5 Stitch two rows of gathering, one row 5 mm and the other row 7 mm from the raw edge. Pull up the gathering to fit around the outside of the tieback. Pin the ruffle to the right side of the main fabric piece without the interfacing, with the raw edges matching. Baste (fig. 2).

6 Pin the interfaced fabric piece over the one with the ruffle with the right sides facing. Baste. Stitch, leaving a 10 cm opening on the longest edge for turning. Clip the seam allowances for ease (fig. 3). Press. Slipstitch the opening closed.

7 Slipstitch one metal ring to each end of the inside back of each tieback.

Fig. 1

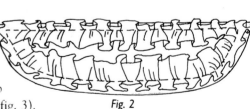

Fig. 2

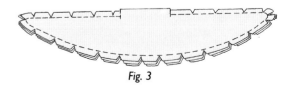

Fig. 3

Appliquéd tieback

Before you begin Fusible interfacing can be used to give the tieback stability and support, especially for a larger tieback or where the fabric drapes to be supported are heavy.

MATERIALS
25 cm main fabric
25 cm fusible interfacing
20 cm contrasting fabric
four metal rings
matching sewing machine thread
pins
cardboard for the template
pencil
scissors

Method

1 Draw the shape of the tieback to the required size, using the cardboard and pencil. Cut out the shape to use as your template.

2 Using the template, cut out two main fabric pieces and the interfacing for each tieback.

3 Make a second template 3 cm smaller all around than the first template. Cut one piece of the contrasting fabric, using the second template, for each tieback.

4 Fuse the interfacing to the wrong side of one main fabric piece. Pin the two main fabric pieces together with the right sides facing and the raw edges matching. Stitch around the outside edge, leaving an opening for turning. Clip the seam allowances at the curves for ease. Trim the seam. Turn the tieback through to the right side and slipstitch the opening closed.

5 Pin the contrasting fabric piece to the centre of the main tieback so that both right sides are facing out. There should be an even amount of the main fabric showing all around the edges of the contrast fabric. Baste, then satin stitch the contrasting piece on to the main fabric through all thicknesses. Trim any excess fabric and sew another row of zigzag stitches if necessary.

6 Slipstitch one metal ring to each end of each tieback.

The unusual edging effect has actually been achieved with appliqué

Pelmets

PELMETS ARE ANOTHER WONDERFUL WAY TO FINISH OFF A WINDOW TREATMENT.

A pelmet can cover an unattractive curtain track, add interest to a dull window, or alter the shape and proportion of a window to better suit your room. Whether you choose a simple ruffle or a padded and shaped buckram pelmet, you will enjoy the decorative effect as well as the practical benefit.

Choosing the right shape and style of pelmet to complement your curtains and your room is a matter of assessing the proportions of your room and window and the look you wish to achieve.

Ruffled piped pelmet

Before you begin This pelmet is attached to the window frame on a wall-mounted track, and does not require any additional hardware. Allow enough fabric for the returns (sides), so that the fabric covers the entire tracking system.

Measuring

To calculate how much fabric you will require, measure the track and the returns and double this figure. If you need to join pieces to achieve this length, add 1.5 cm for each seam allowance and 2.5 cm for each side hem.

Decide on the depth of your pelmet after considering the proportions of your window and the type of fabric you are using. If your fabric has a printed border, take advantage of this feature and incorporate it into your design.

The amount of pleating tape will be twice the length of your curtain rod or track plus 5 cm for side hems.

MATERIALS
sufficient fabric
sufficient contrasting piping
sufficient pleating tape
matching sewing machine thread
pins
sewing machine
tailors chalk
tape measure
scissors
*hooks or rings, one for each pleat
or every 10 cm of tape*

Method

1 Cut and stitch the fabric widths together with a flat fell seam to achieve the length required. Press. Turn in and press 5 mm, then turn in and press another 2 cm on both sides. Stitch and press the side hems. Turn in and press 2.5 cm on the top edge.
2 Pin the tape into place along the top edge on the wrong side of the fabric,

A ruffled pelmet is the perfect addition to a nursery curtain

covering the raw edge. At one end, fold under the raw edge of the tape and knot the cords together.

3 Stitch the tape in place with two rows of stitching, one at the top of the tape and one at the bottom. Do not pull up the tape.

4 Place the piping along the bottom edge of the right side of the pelmet fabric, so that the raw edges are matching. Using the zipper foot on your sewing machine, stitch as close to the piping cord as possible.

5 Cut the ruffle strip to the desired length, joining pieces if necessary. With the right sides together, fold the ruffle over double, lengthways. Stitch across the ends and trim the seam allowance

before turning the ruffle back through to the right side.

6 Stitch two rows of gathering, one 5 mm and the other 7 mm from the raw edge, catching both layers of fabric. Pull up the gathering to fit the bottom edge of the pelmet.

7 Pin the gathered ruffle over the piping, with the right sides facing and the raw edges matching. Stitch along the previous stitch line, using the zipper foot of your sewing machine. Trim the seam allowances, if necessary. Press.

8 Insert the hooks or rings in the pelmet tape. Draw up the cords to fit the pelmet track, tie off the cords and cut off the excess.

If the pelmet is on a separate track, you can open and close the curtain beneath the pelmet

---

Pelmet with jumbo piping

Before you begin This pelmet shape was cut from craft wood, and the fabric and wadding was applied over the wood. Follow the instruc-for measuring and calculating fabric quantities given for the buckram pelmet on page 68.

MATERIALS
piece of 16 mm thick craft wood, the desired width and 30 cm deep, for the front piece
two pieces of 16 mm thick craft wood, 15 cm wide x 30 cm, for the side pieces
pencil
two L-brackets and screws
bullet-head nails and hammer to join the sides of the box to the front
jigsaw
large sheet of paper for the pattern
felt tip marker pen
sufficient fabric

10 cm wide piping
piping cord, size 10
two pieces of fabric, 15 cm x 30 cm, to cover the inside of the box sides
sufficient 30 cm wide wadding
staple gun and staples
all-purpose glue
spray adhesive

Method

1 Draw the shape of your pelmet on to the large sheet of paper, using the grid pattern method to enlarge the pattern given here to fit the size of your pelmet.

Match a brightly coloured pelmet to a blind for an all-over effect

Draw up a grid the same length as your mounting board and with suitably sized squares. Now copy into each square that part of the pattern which appears in the corresponding square of the small grid pattern (fig. 1).

2 Draw the pattern on to the front piece of the pelmet box. Using the jigsaw, cut out the shape of the pelmet.

3 Using the bullet-head nails, make up the box so that the sides are butted to the front.

4 Cut out the wadding and the fabric roughly to the size and shape of the box. Glue the wadding to the sides and the

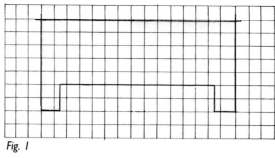

Fig. I

front of the box. Trim away any excess wadding.

5 Spray adhesive over the back of the fabric and glue it over the wadding. Trim the fabric, leaving a 5 cm allowance extending on all sides.

6 Staple or tack the fabric to the inside

of the box, pulling the fabric quite taut over the wadding. Trim any excess fabric bulk.

7 Turn in and press 1 cm around the raw edges of the contrasting fabric pieces for the side panel linings. Glue the folded edges in place inside the box.

8 Glue or staple the piping to the inside edge of the front of the pelmet box. You can cover the staples with a length of masking tape, if you wish.

9 Attach the box to the wall with the L-brackets.

Buckram pelmet

Before you begin

A buckram pelmet is fixed to a mounting board made of particle board or craft wood, depending on the weight of the pelmet. The pelmet is fixed to the board with Velcro tape, allowing it to be easily taken down for cleaning.

The pelmet is most effective when it is padded and quilted in any one of a number of quilting patterns.

As for all drapes, the mounting board for a buckram pelmet should be installed first. You will need a piece of board 16 mm thick x 15 cm deep x the width of the window frame plus an extra 6 cm on each side of the window frame. You will need two right-angled brackets to mount the board on the wall (fig. 2).

Simplicity is the key to quilting. If you are working with a large print, use a simple quilting pattern; if working with a plain fabric, use a more elaborate quilting design. Outline quilting some of the elements of the features of a fabric print is very effective.

Measuring

Measure the required width and depth of your pelmet. To measure the width of your pelmet, add the front width B plus the returns (sides) A plus 5 cm on each side for the lug returns; the lugs stop the sides of the pelmet from splaying. The finished depth of a pelmet should be approximately 30 to 40 cm. Add 2.5 cm to the length for turning.

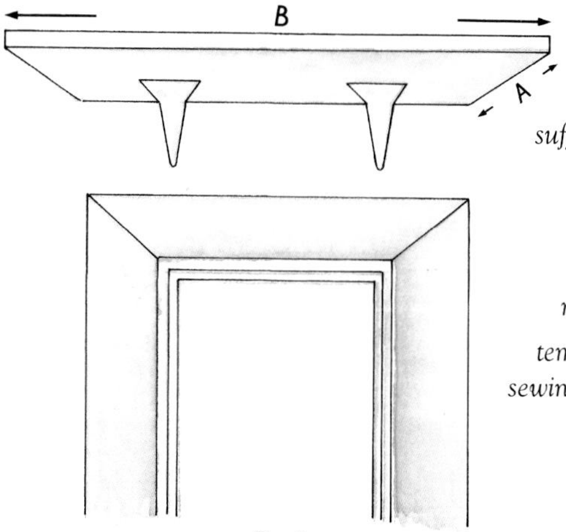

Fig. 2

Another advantage of the buckram pelmet is that the fabric can be turned sideways, so that no seams or joins in the fabric are necessary. There are a few instances when the actual print on the fabric makes this impossible, but by turning your fabric sideways you will see if you can make it work.

MATERIALS
mounting board

screws

electric drill

two right-angled brackets

sufficient fabric and an equal amount of 100 g fibrefill wadding

cotton lining

tailors chalk

matching sewing machine thread

template of the quilting pattern (your sewing machine may even have a program for special quilting patterns)

sewing machine

tape measure

scissors

Velcro

fabric glue or staples and a staple gun

The simple checked fabric makes a charming statement in these country-style pelmets

Method

1 Screw the corner brackets securely to the wall; an electric drill makes the job a breeze. The board can be painted or some of your pelmet fabric glued or stapled over it, if you wish. Place the mounting board on top of the brackets and secure it in place.

2 Cut the fabric, wadding and lining to the desired size. For a 30 cm finished depth, you will need to quilt up 40 cm of fabric and you will need to add 10 cm to the length. Place them together with the lining on the bottom, face down, then the wadding and finally the fabric on top, facing upwards. Pin all the layers together securely, then baste them together around all the edges and at 10 cm intervals across the width of the fabric.

3 Transfer the quilting design to the fabric and quilt it by hand or machine.

4 Cut the quilted fabric to the correct length for the pelmet plus 1 cm on each end for turnings.

5 Turn in 1 cm on the short sides and 2.5 cm on the bottom edge. Stitch the turnings in place.

6 Attach the hook side of the Velcro tape to the front edge of the mounting board with glue or staples. Pin the loop half of the Velcro to the top edge of the wrong side of the pelmet. Stitch both the top and bottom edges of the Velcro in place along the length of the pelmet. If necessary, press the pelmet before attaching it to the mounting board with the Velcro tape.

Draped rectangular pelmet

Before you begin

Determine the depth of your pelmet; ours measured approximately 30 cm finished size. To this measurement, add 1.5 cm for the bottom hem and 5 cm to the top for stapling to the mounting board. Cut the width of the pelmet 1 m wider than the width of your window, allowing a 50 cm drop on either side. Add a further 3 cm for hems. It may seem wasteful but it is best to cut the entire length in one piece so there are no visible joins. If you are making two or three pelmets, cut the fabric through the width.

MATERIALS

sufficient main fabric
50 cm main fabric for the bias strips
sufficient contrasting fabric
scissors
matching sewing machine thread
tape measure
sewing machine
pins
staples and staple gun, or thumb tacks
16 mm thick mounting board cut to the width of your window and 15 cm deep
two L-brackets
screws
electric drill or screwdriver

Method

1 Decide on the height of the pelmet and attach a mounting board at that height above the window.

2 Cut the main fabric and the contrasting fabric in two strips to the required length and width. Place the two fabrics together with right sides facing and the raw edges matching. Stitch down one long side, then turn it through to the right side. Press the fabric so that all the raw edges are now matching.

3 Make sufficient continuous 6 cm wide bias binding, joining the lengths with flat seams. (See pages 20 to 21 for how to make continuous bias binding.)

A simple draped pelmet lined with a contrasting fabric can tie a colour scheme together

4 Turn in and press 5 mm on both long sides of the bias binding, then press the bias binding over double with the wrong sides together. Pin and stitch a length of the bias binding over the long raw edge, then bind the two short ends, folding under the raw ends.

5 Centre the pelmet on the mounting board, ensuring that equal lengths drape down either side. Use the staples or thumb tacks to attach the top of the pelmet to the board, 5 cm in from the front edge. At the corners, fold the pelmet into three soft folds and secure these in place with staples or tacks.

❖

Rod pocket pelmets are so easy to make

Rod pocket pelmet

Before you begin To calculate the total width of fabric you will require for the pelmet, measure the length of your rod. Double that length to allow for gathering and add 1.5 cm for each joining seam and 2.5 cm for each side hem. Add 10 cm to the length for the casing and 6 cm for the bottom hem. The length should suit the size of the window. This one is approximately 40 cm.

MATERIALS
sufficient fabric
matching sewing machine thread
pins
scissors
tape measure
sewing machine

Method

1 Cut the number of drops required to achieve the total width of your pelmet. Cut off the selvages. Pin, then stitch the drops together with a flat fell seam.

2 Turn in and press 1 cm, then turn in and press another 1.5 cm on the side edges. Pin and stitch the side hems.

3 Measure the diameter of your rod. Turn in and press 1 cm at the top edge of your pelmet, then turn in and press another 9 cm. Stitch along the folded edge; this line of stitching will fall underneath the rod. Stitch a second line of stitching the diameter of the rod plus 1 cm above the row just stitched, to form the casing.

4 Turn in and press 1 cm on the bottom edge, then turn in and press another 5 cm. Pin and stitch the hem into place.

5 Slip the rod into the casing and adjust the gathering.

Blinds

BONDED ROLLER BLINDS

ROMAN BLIND

AUSTRIAN BLINDS

TIE-UP BLIND

Blinds

A blind will reflect the sun during the summer and help to stop the heat inside your home from escaping during the winter.

A blind also increases privacy, particularly if it is backed with a stiffened or lined fabric. Where privacy is not required, the blind can be purely decorative when it is made from lace or a lightweight fabric.

Blinds add affordable style to a room and their easy application and relatively low cost mean that seasonal changes become possible.

There are various types and styles of blinds, so finding one to suit your own situation is not difficult. For example, the classic lines of roller and Roman blinds fit well with a contemporary feel. Both blinds use approximately the same amount of fabric and both must be perfectly 'square' in order to hang straight in the window. When lowered, both blinds appear to be flat to the window, but a roller blind virtually disappears when raised, whilst a Roman blind falls into pleated folds, creating a smart geometric look.

Festoons and Austrian blinds, on the other hand, feature folds of fabric that can be used to filter the flow of light. These two types of blinds have lines of gather tape sewn vertically, evenly spaced, across the reverse side of the blind. Thin cords running through the tapes to the top of the blind allow the blind to be pulled up to form elegant swags or scallops. Austrian blinds differ from festoon blinds in that there is an additional row of tape at the top of the Austrian blind and the cords are pulled through it to one side in order to raise and lower the blind.

Your blinds can be simple or very ornate, depending on your choice of trims and finishing treatments. A stencilled motif on a plain roller blind gives it a touch of country charm, whilst a single ornate tassel as the draw cord adds a classic touch to the same roller blind. Ruffles are a great way to trim any gathered blind.

Blinds can be a very practical way to cover your windows. They don't take up a lot of room and are ideal for windows where the covering should only be sill length, such as above a sink or basin, above a desk or in a playroom – any place where there is a working area below the window.

With so many ideas to choose from, take the time to consider them all before making a decision.

Equipment

❖

A good first step when making your own blinds is to make a small drawing of the finished blind. On the drawing, note all the dimensions, including the base hem, eyelet spaces and the size and depth of the mounting board. This small drawing does not need to be a masterpiece, but as long as all the correct measurements are there, it will serve as a handy reference for checking your work as you go.

You will need an adequate working area – large enough to spread your fabric out flat. If the blind is allowed to hang over the edge of table while you are working on it, it may stretch, distorting your final measurements.

As blinds need to be as square as possible, always use a metal ruler and a T-square when marking the pattern.

A dressmakers cutting board will be invaluable for marking the position of pleats, tapes, tucks rings or slats and will also allow you to pin and secure fabric with ease.

Quick-drying tacky fabric glue will allow you to take many short cuts when making blinds. Trims, tapes and facings can all be glued into position, sometimes avoiding altogether the need for sewing. Glue will also keep raw edges from fraying and will hold knots secure.

Fusible webbing is another practical product which will save you a lot of time and effort. Used between two layers of fabric, the webbing fuses and bonds the fabrics when heat is applied, usually with an iron. Fusible webbing can be bought by the metre and cut to any shape or size. It can be used for hemming; for attaching appliqués, trims and braids; and as a stiffening agent for backing. It will be one of your most valuable aids when making roller blinds.

Gather and shirring tapes are sold by the metre in a variety of styles and can be purchased from your local fabric store or department.

*The right blind can add a focal point
to the room*

Measuring for blinds

❖

You must take accurate measurements when making blinds. Even a one centimetre discrepancy can interfere with the smooth running action of the blind or allow light to filter through.

Windows often look to be the same in size at a glance but seldom are; a window frame can even vary in size from the top to the bottom of the window. It is therefore critical that each window is measured separately and carefully.

For roller blinds, first mark the positions where the brackets are to be installed. Note that the mounting position of the bracket foot is not the point from which you take the measurements. It may be best not to mount the brackets at this stage, because you will not know the diameter of the roller until the blind is complete. If this is the case, use the measuring point as your guide.

Mounting blinds

There are three ways to mount roller blinds: inside the recess (A to B), outside the recess (C to D) and from the ceiling. Blinds on tracks are mounted above the window frame.

Blinds hung inside the recess give a tighter fit, allowing less light to escape. If you are going to hang your blinds inside the recess, measure the width and length of the recess. It is a good idea to take measurements at various points inside the recess to ensure that dimensions do not vary significantly.

If the blind is to be mounted outside the recess, you are less likely to be troubled by variations in the window measurement and can compensate more easily for the variations that do exist. When taking your measurements, add at least 7.5 cm on each side to the width of the recess and 10 cm above and below the recess to the length.

When a blind is to be hung from ceiling brackets, it should overlap the window frame by at least 2.5 cm on all sides to avoid gaps.

As a general rule, add 30 cm to the measured length of your window frame to allow for the roll-over so that the blind will not tear when the roller is pulled down. If your roller blind has a decorative finish added to the bottom, allow 40 cm for the roll-over.

Selecting fabrics

Just as for curtains, there are many beautiful fabrics to choose from when making blinds, but the appearance of the fabric is not the only consideration. For roller blinds, the construction of the fabric is also important. A tightly woven cotton is ideal for a bonded blind because it will hang smoothly and roll up evenly. Cotton fabrics are usually fused to a layer of backing for extra stiffness, but there are also

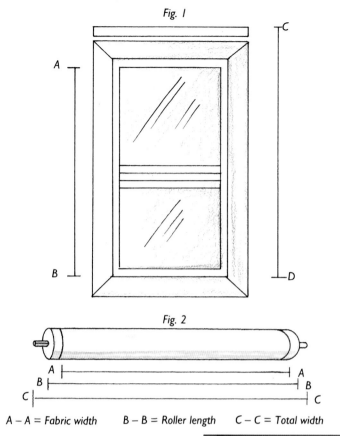

Fig. 1

Fig. 2

A – A = *Fabric width*   B – B = *Roller length*   C – C = *Total width*

fabrics, such as heavyweight chintz, that can be used without lining.

Roman blinds can be made from any cotton fabric of tight construction, but they are especially suited to heavier woven fabrics, such as Indian cottons or jacquards, particularly if the blind is to be unlined.

Austrian and festoon blinds are commonly used to filter light rather than to block it out altogether. Because they are often purely decorative, the range of suitable fabrics is much more extensive. Laces, light voiles, fine cottons and silks are used for soft, romantic effects; cotton chintz, cotton sateens and polyviscose give a crisper, more sophisticated look. Heavy fabrics are not suitable for Austrian and festoon blinds because the weight of the fabric may cause the blind to droop if the tapes and rings are not strong enough to accommodate the weight. Choose a fabric that drapes and gathers well.

Lace makes a lovely soft effect on an Austrian blind. For privacy, add a screening blind or a curtain which can be drawn

Trimming

A simple blind can become a work of art with the addition of a well-chosen braid or trim detail. Contrasting colours on a plain blind will create an interesting focal point; exotic braids will add interesting textures, and ruffles can add a touch of elegance.

It is important to consider the structure of your blind, when selecting a trim. The simplicity and clean lines of a Roman blind should be maintained with simple trimming. A deep border around three sides or a thick braid added only to the bottom hem will give a neat finish. Austrian and festoon blinds, on the other hand, suit a more fussy style with lace trims, tassels and bobbles to emphasise the elegant curved lines.

Bonded blinds lend themselves to interesting shaping on the bottom edge, highlighted with contrasting or coordinating flat braids. Add an elegant tassel for the blind pull, a covered ring or, for a more casual look, a plaited length of contrast fabric can be wound into a knot and a ring sewn behind it.

You can even change the look of an existing roller blind with a little imagination and some clever trimming.

Cut off the bottom of the blind, leaving a raw end (fig. 3). Draw the outline for the new shape onto the blind and cut it out with no allowance (fig. 4). Glue on an attractive braid to follow the shape you have cut, then bind the raw edge with bias binding (fig. 5). Add a new tassel or ring to pull the blind up and down.

Ruffles, braids and contrasting fabrics can all be used to great effect on blinds

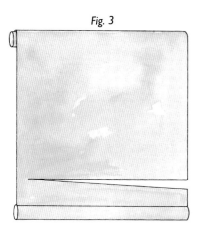

Fig. 3

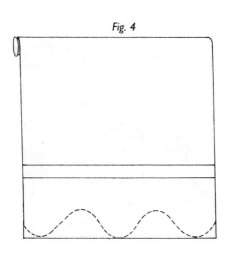

Fig. 4

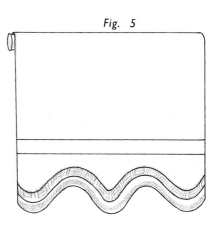

Fig. 5

Bonded Roller Blinds

Before you begin A roller blind kit can be purchased from shops which specialise in soft furnishings and from major hardware stores. The kits contain a roller which encases the winding mechanism or spring (figs 1 and 2). It has a square pin on one end and a round pin and cap on the other end. Once you have established the finished width of the blind, you can cut the roller down to size and fit the round cap.

A wooden or plastic batten which is inserted at the base of the blind for added stability is also included in the kit. If your design requires a second batten, have one cut to the size you need. A cord pull, ring or tassel can be attached to this batten. All kits come with instructions and sometimes diagrams as well. Always read all the instructions before you begin.

The slotted bracket for the square pin should be fitted to the left-hand side of the window and the round bracket to the right-hand side for a conventional roll. In a conventional roll, the fabric comes off the back of the roller, making the blind fit closely to the window (fig. 3). Reverse roll blinds are mounted with the winding mechanism (the square pin end) to the right-hand side. The blind fabric rolls off the front of the blind so that the blind sits slightly out from the window sill, avoiding any handles or locks (fig. 4).

When measuring the positions for the brackets and rollers, measure from tip to tip.

The fabric is fixed to the roller with staples, heavy duty glue or tacks.

Stiffened blind

Before you begin Decide where your blind is to be mounted – inside or outside the recess or on the ceiling. For an inside or ceiling-mounted blind, measure the recess and add 2.5 cm on each side for the side hems and 10 cm for the bottom hem. If the blind is to be outside mounted, add 7.5 cm on each side and on the bottom. If you need to join widths add 1.5 cm for each joining seam. In all cases allow an additional 30 to 35 cm for the roll-over (the fabric can be trimmed more exactly later to fit the roller and window).

MATERIALS
roller blind kit

second batten

sufficient main fabric

20 cm of contrasting fabric the same width as the blind

bias-cut strips of the main fabric for binding the contrast panel and covering the ring

fabric scrap for the pull tab

large wooden ring

spray stiffener

staples and staple gun, tacks or heavy-duty glue

scissors

T-square

metal ruler

tacky fabric glue to prevent fraying (optional)

dressmakers cutting board

sheet of paper as wide as the blind to draw the grid on

tailors chalk

Method

1 Cut the main fabric to the width you have calculated. If you need to join fabric widths, take care to match the pattern carefully, allowing for the 1 cm overlap. Use a flat fell seam for joining.

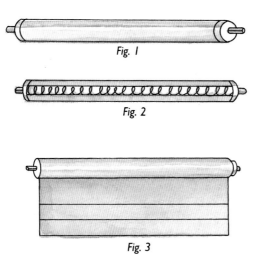

Fig. 1

Fig. 2

Fig. 3

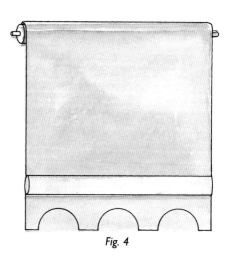

Fig. 4

A simple shape, bias bound, makes a striking finish on a roller blind

2 Turn in and press 2.5 cm on each side. Apply fabric glue if the raw edges begin to fray. Stitch the side hems in place.

3 Apply fabric glue if the bottom edge begins to fray. On the wrong side of the fabric, mark a line 8 cm from the bottom edge, using the tailors chalk and the metal ruler. Lightly spray the area below the mark with stiffener, then fold the bottom edge up to meet this line, forming a casing. Press and stitch the casing in place.

4 On the sheet of paper, draw up a 5 cm squared grid, using the metal ruler and T-square. On the grid, draw the pattern for the bottom edge of the contrast panel. Cut the contrast panel

17 cm x the width of the blind. Place the pattern on the bottom edge of the contrast panel and cut out the shape.

5 Spray the wrong side of the contrasting panel with the stiffener. Allow it to dry. Stitch the side hems as for the main fabric.

6 Make up sufficient bias binding for the bottom edge of the contrasting panel. (See pages 20 to 21 for how to make and apply bias binding.) Bind the lower edge of the contrasting panel with the bias binding, folding in any raw edges and pleating and folding fabric at the corners and curves.

7 Press the fabric well, then spray stiffener on the rest of the blind. Spray again, if necessary, to achieve

sufficient stiffness.

8 On the back of the blind, using the tailors chalk and the metal ruler, mark a line 18 cm up from the bottom of the casing. Draw another line 8 cm above the first one. Fold the fabric so that the lines are matching on the wrong side. Stitch, forming a casing.

9 Cover the wooden ring with a bias strip of the main fabric. For the pull, cut a scrap of the main fabric 10 cm wide. Fold the strip over double with the right sides together and the raw edges even. Stitch down the long side then turn the strip to the right side. Press. Fold the strip around the covered ring, so that the raw ends of the strip are matching. Pin and baste the raw ends to the top edge of the contrasting panel, in the centre.

10 Place the contrasting panel on the blind with the side edges and the bottom corners matching, slipping the contrasting panel under the upper casing. Stitch the top edge of the panel to the blind under the casing, catching the pull strip into the seam.

11 Trim the wooden battens to be 2 cm shorter than the finished width of the blind. Insert the battens into the casings. Stitch over the ends of the casings to hold the battens in place.

12 Place the roller on the front or back of the fabric, depending on whether you want a conventional or reverse roll. Fold over the top edge of the blind and place the folded edge on the marked line and staple, tack or glue into position.

13 Wind up the blind by hand to ensure that the winding mechanism is at the right tension. Screw the mounting brackets to the window frame. Install the blind on the mounting brackets, then pull up the blind to check the tension again. If it is not correct, remove the blind and wind the roller up by hand again.

❖

Lined blind

Before you begin Decide where your blind is to be mounted – inside or outside the recess or on the ceiling. For an inside or ceiling-mounted blind, measure the recess and add 5 cm on each side and the bottom. If the blind is to be outside mounted, add 7.5 cm on each side and on the bottom. If you need to join widths add 1.5 cm on both sides for each joining seam. In all cases allow an additional 30 to 35 cm for rollover (the fabric can be trimmed more exactly later to fit the roller and window) and an additional 10 to 15 cm for the bottom hem if you are shaping the bottom of your blind.

MATERIALS
roller blind kit

sufficient fabric and the same amount of fusible webbing and backing fabric (if the webbing is not wide enough to cover your fabric, use two lengths with a 1 cm overlap)

staples and staple gun, tacks or heavy-duty glue

scissors

T-square

metal ruler

tacky fabric glue to prevent fraying (optional)

dressmakers cutting board

tailors chalk

6 cm diameter metal ring

contrasting fabric, 40 cm x the width of the blind plus 5 cm for turnings and the same quantity of fusible interfacing

contrasting piping

6 cm wide bias binding for the ring pull

Method

1 Cut the fabric to the width you have calculated. If you need to join fabric widths, take care to match the pattern carefully, allowing for the 1 cm overlap. Use a flat seam to join the fabric lengths.

2 Cut the fusible webbing and the backing fabric to the desired size. Join lengths of the backing fabric in the same way as the main fabric, if necessary.

3 Lay the fabric face down on the work area with the webbing in the middle and the lining on top with the right side facing upwards.

4 Press firmly, using a damp pressing cloth to apply additional moisture and create greater steam. Work from the centre to the outsides and allow the fabrics to cool completely before continuing.

5 Using tailors chalk, mark a line 60 cm from the bottom edge on the right side of the main fabric.

6 Fuse the interfacing to the wrong side of the contrasting panel. With the right sides facing and the raw edges even, apply the piping to the top and bottom edges of the contrasting fabric panel.

7 Place the contrasting panel on the right side of the main fabric piece, with the right sides together and the piping stitching line at the top of the contrasting panel matching with the chalk line. Pin and stitch the contrasting panel to the main fabric along this line. Press the contrasting panel down.

8 For the ring pull, fold a length of bias binding in half and stitch down one long side. Thread the metal ring on to the pull and make a knot, leaving the tails of the bias binding free.

9 Turn in and press the bottom raw edge on the contrasting panel. Baste the tails of the ring pull into position under the centre point of the pressed edge. Topstitch the bottom edge of the panel into place on the main fabric, stitching in the piping stitching line and catching the ring pull into the seam. Topstitch along the top piping stitching line in the same way.

10 Turn in and press 2.5 cm on each side edge. Turn in and press another 2.5 cm. Stitch the side hems in place.

11 Turn in and press 1.5 cm on the bottom of the blind, then turn in and press another 8.5 cm. Stitch close to both folds, forming a casing.

12 Trim the wooden batten to be 2 cm shorter than the width of the blind. Slip the batten into the casing. Stitch over the ends of the casing to hold the batten in place.

13 Place the roller on the front or back of the fabric, depending on whether you want a conventional or reverse roll. Place the folded edge of the fabric on the marked line and staple, tack or glue into position.

14 Wind up the blind by hand to ensure that the winding mechanism is at the right tension. Install the mounting brackets on the window frame. Install the blind on the mounting brackets, then pull up the blind to check the tension again. If it is not correct, remove the blind and again wind the roller up by hand.

Right: Use contrasting fabrics and coloured piping for highlights
Below: A colour scheme and fabric that will delight a young child

Roman Blinds

A ROMAN BLIND IS FIXED TO A MOUNTING BOARD OR BATTEN AT THE TOP OF
THE WINDOW FRAME. WHEN RAISED, IT FOLDS INTO SOFT HORIZONTAL DRAPES.
WHEN IT IS LOWERED, IT LIES FLAT AGAINST THE WINDOW FRAME.

Before you begin

The manner of mounting your Roman blind will influence the measurements you take. Roman blinds can be mounted inside the window recess or above the window frame.

You will need a mounting board 16 mm thick x 5 cm deep x the length required for mounting the blind. The board can be painted or covered in fabric if you wish. (See the mounting instructions on page 76.)

Right-angled brackets are used to support the board with screw-in eye hooks spaced evenly at approximately 30 cm intervals along the bottom of the board (fig. 1).

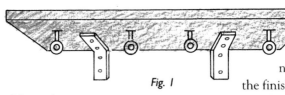

Fig. 1

Measuring

To calculate the amount of fabric and lining required, use the following calculations:

Total width = measured width + 5 cm + 1.5 cm seam allowance on both sides of any joining seam

Total length = measured length + 7.5 cm

If you need to join drops to achieve the total width, allow an additional

Roman blinds give a very neatly tailored finish

1.5 cm on both sides for each joining seam. For the facing, you will need a strip of fabric 12.5 cm x the finished width plus 8 cm.

To determine the amount of cord, add 20 cm to the finished length of the blind and multiply that figure by the required number of vertical draw cords, placing one cord about every 30 cm across the width of the blind. Alternatively, you can purchase threaded ring tape for Roman blinds as a unit.

MATERIALS

mounting board

5 cm thick wooden batten, the same width as the blind

right-angled brackets and screws

screw-in eye hooks (see Before you begin)

sufficient main fabric and an equal amount of cotton lining

strip of cotton lining for the facing

matching sewing machine thread

fusible webbing (optional)

30 to 40 rings

metal ruler

tailors chalk

staples and staple gun, tacks or heavy-duty glue

thin nylon or cotton cord

brass cleat

decorative acorn or toggle

tape measure

pins

scissors

dressmakers cutting board

sewing machine

Method

1 Cut the required number of drops, joining them with flat fell seams to achieve the total width. Press.

2 Lay the main fabric right side down on the cutting board and check that it is square. Turn in and press 5 mm on the side edges, then turn in and press another 2 cm.

3 Lay the lining fabric on top of the main fabric and slip the side edges of the lining under the pressed side hems of the main fabric. Pin the side hems in place over the lining.

4 Place the facing strip on the bottom edge of the main fabric, with the right sides facing and the bottom raw edges even. Note that the facing extends 2.5 cm on each side of the blind. Pin the facing to the blind along the bottom edge, then stitch with a 1 cm seam allowance. Press the facing strip to the wrong side of the blind. Turn in and press the 2.5 cm on each side. Insert a layer of fusible webbing (if you are using it) between the layers and press the extensions into place or sew them into place, if you prefer (fig. 2).

5 Turn in and press the raw top edge of the facing strip, then stitch a 7.5 cm hem. Stitch again 2.5 cm down from the previous stitching to form a casing.

6 Place the blind on the work surface or cutting board with the wrong side up. Determine the positions for the tapes on the back of the blind. Using the metal ruler and the tailors chalk, mark the width every 30 cm, rounding up or down to the nearest whole number to give you the same positions as the screw-in eye hooks in your mounting board. Mark every 10 cm from the top to the bottom of the blind. Mark the folds with a warm iron as guidelines to ensure they remain straight.

7 Cut one tape for each side hem and one each for every marked vertical line across the width of the blind. Make sure that the position of the bottom ring on the tape is close to the rod pocket (fig. 3). Pin the tapes to the blind,

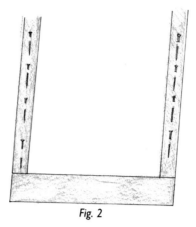

Fig. 2

pinning along the centre of the tapes. Make sure all the tapes are perfectly straight then stitch them into place.

8 Secure the tapes at the bottom ring or tape position with a sturdy knot. Thread the cords up through the tapes or rings to the top of the tape or to the highest ring position, allowing an extra 5 cm at the top. These top positions should all line up across the blind.

9 Take the tapes right up to the raw top edge, placing the last ring 8 cm from the top. On the top edge of the blind, turn in and press 5 mm, then turn in and press another 2 cm, treating the main fabric and the lining as a single layer. Stitch the top hem into place.

10 Attach the blind to the mounting board with tacks, staples or glue.

11 Insert the batten into the casing at the back of the blind. Slipstitch the ends of the casing closed (fig. 4).

12 Thread the cords from the top of the blind, through each of the screw-in eye hooks and over to one side, each time taking the cord across the top edge through each screw-in eye hook as it appears and down the edge of the blind. Knot the cords together at the top. Pull up the blind to check that it works smoothly and make any adjustments necessary before knotting the cords together lower down the blind (fig. 5).

13 Screw the cleat into the window frame. Pass the cord ends through the acorn or toggle and knot them together. Trim the ends close to the knot and pull the knob down to cover the knot. Wind the cord around the cleat to fix the height of the blind.

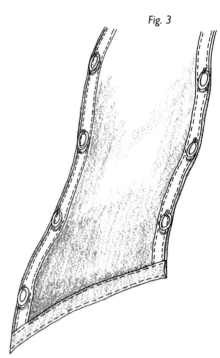

Fig. 3

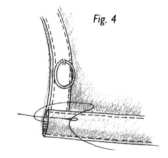

Fig. 4

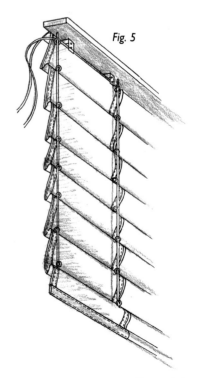

Fig. 5

Austrian Blinds

THE IMPACT OF AN AUSTRIAN BLIND DEPENDS A GREAT DEAL ON THE FABRIC
AND ITS SETTING. EVEN THE SIMPLEST FABRICS, SUCH AS VOILE OR
CALICO, CAN LOOK VERY STYLISH MADE UP THIS WAY.

Before you begin

These blinds are the easiest to make, because accurate measurements are not so important. Austrian blinds should be very full and luxurious – do not skimp on fabric.

There are two types of tape available for Austrian blinds. Both types have rings through which the draw cords are threaded. One type of tape has thin cords on either side which you pull up to gather the blind. The other type has no gathering cords. Check out the blinds shown here or in decorator magazines to help you decide whether you want a gathered or flat effect up the corded lines and this will tell you which tape to buy. Whichever design you choose, the tape and cord quantities are the same.

How far apart you place the vertical tapes will determine the draping effect you achieve. Placing the tape approximately 30 cm apart, will result in small scallops; placing them further apart will produce swag-like scallops. You will require at least three tapes, each one as long as your blind.

MATERIALS
fabric piece, twice the width x twice the length of the window

ruffle strips, 11 cm wide and which when joined should be sufficient for twice the width of the blind

sufficient piping

gather tape, the same length as the fabric width

cord for each tape

brass cleat

sufficient Austrian blind tape

An otherwise uninteresting bathroom window becomes a feature if you add a ruffled Austrian blind

Method

1 Cut the fabric to the required size. If it is necessary to join pieces to achieve the correct width, allow 1.5 cm on each side of all joining seams. Join drops with flat fell seams.

2 Turn in and press 5 mm, then turn in and press another 2 cm on the sides of the blind. Stitch the side hems in place.

3 Mark the tape positions on the wrong side of the fabric. Fold the fabric along these lines and press lightly. Use the pressed creases for guidelines.

4 Join the ruffle strips together to achieve the desired length. Turn in and press 5 mm, then turn in and press another 1 cm on one long edge and the sides of the ruffle. Gather the other raw long edge. Draw up the gathering to fit the bottom edge of the blind. Pin the piping to the bottom edge of the blind with right sides facing and raw edges matching. Pin the ruffle to the blind with the right sides facing and the raw edges matching. Baste. Stitch the ruffle in place through all thicknesses, catching the piping in the seam.

5 Turn in and press 2 cm on the upper edge. Stitch the gather tape along the top edge 1 cm from the top (fig. 1).

6 Stitch the lengths of Austrian blind tape along the pressed guidelines, starting just above the ruffle and finishing just below the top. Make sure you have a cord ring just above the ruffle on each tape (fig. 2).

7 Mount the Austrian blind track. Attach the blind to the track with appropriate hooks.

8 If you are using tape which draws up, draw up the gathering cords on the tape and secure them when the blind is gathered in the way you wish. Secure the cord in the bottom ring on each tape and then thread the cords up through the rings on each tape. Thread all the cords through the brass cleat in the window frame.

A combination of an Austrian blind with a curtain and pelmet offers a great opportunity for creative use of fabric. See how the ruffle on the Austrian blind has been cut across the fabric to make best use of the striped pattern.

Fig. 2

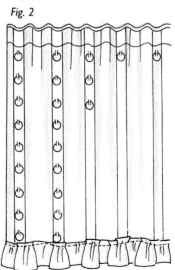

Fig. 1

Tie-up Blind

FOR A LIVING AREA WHERE YOU NEED TO BALANCE A CERTAIN DEGREE OF
PRIVACY WITH ALLOWING THE WARMTH OF THE SUN AND DAYLIGHT TO
ENTER, THIS SIMPLE TIE-UP BLIND COULD BE THE ANSWER.

Charming tie-up blinds can be combined with simple matching curtains for a total window treatment

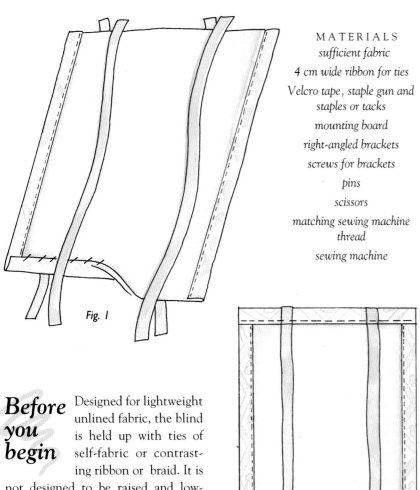

Fig. 1

MATERIALS

sufficient fabric

4 cm wide ribbon for ties

Velcro tape, staple gun and staples or tacks

mounting board

right-angled brackets

screws for brackets

pins

scissors

matching sewing machine thread

sewing machine

Fig. 2

Before you begin

Designed for lightweight unlined fabric, the blind is held up with ties of self-fabric or contrasting ribbon or braid. It is not designed to be raised and lowered frequently and is only suitable for a relatively narrow window.

You will need two ties for each blind. Decide where you wish the ties to be placed. In our blind, they line up neatly with the window frames.

This blind is mounted on a board (approximately 16 mm thick x 5 cm deep x the width of the blind) which is attached to the wall with right-angled brackets. The board may be painted or covered in fabric or lining if desired.

Measuring

The total width of the fabric required must be the width of the window plus 5 cm for each side hem, 5 cm for the bottom hem and 10 cm for the top hem.

Method

1 Turn in and press 1 cm on the sides of the blind, then turn in and press another 4 cm. Stitch the side hems.

2 Turn in and press 1 cm on the bottom hem, then turn in and press another 4 cm. Stitch the bottom hem in place.

3 Mark the position of each tie on both the right and wrong sides of the blind.

4 Cut each ribbon tie to be the length of the blind plus 30 cm for the bows. Lay one tie on the wrong side of the fabric along the guideline and pin it in position. On the front of the blind, pin another tie in the same position (fig. 1). Pin all the layers together down the middle of the tie. Baste through all thicknesses. Stitch down each side of the tie, beginning at the top and ending between one-third and halfway down the blind. The further down the blind you sew the ties, the lower will be the height the blind can be drawn up.

5 Turn in and press 5 cm on the top hem, turning in the ends of the ties at the same time, then turn in and press another 5 cm. Stitch the hem in place (fig. 2).

6 Sew the hook side of the Velcro tape across the width of the top hem. Attach the other half (loop) side of the Velcro to the mounting board with glue or staples. Alternatively, staple or tack the blind directly to the top of the mounting board (fig. 3).

Fig. 3

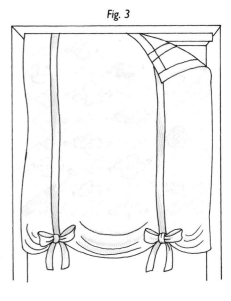

Cushions

PIPED CUSHIONS

HEIRLOOM CUSHIONS

STENCILLED CUSHIONS

BOLSTERS

CHAIR CUSHIONS

ROUND BUTTONED CUSHION

Cushions

A SIMPLE CUSHION HAS THE POTENTIAL TO PULL A DECORATIVE SCHEME TOGETHER THROUGH ITS COLOUR, PRINT, STYLE AND EMBELLISHMENTS.

Versatile cushions will transform a tired corner into a focal point of the room, give your chair or sofa a new look, or make a hard chair inviting and comfortable. As well as adding finishing touches, large cushions can provide valuable extra seating.

Choosing the style for your cushions is a matter of personal taste combined with consideration of the intended use of the cushion. This balance will determine whether you are trying to achieve a crisp, neatly defined look with straight piping or single lengths of braid, or a totally feminine look with ruffles and lace frills. Your choice of trims will give your cushion a unique touch. Experiment with some of the ideas in this chapter, mixing and matching ideas for different effects.

Cushions can also help you highlight attractive features of a room or camouflage the ones you would rather forget. Round cushions scattered on your high-backed lounge suite will de-emphasise the harshness of high ceilings and soften the line of tall pieces of furniture. On the other hand, irregular or asymmetrically shaped cushions in an array of colours will draw the eye to a particular object, taking the attention away from other less pleasing aspects of a room.

Mix and match cushion styles, fabric and trims to maximise the impact

Fabrics and fillings

The selection of fabric for cushions will depend upon their end use. Durable fabrics are required for floor cushions and loose covers; lace and delicate broderie anglaise should be used only for purely decorative cushions; whilst general furnishing fabrics are ideal for all types of scatter cushions.

For the dining and kitchen areas use easy-care fabrics that can be thrown into the washing machine time and time again. Fabrics that are in constant use, such as in the family room, can be treated with one of the stain-repellent sprays, such as Scotchgard or Teflon. These products need to be reapplied after each wash. Upholstery-weight fabrics often come already impregnated with a similar product, offering immediate protection.

The strength of the fabric should also be considered. A dress fabric would not be recommended for anything but decorative cushions that are placed on a bed cover and removed at night. Heavy cottons and tightly woven fabrics are ideal for floor cushions and loose seating covers. Soft furnishing fabrics are ideal for cushions because they are wide and therefore more economical. Natural fabrics, such as cottons and linens, and man-made fabrics, such as polyester, acrylic and acetate, have beneficial properties. Natural fabrics are easy to clean but can shrink and become distorted; man-made fibres are more likely to attract dirt but are less likely to lose their shape when cleaned. A fabric such as a polycotton, which is a combination of polyester and cotton, possesses qualities from both groups, being easy to clean and less likely to lose its shape.

Fillings should be chosen carefully. Use feather or down fillings only with tightly woven fabrics; fabrics which are loosely woven will allow the feathers or down to migrate through. (Fine cotton or chintz is ideal for casings for down or feather fillings.) Foam chips are less expensive than feathers or down, but are lumpy and will crumble over time. Foam blocks can be cut to any shape or size. Polyester fibre is fully washable, inexpensive and easy to work with, giving a final product that is soft and pliable.

Trimming cushions

❖

Cushions can be embellished in numerous ways. Apart from the basic decorative ruffles and piping you can also use ribbon, braid, beading, patchwork, appliqué and stencilling – to name just a few.

In this section, you will find many of these methods of trimming described in detail. Use them alone or combined to create cushions with a unique touch.

Continuous corded piping

To make corded piping, you need to begin by making a length of continuous bias binding. You can, of course, use purchased bias binding or, for that matter, purchased piping, but where you want to use self-fabric trims or match a particular colour, the following simple method will make it so easy:

1 Cut a piece of fabric as shown. Mark the bias strips as shown. The width of the strips will depend on how fat you want your piping to be (fig. 1).
2 Fold the fabric with the right sides together, so that points A and B are matching. Note that one strip width extends at each side. Join AA to BB with a 6 mm seam and press the seam open (fig. 2).
3 Cut along the marked lines. This will give you one continuous strip of bias fabric.
4 Fold this strip over double with the wrong sides together, enclosing a length of the piping cord. Secure the cord inside the bias fabric by stitching close to the cord through all thicknesses, using the zipper foot on your machine.
5 With the right sides of the piping and the fabric facing and the raw edges matching, pin the piping around the edge of the cushion cover front, clipping the piping seam allowances at the corners to allow the piping to curve more easily.
6 Cut 2 cm of the piping cord out of one end of the piping to lessen the bulk at the overlap. Overlap the ends of the piping. Stitch as close to the piping cord as possible, using the zipper foot on your sewing machine.

Using ready-made trims

To save time and still create a truly beautiful cushion, invest in one of the many bullion trims that are available from retail outlets. Heavy braids and trims beautifully complement the heavier fabrics, such as tapestries and jacquards.

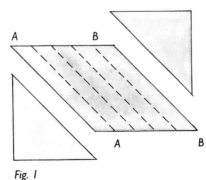

Fig. I

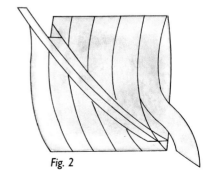

Fig. 2

Braids can also be sewn on by hand to the outside of a finished cushion. All you need to do is to unpick 5 cm in one of the side seams of your cushion cover and poke one end of the braid into the opened seam section. Then handstitch the braid all around the cushion, poke the other end into the opening and slipstitch the opening closed.

How to make a one-colour ruffle
1 Cut the ruffle to double your chosen finished width plus 2 cm for seam allowances, and twice the circumference of your cushion cover in length. For example, for a 10 cm ruffle on a 40 cm cushion cover, your ruffle strip will measure 22 cm x 3.2 m. If necessary, join strips with a flat fell seam to achieve the required length.
2 Join the short ends of the ruffle to form a circle, again using a flat fell seam.
3 Fold the ruffle strip over double, lengthways, with the wrong sides together and the raw edges matching. Press. Gather the ruffle, 1 cm in from the raw edge with two rows of gathering stitches, either by hand or by machine.
4 To ensure that the ruffle is even all around the cushion cover, divide its length into quarters and mark these points with pins. Pull up the gathering to fit around the cushion cover front. Pin the ruffle around the right side of the cushion cover front with the right sides together and the raw edges matching, placing a pin mark at each corner of the cushion cover. Manipulate the ruffle with your fingers to place a little extra gathering at each corner for added fullness. Stitch in the line of the gathering (fig. 1).
5 Place the cushion cover back on top of the cushion cover front with the ruffle attached, with the right sides facing and all the raw edges matching. Baste through all thicknesses. Ensure that the ruffle is properly sandwiched between the cushion cover front and the cushion cover back and then stitch

along the previous stitching line, leaving an opening for turning. Remove any visible basting stitches. Turn the cushion cover to the right side.

How to make a two-colour ruffle
This very clever method produces a frill which works on both sides and gives the appearance of having been bound.
1 Cut two ruffle strips, one 28 cm wide and another in a contrasting fabric, 22 cm wide. The length of both strips should be twice the circumference of your cushion cover plus 3 cm for seams.

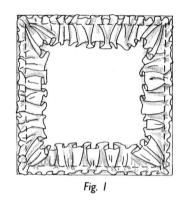

Fig. 1

2 Place the two strips together along one long side with the right sides facing. Stitch 1 cm from the edge. Press the seam to one side. Join the short ends of the combined ruffle to make a circle.
3 Fold the ruffle over double, lengthways, with the wrong sides together and the raw edges matching. Press.
4 Gather both raw edges of the ruffle, 1 cm from the edge. Divide the length of the ruffle into quarters and mark these points with a pin. Draw up the ruffle to fit around the outside edge of the cushion cover front.
5 Pin the ruffle to the cushion cover front with the right sides facing and the raw edges matching, placing a pin mark at each corner. Manipulate the ruffle with your fingers to place a little extra gathering at each corner for added fullness. Stitch in the line of the gathering.
6 Place the cushion cover back on top of the cushion cover front with the ruffle attached, with the right sides facing and all the raw edges matching. Baste through all thicknesses. Ensure that the ruffle is properly sandwiched between the cushion cover front and the cushion cover back and then stitch along the previous stitching line, leaving an opening for turning. Remove any visible basting stitches. Turn the cushion cover to the right side.

Stencilling
Stencilling was one of the first methods of printing on fabric. Pure cotton is the best choice as a fabric for stencilling. As the finish in some fabrics repels paint, wash your fabric thoroughly before applying any paint.

For cutting out a stencil, use a firm, clear plastic sheeting or sheets of thick

Above left: A two-colour ruffle
Left: A one-colour ruffle

Ruffled cushions have an old-world charm which is very appealing

manilla cardboard, coated with a mixture of fifty per cent turpentine and fifty per cent boiled linseed oil. Hang the sheets up to dry and wipe them thoroughly before using them. Choose a paint that is appropriate for the surface you are stencilling. Experiment with the stencil first on scraps of fabric to test absorption and colour strength. Don't judge a colour until it is dry.

When the paint is dry, heat-seal the colours by ironing on the back of the fabric or by using a very hot hairdryer on the paint surface.

If you are repeating a pattern, for example across the top of a sheet, measure out each position before you begin stencilling. Reposition the stencil accurately each time, using masking tape to hold the stencil in place while you

are working. Be sure to keep the tape clear of the area to be stencilled.

Stencil brushes are flat and thick, with a level end surface, because the best way of applying the paint is by tapping the brush down, in a pouncing motion, on to the space to be painted. Brush strokes can blur the outlines. Before painting, remove any excess paint from the brush with a rag.

Appliqué

If your machine can zigzag, you can appliqué beautiful motifs very easily. Think of appliqué as a way of painting a picture with fabric.

Decide on your appliqué motif. Look for clear bunches of flowers or motifs that will be attractive as a feature.

You may find you will have to strengthen the motif with fusible interfacing if it is too flimsy. If interfacing is necessary, cut out your fabric around the general area of the motif, then with a warm iron and a pressing cloth, fuse an equal-sized piece of interfacing to the wrong side of the fabric. Finally cut out the detail of the motif.

When using this appliqué method, choose a sewing thread close to the background colour of the fabric and always use a sharp machine needle.

Bows and ties are the ideal form of closure on these pretty striped cushions

Openings & closures

A cushion cover needs to be fully removable for laundering purposes. Zippers are the most common way to close cushion covers; however, Velcro, buttons and ties are all suitable.

The placement of the opening may vary. A back vent in the middle of the back of the cushion cover is often used when the cushion does not need to be turned over. A side vent opening is concealed in a side seam so that the cushion cover can be reversible.

Decorative items, such as buttons and bows, provide added interest as well as providing a functional method for opening and closing.

The methods given here describe the basic steps in making a back vent opening and various closures. They can all be incorporated into the cushion cover patterns in this chapter.

Back vent opening

This easy method of opening that uses the fabric overlap as its only means of closure is very simple; the only drawback being that if the insert is too full the vent can spread open.

1 Cut the cushion cover front to the finished size plus 1.5 cm all around for seam allowances. Cut out a cushion cover back to the same size, but add 11 cm to two opposite sides to form a rectangle. Cut the rectangle in half across the long sides; these cut edges will be the centre back edges.

2 Turn in and press 1.5 cm to the wrong side along the centre back edges, then turn in and press another 1.5 cm. Stitch.

3 Place the centre back edges together so the hemmed edges overlap by 5 cm to form the back vent. Baste these edges together.

4 Complete the cushion cover as described in the instructions for the cushion you have chosen.

5 Once the cushion cover is right side out, remove the basting, put the cushion insert in the cover and slip-stitch the vent closed.

Velcro closure

1 Cut the cushion cover front to the finished size plus 1.5 cm seam allowances all around. Cut out a cushion cover back to the same size, but add 11 cm to two opposite sides to form a rectangle. Cut the rectangle in half across the long sides; these cut edges will be the centre back edges.

2 Turn in and press 1.5 cm to the wrong side along the centre back edges, then turn in and press another 1.5 cm. Stitch.

3 Pin one half of the Velcro strip on to the right side of one half of the cushion cover back, over the hem just stitched. Pin the other half of the Velcro strip to the wrong side of the remaining half of the cushion cover back, over the hem just stitched. Test the closure to ensure the back will close in a perfect square before stitching the Velcro into place.

4 Complete the cushion cover as described in the instructions for the cushion you have chosen.

Buttons

1 Cut the cushion cover front to the finished size plus 1.5 cm seam allowances all around. Cut out a cushion cover back to the same size, but add 11 cm to two opposite sides to form a rectangle. Cut the rectangle in half across the long sides; these cut edges will be the centre back edges.

2 Turn in and press 1.5 cm to the wrong side along the centre back edges, then turn in and press another 1.5 cm. Stitch.

3 Mark the positions for the buttons and buttonholes on the two hems just stitched.

4 Make the buttonholes on the top half of the opening and sew the buttons to the right side of the bottom half.

5 Complete the cushion cover as described in the instructions for the cushion you have chosen.

Bows or ties

In addition to your main fabric, you will need to allow approximately 6 cm x 20 cm fabric for each tie. These can be cut on the bias or on the grain.

1 Decide how many pairs of ties you need and cut out the required pieces.

2 For each tie, fold the fabric strip over double with the right sides together and the raw edges even. Sew down the long side and one end. Turn the tie through to the right side. Press.

3 Cut out a cushion cover front and a cushion cover back with a 1.5 cm seam allowance all around. Pin the raw ends of the ties on to the right side of the cushion cover back and front, so that the raw ends of the ties match the raw edge of the cushion cover. Make sure the pairs of ties are also matching.

4 Cut two pieces of fabric for the facings, each 5 cm wide by the width of the cushion. Place one facing piece on each half of the cushion cover over the ties with the right sides facing and with the raw edge of the facing matching the

raw edge of the cushion cover on the opening edge. Stitch along the opening edge. Turn the facing to the wrong side. Press.

5 Complete the cushion cover as described in the instructions for the cushion you have chosen.

Inserting a zipper

❖

Zippers are most commonly used for cushion covers. Always use a good quality zipper.

Inserting a centred zipper

1 Measure and mark on the opening the length of the zipper teeth plus 5 mm. Close the zipper seam with a basting stitch and press the seam open.

2 Open the zipper and position it face down on the seam allowance so that the zipper teeth are along the seam line. Baste the zipper into place along one side of the zipper tape. Close the zipper and baste the other side into place.

3 Turn the fabric right side up with the zipper underneath. Using the zipper foot on your sewing machine and commencing at the top of the zipper, stitch down one side, then across the bottom of the zipper and back up to the top. Remove the basting stitches.

Lapped zipper in a piped seam

1 Press the seam allowance of the opening under, along the seam line.

2 With the piped pieces together, pull back the top seam allowance to view the piping allowance.

3 Open the zipper, lay it face down over the seam allowance with the zipper teeth resting on the top of the piping. Baste along the zipper tape close to the zipper teeth. Check that the zipper will open and close smoothly, before stitching it in place. Remove the basting.

Offset zipper

This method is used to conceal a zipper from view.

Top: The centred zipper

Centre: The offset zipper

Above: The zipper in the side seam

1 With the zipper open, position it over the opening so that the zipper teeth are centred over the right-hand seam allowance. Baste one side of the tape into position 5 mm from the zipper teeth.

2 Close the zipper and baste the other side of the zipper to the other seam allowance.

3 Turn the fabric right side up and topstitch the zipper in place through all the layers of fabric, using the zipper foot on your sewing machine and stitching close to the ends of the zipper. Remove the basting.

Piped Cushions

Basic piped cushion

MATERIALS

40 cm square of fabric for the cushion cover front

two pieces of fabric, each 22 cm x 40 cm, for the cushion cover backs

40 cm square cushion insert

30 cm zipper

1.7 m of corded piping (see how to make and apply piping on page 91)

matching sewing machine thread

scissors

pins

tape measure

sewing machine

Method

1 Place the two 40 cm edges of the back pieces together with the right sides facing and the raw edges even. Stitch a 5 cm long seam at each end, leaving an opening in the centre for the zipper. Insert the zipper. Open the zipper to allow for turning the cushion cover.

2 With right sides facing and the raw edges matching, pin the piping around the edge of the cushion cover front, clipping the piping seam allowances at the corners to allow it to curve gently. Cut 2 cm of the piping cord out of one end of the piping to lessen the bulk at the overlap. Overlap the piping ends.

Sew on the piping using the zipper foot on your sewing machine and stitching as close as possible to the piping.

3 Pin and baste the cushion cover back and cushion cover front together with the right sides facing and all the raw edges matching. Stitch around all sides, stitching in the piping stitching line. Trim the seams and clip the corners.

4 Turn the cushion cover right side out through the zipper opening. Remove any basting stitches that are visible. Press.

An interesting fabric, such as this one, needs only very simple trimming to make an attractive cushion

A contrasting ruffle makes a strong decorative statement

Frilled piped cushion

MATERIALS

40 cm square of fabric for the cushion cover front

two pieces of fabric, each 22 cm x 40 cm, for the cushion cover backs

1.7 m of contrasting piping

30 cm zipper

3.2 m fabric strip for the ruffle

40 cm square cushion insert

matching sewing machine thread

scissors

pins

tape measure

sewing machine

Method

1 Make a two-colour ruffle as instructed on page 92. Make the piping as instructed on page 91 or purchase ready-made piping.

2 With the right sides of the fabric facing and the raw edges matching, sew the piping and then the completed ruffle around the edge of the cushion cover front. If you are attaching the ruffle separately, after the piping, sew in the piping stitching line.

3 Place the two 40 cm edges of the back pieces together with the right sides facing and the raw edges even. Stitch a 5 cm long seam at each end, leaving an opening in the centre for the zipper. Insert the zipper. Open the zipper to allow for turning the cushion cover to the right side.

4 Place the cushion cover back and front together with the right sides facing and the raw edges even. Sew around the outside edge following the piping stitching line. Trim the seams and clip the corners to reduce bulk. Turn the cushion cover to the right side through the zipper opening and press.

Cushion with contrast band

MATERIALS

40 cm square of fabric for the cushion cover front

two pieces of fabric, each 22 cm x 40 cm, for the cushion cover back

four strips of border fabric, each 5 cm x 32 cm

1.7 m of contrasting corded piping (see how to make corded piping on page 91)

30 cm zipper

40 cm square cushion insert

matching sewing machine thread

tape measure

scissors

pins

sewing machine

Method

1 Trim the short ends of the border strips to perfect diagonals (fig. 1). Join the strips with mitred corners to form a square (fig. 2) which fits the cushion cover, 4 cm from the outside edge, as shown. Clip in 1 cm on the inner corner seams. Press the seams open.

2 Press under 1 cm on the inside and outside edges of the square. Pin the square on to the cushion cover front. Edgestitch into place. Press.

3 Attach the piping to the cushion cover front. Insert the zipper into the cushion cover back as instructed on page 94.

4 Place the cushion cover front and cushion cover back together with the right sides facing and the raw edges matching. Stitch around the outside edge. Trim excess bulk from the corners and seams. Turn the cushion cover to the right side through the zipper opening. Press.

Simple trimmings, cleverly applied, make a plain cushion into a unique one

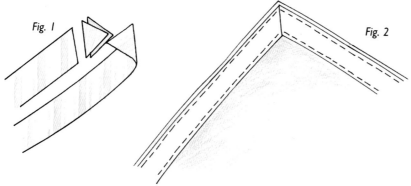

Fig. 1

Fig. 2

Machine-appliquéd cushion

MATERIALS

fabric, featuring flowers, animals, borders or any motif that will lend itself to being cut out

30 cm square of fabric for the cushion cover front

two pieces of fabric, each 17 cm x 30 cm, for the cushion cover backs

fabric strip for the ruffle, 12 cm x 2.4 m

25 cm zipper

30 cm square cushion insert

fusible interfacing (optional)

pins

scissors

matching sewing machine thread

sewing machine

warm iron

pressing cloth

Method

1 Cut out around the motif, leaving a 2 cm margin all around. Interface the motif if necessary. Pin or baste the motif on the area to be appliquéd.

2 Zigzag around the motif 5 mm in from the cut edge. Trim away the excess fabric, close to the stitching. Stitch again over the first zigzag stitching, using a slightly wider satin stitch.

3 Join the short ends of the ruffle strip. Fold the ruffle over double with wrong sides together and raw edges matching. Press. Gather the raw edges together. Apply the ruffle to the cushion front as instructed on page 92.

4 Insert the zipper into the cushion cover back as instructed on page 95, remembering to leave the zipper open.

5 Place the cushion cover back on the front, with the right sides facing. Stitch around the outside edge, through all thicknesses, following the piping stitching line. Turn the cushion cover to the right side through the zipper opening and press.

Triangular cushion

Before you begin You can make a triangular insert for this cushion from calico, following these instructions but omitting the zipper; or simply stuff the cushion cover with polyester fibre fill.

MATERIALS

60 cm of 140 cm wide fabric

2.6 m of 6 cm wide contrasting bias binding

2.6 m of piping cord

matching sewing machine thread

30 cm zipper

polyester fibre fill

scissors

pins

tape measure

sewing machine

This triangular cushion with its bright contrasting piping is the perfect foil for the checked slipcover

Method

1 Cut out two triangles with each side measuring 42 cm including a 1.5 cm seam allowance.

2 Make two lengths of piping, each one 130 cm. (See page 91.)

3 Cut a piece of fabric for the wall, 13 cm x 129 cm including seam allowances. If you need to join lengths to achieve the total length, add 1.5 cm for seam allowances on joining seams.

4 Pin the piping around the right side of the top and bottom pieces with the raw edges matching and the right sides together. Clip into the seam allowance of the piping to allow it to curve around the corners. Overlap the piping as neatly as possible at the ends, pulling the ends into the seam allowances. Stitch.

5 To attach the wall, pin and baste the ends of the strip together to form a circle. Check the fit. You may have to make a slight adjustment. Pin the wall to the top cushion piece with the right sides facing and the raw edges even. Stitch in the piping stitching line. Trim

the seam allowance.

6 Stitch the wall to the bottom cushion piece in the same way as for the top, leaving a 30 cm opening along one side for the zipper. Trim any excess bulk around the corners and at the seams.

7 Insert the zipper and leave it open. (See page 95 for how to insert a zipper.) Turn the cushion to the right side through the open zipper and press.

8 Stuff the cushion firmly and evenly with the fibre fill, ensuring that the corners are well filled. Close the zipper.

Heirloom Cushions

MADE FROM SILK AND LACE, THESE CUSHIONS USE BASIC PATCHWORK
SKILLS AND HAND-APPLIQUE TO GIVE THEM A LOOK OF DISTINCTION
THAT WILL BECOME MORE CHARMING WITH AGE.

Lace patchwork cushion

MATERIALS
2 m of 5 cm wide lace
12 cm x 192 cm of natural-coloured silk
for the cushion cover front
two pieces of silk, each 22 cm x 40 cm, for
the cushion cover backs
30 cm zipper
40 cm square cushion insert
pins
needles
matching sewing machine thread
tape measure
sewing machine

Method

1 Stitch both sides of the lace down the centre of the fabric strip, stitching close to the edge of the lace. Carefully press the seams flat, then cut the strip into sixteen 12 cm squares.

2 Sew the squares together in four rows of four squares each, noting that the direction of the lace must be alternately horizontal and vertical. Sew the four rows together to form the front of the cushion cover.

3 Complete the cushion, using the cushion cover method of your choice and embellish it with your choice of trims. We have added a ruffle.

These cushions are the heirlooms of tomorrow (Make the Battenburg lace cushion in the same way as a ruffled cushion, using a lace edging instead of the ruffle.)

Hand-appliquéd cushion

Before you begin

The traditional hand-appliqué method is ideal for delicate voile pillow-cases and lightweight cotton cushion covers, as well as chintz motifs that can be cut out and appliquéd on to softer coloured backgrounds.

MATERIALS
cushion cover of your choice

tracing paper

pencil

fabric in a contrasting colour or texture for the bow

dressmakers marker pen

needle

pins

scissors

matching sewing thread

Method

1 Trace the bow motif, using the tracing paper and pencil. Cut out the pattern pieces.

2 Pin the pattern pieces on to the right side of the cushion front and trace around each element.

3 Cut out the bow elements from the contrasting fabric, allowing an additional 5 mm around each one. Turn in and press the 5 mm allowance to the back of each piece and baste it in place. When you are working around curved shapes, gather in the basting stitch slightly so that the edge will lie flat. Snip into the corners and curves where necessary.

4 Pin the motif into position right side up and baste. Working from the back and using small slipstitches, stitch the motif in place. Remove the basting.

If you are making your own cushion cover, you can use the appliqué fabric for a ruffle or a bias trim

Stencilled Cushions

MATERIALS

firm plastic sheet for the stencil

fineline marker pen

sharp craft knife or scalpel

bread board or similar cutting board

stencil brushes

paints

masking tape

fabric for practice and testing colours

40 cm square of calico for the
cushion cover front

two pieces of calico, each 22 cm x 40 cm,
for the cushion cover back

calico strip for the ruffle

checked cotton fabric strip for
the second ruffle

40 cm square cushion insert

matching sewing machine thread

pins

scissors

tape measure

sewing machine

Method

1 Place the plastic sheet over the motif and trace around the design, using the marker pen. Cut the stencil out on the cutting board, using the sharp knife or scalpel. Remember to leave 'bridges' in the design that are not cut through.

2 Place the stencil on the cushion cover front. Define the stencil areas that will be the same colour by covering all other areas with masking tape. Taking care to paint the elements in their logical order (main colour first, then details), start stencilling from the outside, gradually filling in the entire area until you are happy with the depth of colour. Each time you finish stencilling a colour, you can cover it with tape and uncover the next area to be painted. It is a good idea to let each section of colour dry before you begin applying the next one, to avoid them bleeding into one another. Allow all the paint to dry before you begin sewing.

3 Make the two ruffles as instructed on page 92.

4 Complete the cushion in the same way as the two-colour ruffled cushion on page 92.

The stencil below provides a basic outline. Change any detail to please yourself.

For a fresh country look, stencil calico cushions with farmyard motifs

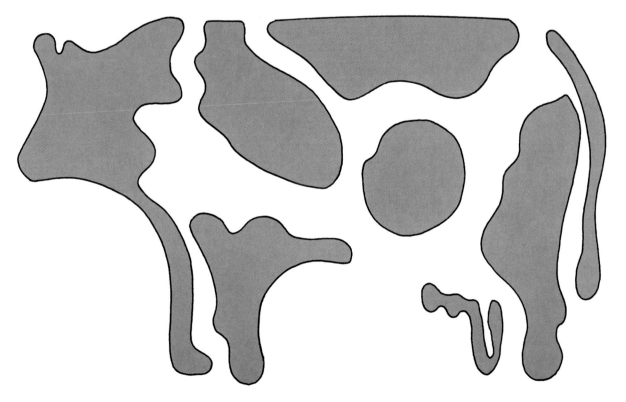

Bolsters

LARGE BOLSTERS ARE OFTEN USED AS NECK ROLLS ON A BED, WHILE SMALLER
VERSIONS ARE USED PURELY AS DECORATION FOR A WINDOW SEAT OR
TO COMPLEMENT OTHER CUSHIONS ON A LOUNGE OR A BED.

Before you begin Like cushions, bolsters can also be uniquely embellished with embroidery and a variety of trims. There are two styles of bolsters: one has a gathered end and the other has a flat end. The materials required vary slightly for the two styles.

Gathered-end bolster

MATERIALS
sufficient main fabric
bolster pad
two buttons for covering and a 5 cm square of fabric for covering each button
matching sewing machine thread
scissors
pins
tailors chalk
quilting thread
long needle
tape measure
sewing machine

Bolsters, such as these, are a charming feature on a traditional day bed

Method

1 Cut a rectangle of fabric 3 cm wider than the circumference of the bolster pad and 4.5 cm longer than the length of the bolster pad.

2 Sew the long edges together with a 1.5 cm seam and the right sides facing. Press the seam open and turn the tube right side out.

3 Position the pad in the centre of the fabric tube, so that equal amounts of fabric extend on either end. Mark the

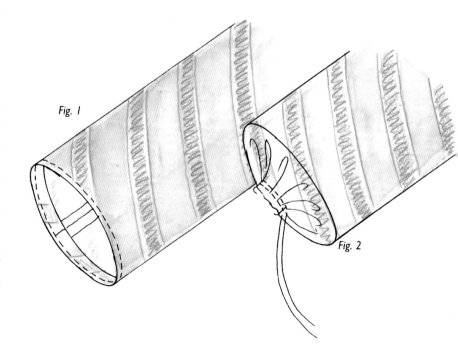

Fig. 1

Fig. 2

position of the pad with pins or chalk and remove the cover.

4 Turn in and press 1.5 cm on each end (fig. 1). Gather around the circumference of each end close to the folded edge. Replace the pad in the cover. Gather in the fabric tightly at each end and secure (fig. 2).

5 Cut out the fabric for covering the buttons, 1 cm larger than the circumference of the button. Gather around the circumference of the fabric, draw up the fabric around the button, then tie off the ends of the thread. Attach the buttons with the quilting thread and the long needle to the centre of each end, covering the gathering.

Bolsters can be quite simple or lavishly trimmed with piping and a tassel

Piped flat-end bolster

MATERIALS
sufficient main fabric

twice the circumference of the ends of the bolster plus 3 cm for seams in contrasting corded piping (see how to make and attach corded piping on page 91)

bolster pad

25 cm zipper

two decorative tassels

matching sewing machine thread

scissors

pins

tape measure

tailors chalk

sewing machine

Method

1 Cut a rectangle of the main fabric 3 cm longer than the bolster pad and 3 cm wider than the circumference of the pad.

2 Cut two circles for the ends of the bolster, the same diameter as the bolster pad plus 3 cm for seams.

3 Pin the piping to the right side of the fabric on the short edges of the rectangle, with the raw edges matching. Clip into the seam allowance of the piping to allow it to curve.

4 Pin the long edges of the rectangle together with the right sides facing. With a 1.5 cm seam allowance, stitch each end, leaving a 25 cm opening in the centre for the zipper. Baste the rest of the seam closed along the seam line.

5 Press the seam open. Remove the basting stitches and insert the zipper as

instructed on page 95, following the method for a centred zipper (fig. 3). Undo the basting and open the zipper.

6 Cut notches into the seam allowances of the two circles. Baste the ends into place over the piping. Check that all the edges are secured in the basting, then stitch with the zipper foot on your sewing machine (fig. 4). Trim and clip the seam allowances. Turn to the right side through the zipper opening.

7 Stitch a decorative tassel into place in the centre of each end. Insert the bolster pad and close the zipper.

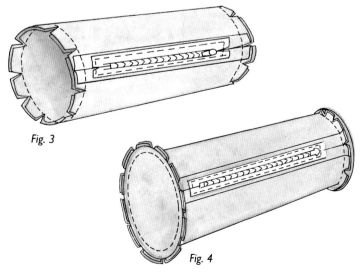

Fig. 3

Fig. 4

Chair Cushions

CHAIR CUSHIONS ARE AN EASY WAY TO ADD COMFORT AND STYLE TO
WOODEN CHAIRS. CHOOSE A WASHABLE FABRIC AND ONE THAT WILL
COMPLEMENT YOUR COLOUR SCHEME.

The shape of these two cushions will vary according to the shape of your chair, so you will need to make a pattern

Walled chair cushions

MATERIALS
*two pieces of sturdy fabric, each
45 cm x 50 cm, for the seat cushion
cover, and two pieces approximately
50 cm x 50 cm for the back rest*

*50 cm of 6 cm wide fabric strip
for the wall*

*5 m of contrasting piping (see how to make
and apply piping on page 91)*

polyester fibre fill

large sheets of paper

pencil

ten matching covered buttons

matching sewing machine thread

tailors chalk

pins

scissors

sewing machine

Method

1 To make the pattern, trace the shape of the chair seat and the back rest on to the large sheets of paper. Following the paper pattern, cut two seat cushion pieces and two back rest pieces adding 1.5 cm seam allowance.

2 Stitch the piping around the right side of each seat cushion cover piece, clipping the seam allowance of the piping at the corners. Stitch the piping around the right side of the front of the back rest in the same way.

3 Determine where the back seam should be in the wall of the seat cushion. Starting at that point, pin the wall around the edge of one cushion cover piece, over the piping, with the right sides together and the raw edges matching. Stitch the back seam, then stitch the pinned edge of the wall to the cushion cover, following the piping stitching line.

4 With the right sides facing, pin the remaining cushion cover piece to the wall, then stitch, following the piping stitching line and leaving an opening at the back for stuffing. Turn to the right side and press. Stuff the cushion with the fibre fill, distributing the stuffing evenly.

5 Fold in the wall seam allowance at the opening. Pin it to the piping stitching line, then stitch.

6 For the back rest, place the front and back together with right sides facing and raw edges even. Stitch around the outside edge, leaving a 15 cm opening at the bottom for stuffing. Turn to the right side and press.

7 Stuff loosely. Stitch three buttons on each side, roughly corresponding to where the chair arms begin, pulling the thread firmly through the button and the stuffing to the back of the back rest. Stitch four buttons to the seat cushion in the same way.

Walled chair cushions can be made to any size or shape following these instructions

Chair cushion with deep ruffle

Before you begin

You will need two fabric strips for the ruffles: one should be one and a half times the length of the back edge of the chair, the other one should be one and a half times the length of the three remaining sides of the chair allowing an extra 3 cm on each piece for hems. Decide how wide you wish your ruffle to be and add 1.5 cm for the top and bottom seam/hem allowance.

MATERIALS

two pieces of sturdy fabric, each
45 cm x 50 cm, for the cushion cover
polyester fibre fill
2 m of 6 cm wide fabric strips for ties
fabric for the ruffle strips
large sheet of paper
pencil
matching sewing machine thread
pins
scissors
tape measure
turning hook or knitting needle
sewing machine

Method

1 To make the pattern, trace the shape of the chair seat on to the large sheet of paper. Following the paper pattern, cut two cushion cover pieces.

2 To make the ruffle: Turn in and press 5 mm on the sides and ends of the two ruffle strips and then turn in and press another 5 mm. Stitch. Gather the top edge of each strip.

3 Pin and then baste the smaller ruffle to the back edge of the cushion cover front with the right sides facing and the raw edges matching, starting 2.5 cm in from both back corners. Pull up the gathering to fit. Pin and baste the longer piece around the front and side edges of the cushion cover front with the right sides facing and the raw edges matching, starting 2.5 cm in from both back corners.

4 Cut the 6 cm wide strip into four 50 cm lengths. Fold each length over double with the right sides facing and the raw edges matching. Stitch down the long side and across one short end. Turn the ties to the right side with the turning hook or knitting needle and press. Pin the ties at the four corners so that the raw edges are matching. Baste.

5 Place the cushion cover back and front together with the right sides facing and the raw edges matching and the ruffle in between. Stitch around the outside edge in the ruffle basting line, leaving an opening at the centre back.

Turn the cushion cover to the right side and press.

6 Stuff the cushion, distributing the stuffing evenly. Close the opening by hand.

Above and below: Make a ruffled chair cushion in a washable fabric to coordinate with the blinds

Piped chair cushion

MATERIALS

*two pieces of sturdy fabric, each
45 cm x 50 cm, for the cushion cover*

polyester fibre fill

*1.5 m of corded piping (see how to make
and apply corded piping on page 91)*

2 m of 14 cm wide fabric strips for ties

large sheet of paper

pencil

matching sewing machine thread

pins

scissors

tape measure

turning hook or knitting needle

sewing machine

Method

1 To make the pattern, trace the shape of the chair seat on to the large sheet of paper. Following the paper pattern, cut two cushion cover pieces.

2 Apply the corded piping to the right side of one cushion piece.

3 Cut the 14 cm wide strip of fabric into four 50 cm lengths. Fold each length over double with the right sides facing and the raw edges matching.

A cushion adds comfort as well as charm to a wooden chair

Stitch down the long side and across one short end. Turn the ties to the right side with the turning hook or knitting needle and press. Place the ties on the right side of the front cushion cover,

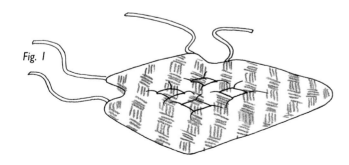

Fig. 1

matching the raw edges. Baste.

4 Place the cushion cover back and front together with the right sides facing and the raw edges matching. Stitch around the outside edge in the piping stitching line, leaving an opening for stuffing at the centre back. Turn the cushion cover to the right side. Press.

5 Stitch around four little squares evenly spaced in the centre of the cushion (fig. 1). Stuff the cushion with the fibre fill, distributing the stuffing evenly. Close the opening by hand.

Round Buttoned Cushion

MATERIALS

1 m of 120 cm wide fabric plus fabric
to cover the buttons (approximately
10 cm square for each button)

2.4 m of corded piping (see how to make
corded piping on page 91)

two buttons

matching sewing machine thread

quilting thread

quilting needle

polyester fibre fill

pins

tape measure

scissors

sewing machine

brown paper

pencil

string

thumb tack

dressmakers cutting board

Method

1 To make a paper pattern for the circles, cut a square of brown paper larger than the area of your cushion, then fold the paper into quarters so that the folded centre of the paper is at the upper left corner. With the thumb tack, pin the piece of string to the corner at the folded centre, pushing the thumb tack through into the cutting board underneath. Tie the pencil to the other end of the string at a distance equal to the radius of the circle required. (The radius is the distance from the centre of a circle to its circumference.) In the cushion shown here the radius is 20 cm. Draw the quarter of the circle on the paper and cut along the drawn line through all the thicknesses of paper. Unfold the paper and you should have a perfect circle of the size you need (figs 1 and 2).

2 Trace the circle pattern on to your fabric to give you two equal circles.

3 Sew the piping around the right sides of the front and back of the cushion cover with right sides together and raw edges matching, clipping into the seam allowance of the piping to allow it to curve.

4 Cut a strip of fabric, 10 cm x 1.26 m, for the cushion wall.

5 If it is necessary to join fabric for the wall strip, ensure that all pieces are cut in the same direction on the fabric with the grain running in the same direction. Join the pieces into a circle with flat fell seams and trim away any excess fabric. Press the seam open.

6 With the right sides together, pin one edge of the wall to the cushion cover front, sandwiching the piping in between, and stitch it into place through all thicknesses. Trim the excess fabric, clip into the curve all the way around and press the seam open.

7 Pin and stitch the other edge of the wall to the back of the cushion cover as for the front, leaving an opening for turning. Trim the seam as for the front and press the seam open.

8 Turn the cushion cover right side out. Insert the filling and slipstitch the opening closed.

9 Cut out the fabric for covering the buttons, 1 cm larger than the circumference of the button. Gather around the circumference of the fabric, draw up the fabric around the button, then tie off the ends of the thread.

10 With the quilting thread and the quilting needle, attach one button to the cushion front and one button to the cushion back, drawing the needle through the cushion cover at least three times from button to button to ensure they are securely attached.

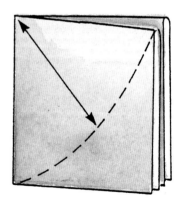

Fig. 1

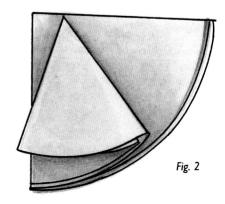

Fig. 2

A pretty brocade works very well for this style of cushion

New Covers

EDGE TREATMENTS
ARMCHAIR COVER
DROP-IN SEAT COVER
DIRECTORS CHAIR COVERS
TAILORED CHAIR COVER
RUFFLED CHAIR COVER
INSTANT SOFA COVER-UP

New Covers

IT IS USUALLY BEST TO LEAVE TRADITIONAL UPHOLSTERY TO THE PROFESSIONALS, BUT THERE ARE LOTS OF QUICK AND EASY FURNITURE-COVERING PROJECTS SUITABLE FOR THE ENTHUSIAST.

Wouldn't that old sofa that you bought at the last jumble sale look great with a smart new cover? A few metres of fabric and a couple of weekends' work and hey presto, a new sofa! If only it were that easy. Traditional furniture upholstery can be a minefield of pitfalls for the amateur. Furnishing fabrics are expensive and mistakes can quickly swallow up your decorating budget. Even the simplest type of upholstery involves fixing a covering fabric over a tightly stretched calico cover which itself covers padding of some kind and possibly springs. The variety of furniture shapes and styles is almost endless. Some furniture pieces have shapes which create particular problems and awkward corners to work around.

There are very simple cover projects – such as renewing dining-room chairs, or recovering cushions – that are perfect 'Do It Yourself' projects. There are step-by-step instructions for these in the following pages. These projects are not 'upholstery' in the traditional sense – no repairs, new stuffing, webbing or springs are required. They do, however, provide decorative solutions to tired and worn-out chairs, or practical removable covers where laundering is required.

Choosing fabric

Choosing the right fabric for the job and the room is crucial to the success of the project, but the great variety of fabrics available can be daunting for the home decorator. The four natural fibres – cotton, wool, silk and linen – are widely used in upholstery. Cotton, which is mass-produced and generally economical, is a popular choice for slipcovers and cushions. Prewash all cottons to allow any shrinkage to take place before cutting out your pattern. Wool is very hard-wearing, flame-resistant, light and relatively waterproof. It has been popular for furniture coverings from time to time. Silk is the glamour fabric, but because of its relatively high cost is usually reserved for trimming, cushions or luxury pieces. Linen is one of the oldest domestic fibres and because of its long-wearing qualities has always been a popular choice for loose covers – especially in high-traffic areas. Many synthetic fibres are also available these days and are often blended with natural fibres. This reduces fabric cost and takes advantage of the good wearing and washing qualities of polyester and viscose.

Colour and pattern

The choice of colour and pattern for a particular loose cover or upholstery project will be determined by a number of factors. Are you re-covering an entire suite or will your new cover have to fit in with existing pieces? Is your room big enough to cope with that large splashy floral or will your print be overwhelmed by other objects in the room? Do you need to warm up a room with yellows, pinks and reds or do you need to cool it down with blue? Remember that colours can be very affected by the light in a room, both natural and artificial. Working with a story board of the total room colour and pattern concept will be a big help. Before buying metres of fabric, it is a good idea to take home a large sample piece. Drape it over your sofa or chair and leave it there for a day or two so you can judge the effect of the light in the room and how you think it will fit in with the curtains, wallpaper and other colours and patterns in the room. Generally, the larger your room the more you can get away with. There are exceptions, of course, but as a rule of thumb, it will help you avoid decorating disasters.

Matching patterns, where fabric pieces join in upholstery can be a nightmare. If you are not experienced, or endowed with the patience of Job, you are probably best to stick to plains or all-over small prints which do not need matching. Stripes do need careful matching but provide their own easy-to-follow guidelines. Floral bouquets or medallion patterns are more difficult because the motif has to be centred on seats cushions and backs, wasting a lot of fabric. Checks are the hardest of all, having to be matched in all directions at once.

Before you buy, it's a good idea to assess whether the fabric you like will present pattern-matching problems. Lay two lengths side by side as though they were joined, then move one slightly up or down. Now stand back and see the difference. You can do the same test if patterns are to meet end to end.

Trimming

Piping and trims add the finishing professional touch to your coverings. They also define the line of a piece of furniture and give strength to areas, such as the arms, that receive constant hard wear. When selecting a suitable colour for piping or trims, it is usual to highlight one of the colours used in small amounts found in your fabric. If you use one of the colours from the main colour palette of your fabric the piping will blend in rather than create a decorative highlight.

There are different gauges of piping cord available and the size you should select is determined by the fabric to which it will be attached. As a general rule, a thick fabric requires a thin cord and a thin or fine fabric will require a thicker gauge cord to give the fabric body. Upholstery piping is often called 'welting'; this is simply a trade name for the same product.

On page 21, you will see how to make piping for cushions. The same method can be applied to upholstery piping. Lengths of bias fabric are joined with 5 mm seams, or you can cut continuous bias (see page 20). Lay the piping cord on the wrong side of the fabric. To join the ends of the piping cord, butt the ends together and bind them neatly with a heavy embroidery thread. Fold the fabric in half, enclosing the cord. Stitch close to the cord, using the zipper foot on your sewing machine.

Edge Treatments

CHOOSING THE RIGHT EDGE TREATMENT FOR THE BOTTOM OF YOUR LOOSE
COVERS IS A MATTER OF PERSONAL TASTE AND STYLE.

Before you begin A frilled or ruffled edge creates a look of cottage comfort, informal yet inviting; knife pleats ensure a tailored look; soft scalloped edges are harmonious and feminine; while a flush edge gives a neat and simple finish. Concealed edges show the clean lines of the chair or suite, enhancing the natural characteristics of the fabric. Braids can be used to cover seam lines and can be secured with upholstery tacks.

A staple gun is a handy tool for securing fabrics on to a wooden base. The staples can subsequently be covered with flat braids.

Concealed bottom edge

Before you begin This method will give you a fitted tailored look with four separate flaps (one for each side of the base) that are secured underneath the chair with ties.

You will need four 12 cm wide strips: two that are the same length as the width of the chair base and two that are the same length as the depth of the chair base. Add 5 cm to the length of each flap for the side hems and 2.5 cm for the bottom hem.

MATERIALS
four fabric flaps, the same as the body fabric of the chair cover

sewing machine with a needle suitable for sewing through several layers of fabric

gauge 4 cord

large safety pin

pins

scissors

tape measure

Method

1 Pin the flaps to the bottom edges of the chair cover. Trim away the excess fabric around the chair legs or castors, leaving at least a 2.5 cm seam allowance. Remove the flaps. Turn in and press 5 mm on the side edges, then turn in and press another 2 cm. Machine-stitch the side hems in place.

2 Turn in and press 5 mm along the raw bottom edges of the flaps, then turn in and press another 2 cm. Stitch the bottom hems in place, forming a casing by stitching close to both folds. Stitch the flaps to the chair cover.

3 Using the safety pin, thread the cord loosely through the casing. Fit the cover over the chair. Turning the chair on its side, pull up the cord and tie the two ends of the cord in a bow or knot (fig. 5).

Figs 1 to 4: Various edge treatments

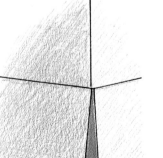

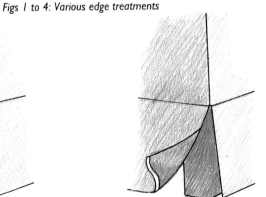

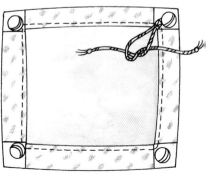

Fig. 5

Ruffled valance

MATERIALS

*fabric, the same as the body
fabric of the cover*

*sewing machine with a needle suitable for
sewing through several layers of fabric*

matching sewing machine thread

*quilting thread for gathering up
the ruffle (optional)*

pins

scissors

tape measure

Before you begin Measure around the bottom edge of the chair cover. For the ruffles, you will need twice this measurement plus 1.5 cm for each seam allowance on any joining seams. Determine the depth of the valance by measuring from the bottom edge of the cover to 1 cm above the floor. Add 2.5 cm for the hem and another 1.5 cm for the gathering and top seam allowance.

Method

1 Cut as many strips of the required depth as you need to achieve the total length, following the grainline of the fabric and matching the pattern. Join the strips together into a long strip with flat fell seams.

2 Hem the bottom edge and the short ends by machine or by hand; the latter method is preferable if a light fabric is being used, so that the stitches are not obvious.

3 Gather along the top edge and pull up the gathers to fit the bottom of the chair cover. With the right sides together, pin and baste the frill to the bottom edge of the chair cover, allowing extra fullness at the corners. Place the cover on the chair and make any final adjustments before machine-stitching the valance into place, placing the opening at the back leg, where the chair cover is also open.

Box-pleated valance

Before you begin The valance must begin and end at the back leg where the chair cover is also open. The pleats should be evenly arranged, preferably with a pleat at each corner, one at the centre front and one at the centre back. Making a newspaper pattern like the ones here is a good idea (figs 6 and 7).

Measure around the bottom edge of the cover. You will need three times this measurement plus 1.5 cm for each seam allowance on any joining seams. Determine the height of the pleat by measuring from the bottom edge of the cover to 1 cm above the floor. Add 2.5 cm for the hem and another 1.5 cm for the top seam allowance.

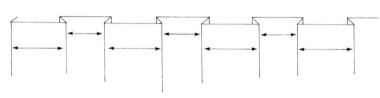

Fig 7: Measure around the bottom of the chair and determine the width of each pleat

MATERIALS

*fabric, the same as the body fabric
of the chair cover*

*sewing machine with a needle suitable for
sewing through several layers of fabric*

matching sewing machine thread

*stiff cardboard, the width of your pleat by
the final depth of the box-pleated edge*

tailors chalk

pins

scissors

pencil

steel ruler

Method

1 Cut as many strips of the required size as you need to achieve the total length, following the grainline of the fabric. Join the strips together into one long strip with flat fell seams.

2 Hem the bottom edge and the two short ends.

3 Cut a cardboard template for the pleats, the width of your pleat (say 20 cm) x the height of the pleat. Moving the template along the length of the fabric, mark the pleats with tailors chalk, marking both the top and bottom edges as shown in the diagram.

4 Fold and pin the pleats, then baste them in place. Press the pleats carefully. Machine-stitch across the top to secure the pleats. Remove the basting.

5 To attach the valance, begin at the back leg where the cover is open and pin the valance to the bottom edge of the chair cover, with the right sides together and the raw edges even. Stitch.

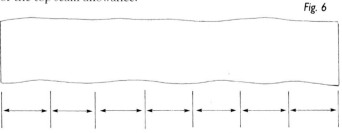

Fig. 6

Armchair Cover

YOU MAY NOT BE ABLE TO RUN UP A NEW ARMCHAIR ON YOUR SEWING
MACHINE, BUT YOU CAN CERTAINLY GIVE THE OLD ONE A TOTALLY FRESH
LOOK WITH NEW FABRIC AND A LITTLE INGENUITY!

Before you begin

Easy covering is all about revamping furniture with minimum fuss and expense. If the frame of your chair is solid, but the fabric is shabby, this type of re-covering is an ideal solution for the home sewer. However, if your chair has stretched, or torn webbing or the odd spring is poking through, a 'bandaid solution' is not enough – you will have to consider using a professional upholsterer.

The instructions given here are for re-covering an armchair, but you can cover a settee in exactly the same way.

Measuring

Measuring and making a pattern for your loose chair or sofa cover is an exacting process. When you are making a large investment in fabric, it is essential that you buy the correct quantity. Remember, it is a good form of insurance to buy an extra 50 cm of fabric. If it is not needed for the cover,

it could be converted into a beautiful throw cushion to complement your loose cover. Time is your best friend when measuring for loose covers – avoid working in a hurry and always recheck all measurements. It is often wise when making a loose cover to make a calico pattern or mock-up first so that any problems or adjustments can be made at this preliminary stage rather than

with your expensive fabric.

Make a sketch or drawing of the piece you are covering, with the measurements for each plane of the chair marked on it (fig. 1). On this same piece of paper keep a running list of all measurements. This list should include measurements for: inside back, seat, inside arms, outside arms, front border, front scrolls, back scrolls, outside back,

Fig. 1

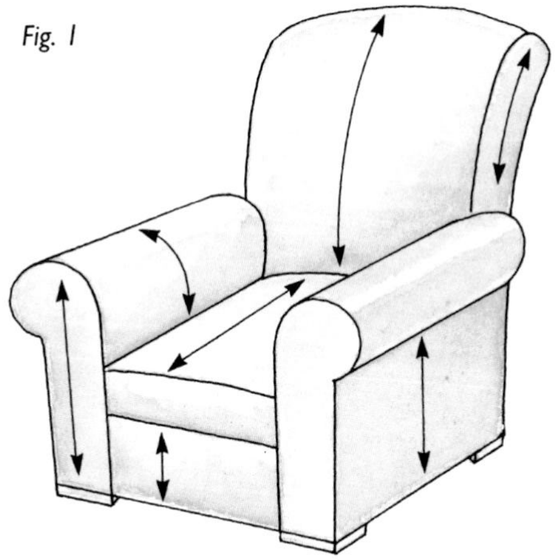

Fig. 2

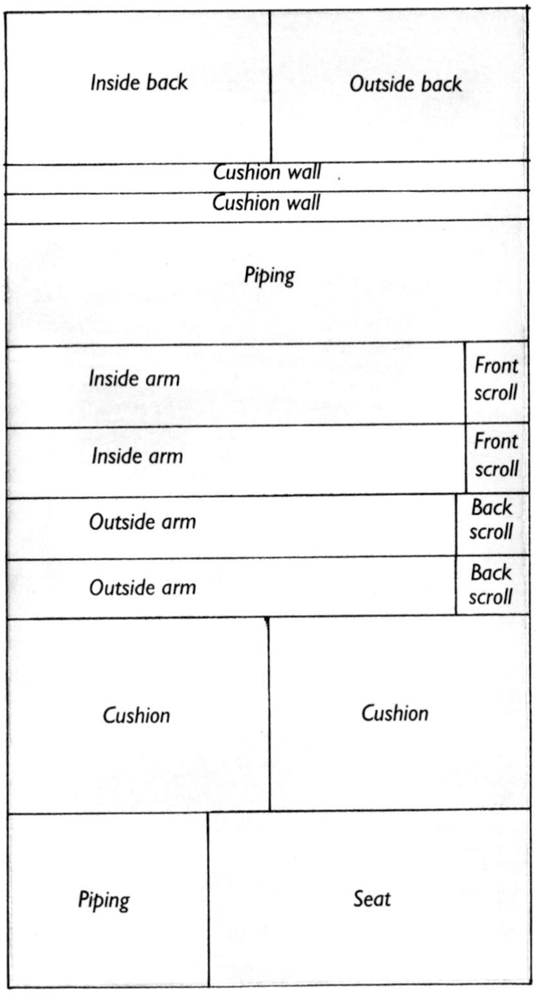

Inside back	Outside back
Cushion wall	
Cushion wall	
Piping	

Inside arm	Front scroll
Inside arm	Front scroll
Outside arm	Back scroll
Outside arm	Back scroll

Cushion	Cushion
Piping	Seat

cushion, cushion borders and piping. Always write the measurements with the length of the fabric shown first, followed by the width. The drawing and the list will prove a handy cross-check system for all your measurement requirements.

Consider the style of the furniture piece as well as the pattern and weave of the fabric. When working with a patterned fabric, the pattern on the arms of the chair should run in line with the centre back, which should in turn be in line with the seat. When working with a fabric that has a raised pile, the pile must always run down the chair. Always take measurements on the widest point of each section and allow 2.5 cm for each seam allowance. Add an additional 10 cm for the tuck-in, the part of the fabric that runs between the seat and the inside back and helps to keep the cover in place.

If the chair has a removable cushion, remember to take the cushion out so that you can measure the cover that sits underneath it. You will also need to decide how you wish to finish the bottom edge of your covers. On pages 116 to 117, you will see a number of options. Allow extra fabric for whichever of these options you choose.

Also, remember to allow fabric for piping. Approximately 6.5 m of piping can be made from 25 cm of 122 cm wide fabric. It is a good idea to allow enough fabric for covers for arm rests or head rests, which will help to protect your chairs from soiling.

When cutting out your pattern, work with rectangles of fabric that are a little larger than you need. They can be trimmed to shape and size as you go.

Linens and cottons should always be cut with pinking shears in order to minimise fraying.

Pattern layout (fig. 2)

To calculate your fabric requirements, draw up a scaled pattern with each separate pattern piece drawn in and its correct positioning (in relation to the

Contrasting piping is a feature of this charming floral armchair slipcover

grain and pattern of the fabric) noted. Where pieces are required that are larger than the width of the fabric, for example on the inside back – try to get the best possible pattern placement. If this is impossible, join two pieces together with a piped seam to disguise the imperfect match.

MATERIALS

sufficient calico, approximately 8 m for an armchair

upholstery weight fabric, the same quantity as the calico, allowing extra for pattern matching (2 to 5 m additional fabric)

upholstery pins or upholstery tape

tailors chalk or masking tape for marking pieces

quilting thread

matching sewing machine thread

upholstery needle

Velcro tape or hook-and-eye tape

felt tip marker pen

sewing machine with a suitable upholstery-gauge needle

sufficient bias-cut fabric strips (the width of the strips will be determined by the gauge of the cord used)

sufficient suitable-gauge piping cord

Method

1 Cut rectangles from the calico for each piece marked on your pattern layout. With the felt tip pen, mark the location of each pattern piece on the calico.

2 Working with one piece at a time, pin with upholstery pins or tape each calico piece to the area to which it belongs. Mark the final shape on each piece. Remove the calico pieces and adjust each shape with a 2.5 cm seam allowance all around. Place each piece back in position to check the fit.

3 Pin all the pieces together.

4 Sewing pieces together in the right order will help to ensure that the finished pattern can be easily worked. Baste with the quilting thread in the following order:

- the outer back piece to the inside back;
- the inside back to the seat;
- the seat to the lower front panel;
- the seat to the arms along the inside edge;
- the inside arm to the outside arm;
- the front of the arms between the inner and outer arms;
- the end of the arm pieces to the back and inside back, leaving an opening on one back seam approximately 35 cm from the base to the back of the inside scroll; and
- the bottom edge treatment.

5 Slip the cover on the chair, inside out. On curved areas, such as the arms, it may now be necessary to take out some fullness. Do this by unpicking the basting stitches and making tiny gathers or pleats on the wrong side, taking up the slack. Make any darts as necessary. Stitch the basting back into place again to ensure a perfect fit. Once you are satisfied with the fit of the pattern, remove it from the chair. Cut through all the basting stitches, making tailors

tacking marks. Highlight all seam lines, gathering and darts with tailors chalk.

6 Lay the fabric on the floor with the right side facing up. Place the calico pattern pieces (right side up) on top of the fabric, checking that the grain is running in the correct direction. Mark out and label the fabric pieces, marking the top and bottom of each piece. Once all the pieces are marked they can be cut out.

7 If you are going to use piping, make up sufficient piping, allowing a little extra. Apply the piping to the right side of all pieces to be piped, with right sides together and raw edges matching. (See page 21 for how to apply piping.)

8 Follow the same method for joining pieces as you did with the calico pattern, inserting the piping between the fabric layers as you work through each section. (See page 21 for how to make and insert piping.)

9 Machine-stitch one half of the Velcro tape to each side of the back opening (fig. 1). Zippers are not recommended because they are often not strong enough, but hooks and eyes, spaced evenly along the opening, can be used.

10 If you wish to add a box-pleated valance like the one pictured, follow the instructions on page 117.

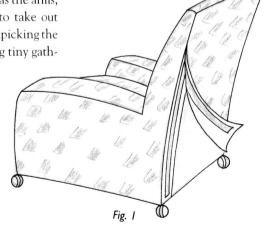

Fig. 1

Shaping around curved backs or arms is possible in a number of ways:

- Handsew gathering stitches along the seam line on the curve. Pull up the gathering to fit and join the pieces together (fig. 2).
- Making small flat pleats is another way to achieve a smooth finish (fig. 3).
- If there is a lot of fullness to be taken out, darts are a good method to consider. Pin the darts as shown to confirm a good fit, before you stitch (fig. 4).
- If your chair back has straight corners, join the pieces as shown in fig. 5.

Fig. 2

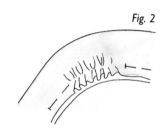

Fig. 3

Fig. 4

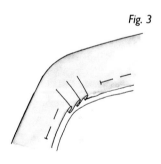

Fig. 5

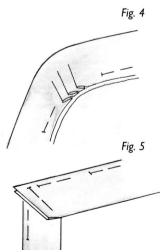

Walled seat cushion

Most sofas and armchairs have loose seat cushions

Before you begin Loose, walled seat cushions are often found on sofas and lounge suites. The method given here is a basic guide for covering a foam block cushion.

The same method can be used for other fillings such as down and feather or foam chips, but a tightly woven cover from calico or cotton should be made first to hold the filling in place.

For most upholstery-weight cushions, it is best to conceal the zipper in the side seam so that the cushion can be reversed to share the wear and tear.

MATERIALS

fabric, the same as the main chair fabric

contrasting fabric for piping

suitable-gauge piping cord

upholstery thread

upholstery needle

sewing machine with a needle suitable for sewing through several layers of fabric

30 to 40 cm metal zipper (depending on the size of the cushion)

tailors chalk

Method

1 Cut two pieces of fabric large enough to cover the top and bottom of the cushion pad with 2.5 cm seam allowances all around.

2 Measure the length of piping you will require. Cut a sufficient number of bias strips from the contrasting fabric to achieve that length and wide enough to wrap around the piping cord you have chosen plus 1 cm on each side for seam allowances. Make the piping and join the lengths as shown on page 91.

3 Pin the piping to the right side of the top and bottom panels with the raw edges matching and right sides together. Cut a square from the seam allowance of the piping to allow it to curve around the corners (fig. 3). Where the two ends of the piping meet, cross them over as neatly as possible, pulling the ends into the seam allowances. Stitch.

4 For the wall of the cushion cover, cut four strips to the required length, allowing a 2.5 cm seam allowance at each end of each one. With the right sides facing, pin and baste all the short ends together, forming a square (fig. 4). This is a good time to check the fit. Stitch and press the seams open.

5 Stitch the bottom panel to the wall, with right sides facing and raw edges even, stitching over the piping stitching line.

6 Insert the zipper between one side wall and the top panel. (See page 26 for how to insert the zipper.)

7 Pin and baste the top panel to the remaining three walls in the same way as for the bottom panel. Try the cushion cover on the pad to check the fit, then stitch the seams. Turn the cover through to the right side through the open zipper. Press.

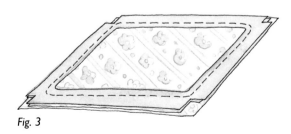

Fig. 3

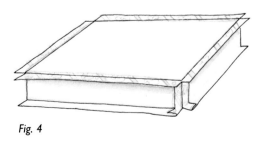

Fig. 4

Drop-in Seat Cover

VERY OFTEN THE SEAT PADDING ON DINING CHAIRS IS QUITE SOUND,
ONLY NEEDING A COVER OF NEW FABRIC TO BE REBORN.

Before you begin

Ensure that your chair frames and padding are in good condition. It does not make much sense to spend time and money recovering the seat of a chair that's on its last legs – literally!

Measuring

Measure the seat of your chair to establish how much new fabric you will need for each seat (fig. 1). Don't forget to allow for the height of the cushioning. If you can, use the old cover as a pattern for the new one. The lining fabric only needs to be sufficient to cover the underside of the chair base.

MATERIALS

sufficient fabric and lining

staples and staple gun or upholstery tacks and a small hammer

braid for the perimeter of the chair seat plus 6 cm for overlap and turns

craft glue

Method

1 Remove the old fabric and lining from your chair seat. Using the tip of a screwdriver or pliers, lift out any remaining tacks or staples.
2 Using the old cover or your measurements, cut out the new covers.
3 Place the new cover over the seat, folding in the corners and fastening the fabric underneath the seat with staples or upholstery tacks (fig. 2).
4 Turn in the edges of the lining piece. Position it over the centre of the underside of the seat, so that the previous stapling is covered. Staple or tack the lining to the frame (fig. 3).
5 Glue the braid over the staples or tacks, overlapping the ends and turning in the upper raw end.

A drop-in seat is very easy to re-cover

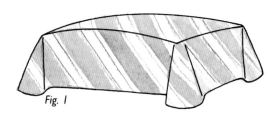

Fig. 1

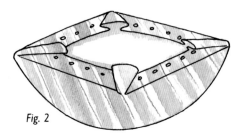

Fig. 2

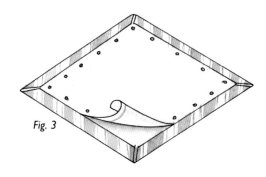

Fig. 3

Directors Chair Covers

DIRECTORS CHAIRS HAVE FOUND A PLACE IN MANY HOUSEHOLDS.
REASONABLY PRICED, COMFORTABLE AND EASY TO STORE, THEY
CAN UNDERGO ENDLESS TRANSFORMATIONS.

Directors chair 1

Before you begin This is a great way to dress up a directors chair. Whether you choose a plain fabric or a bold print, these inexpensive chairs will take on a whole new look.

You may wish to recover your directors chairs to coordinate with the new tablecloth and napkins you have just made for summer, or you may wish to make a statement by stencilling a new seat and back panel for your chairs. Either way, your final project will be a work of art when you paint the woodwork in a coordinating colour.

Measuring

Remove the existing covers from your chair and use them to estimate the fabric you will need for the new covers. Don't forget to add seam and hem allowances and extra fabric for wrapping around the frame and attaching the cover to the chair.

MATERIALS

sufficient fabric, such as lightweight canvas

sewing machine with a heavy-gauge needle suitable for sewing upholstery

upholstery tacks

matching sewing machine thread

tailors chalk

scissors

pins

tape measure

Method

1 Using the old covers as your pattern, cut new back and seat covers for the chairs. To prevent fraying, finish the edges with overlocking, zigzag stitching or as you prefer. Mark the hem turnings with tailors chalk.

2 Pin the hems at the marked turnings and check the fit before sewing. Stitch the seams as marked. Replace the covers on your chairs.

Crisp stripes are the perfect choice for a casual garden setting

Directors chair 2

Before you begin Directors chairs do vary in size so it is important that you measure your chair before you begin. Starting at the front of your chair at ground level, measure the distance up to the seat plus the depth of the seat up to the top of the chair back plus the distance from the top of the chair, then back to ground level. Record the measurement for the depth of the seat and the width of the back rest separately. Measure from the ground level up to and over each arm rest down to the seat. Add 1.5 cm seam allowances to all measurements. Sketch these elements on a sheet of paper and use the sketches as a guide only – you do not need to make a proper pattern. For this chair, the main pattern piece is 60.5 cm x 221.5 cm; the arm pieces measured 51.5 cm x 90 cm.

MATERIALS
pencil and paper

approximately 2.8 m of 120 cm wide fabric

30 cm of contrasting fabric for the ties

matching sewing machine thread

scissors

tape measure

pins

sewing machine

Method

1 Using your drawings as a guide, cut out the three pattern pieces. Cut four 15 cm wide ties, each 40 cm long.

2 Do not remove the existing seat or back rest; the slipcover will slip over the top. Place the main pattern piece over the chair, face downwards. Do the same with each arm piece. Pin the arm pieces to the main piece at the seat level and at the front leg. Pin the front and back of the main piece together down to the arm level of the chair, finishing pinning at this point.

3 Return to the front of the chair and pin a dart across the top of each arm front at right angles to the front seam. This will ensure the drape over the arm sits straight.

4 Remove the slipcover and machine-stitch all the seams into place. Trim the excess seam allowance, if necessary.

5 Return the slipcover to the chair (still inside out). Turn in 5 mm, then turn another 1 cm for the hem around the bottom of the slipcover and at the openings at the back legs.

6 Fold the strip for each tie over double with the right sides together and the raw edges even. Sew one short end and the long side. Turn through to the right side. Pin and baste the raw end of one tie to the hem on the front and back edges of each back opening. Remove the slipcover from the chair and stitch all the hems and seams, catching the ties as you go. Turn the slipcover to the right side and press.

Below: A bold check cotton slipcover gives new life to an old chair

Right: The painted chair frame and the combination of many coordinating fabrics give this setting a decorator's touch

Directors chair 3

Before you begin Applying two coats of high gloss enamel paint will give the frame an instant lift. Sand lightly between coats to give a satin-smooth finish.

If you are working with a heavy sateen or upholstery fabric, use a double thickness of fabric for extra strength. Fusible webbing between the layers of fabric will also add strength and keep the fabrics firmly in place.

Measuring

Measure from the top of the back rest down to the seat and along the seat to the front of the chair. This measurement plus the allowances for turnings at both ends is the total length. Measure the width required and add sufficient length to fold the fabric around the frame on both sides.

On a large sheet of paper, draw a rectangle to the length and width you have calculated. At one end of the rectangle mark the length of the back rest. At the other end, mark the depth of the seat. Do not forget to add sufficient allowance for turnings.

Draw in the shape of the chair cover with a rectangle at one end for the back rest and one rectangle at the other end for the seat, connected by a curved back rest extension.

MATERIALS
large sheet of paper
pencil
ruler
high gloss enamel paint
paintbrush
sufficient fabric
fusible webbing
heavy-gauge sewing machine needle
matching sewing machine thread
pins
heavy duty staples and stapler
scissors
tape measure
sewing machine

Method

1 Remove the existing covers and paint the wooden frame.

2 Cut out the fabric (or fabrics) for the chair cover. If you are using two fabrics, fuse them together with the fusible webbing. Turn in and stitch a double hem at each end of the fabric.

3 Make a narrow double hem along both sides of the fabric.

4 Place the cover on the chair, taking the turnings over to the wrong side, then attaching the cover to the frame with heavy duty staples.

Tailored Chair Cover

IF YOU HAVE WOODEN DINING CHAIRS THAT ARE STILL SOLID BUT HAVE SEEN BETTER DAYS, THIS SLIPCOVER PROJECT IS AN IDEAL REFURBISHING SOLUTION.

This easy-cover project may be the perfect opportunity to convert six odd chairs into a matched set.

This slipcover pattern is designed for chairs which are flat across the top of the back rest and do not have protruding knobs – all the lines and surfaces of the chair should be as straight as possible. Bowed backs and curved seats will not allow the fabric to hang properly. Choose your fabric carefully. You will need a sturdy material that doesn't present too many problems with matching patterns on adjacent surfaces.

Choose a contrasting or complementary fabric for the lining as it is sure to show at the joins. If you like, the slipcover can be lined with the main fabric for an all-over look.

For added comfort you can include a layer of wadding between the main fabric and the lining.

Measuring
You will need to take the measurements of your own chair then draw those rectangles on to a sheet of paper. Mark each rectangle with its position and mark all the measurements on it. The drawings here are intended as a guide only.

• *Pattern piece 1* Measure the length from the seat up the chair back and down to the floor (allowing for the width of the chair frame at the top of the back rest) by the width of the chair (allowing for the width of the chair frame at the sides).

• *Pattern piece 2* Measure the depth of the seat plus the distance to the floor by the width of the chair.

• *Pattern piece 3* Measure the depth of the seat plus the width of the timber frame by the height of the seat from the floor. Cut two.

Once you have established these measurements you can calculate the amount of fabric required.

MATERIALS
sheet of paper
pencil
ruler
main fabric
lining fabric
wadding in the same size (optional)
matching sewing machine thread
pins
scissors
tape measure
sewing machine

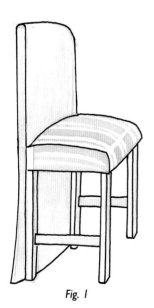

Fig. 1

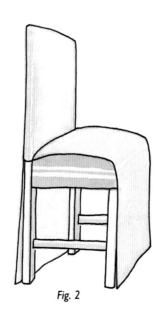

Fig. 2

Fig. 3

Method

1 Cut out the pattern pieces from the main and the lining fabric, allowing 1.5 cm all around for seams. Take care to match and centre any fabric pattern at this point.

2 On pattern piece 1, sew the sides together from the top of the chair back rest to the seat (fig. 1). Press.

3 Sew pattern piece 1 to pattern piece 2 at the seat back edge (fig. 2). Attach a pattern piece 3 at each side (fig. 3). Press.

4 Make eight 30 cm long ties out of scraps of the cover fabric. Pin one end of each tie, with the raw edges matching, on the right side of the fabric front and back edges, just below seat height.

5 Make the lining in the same way as for the cover. Place the lining and the cover together with the right sides facing and the raw edges even. Sew around the outside edge, leaving an opening for turning, and catching the ends of the ties in the seam. Turn the cover right side out, taking care to push the corners out completely. Press.

Match up your odd chairs with a set of tailored slipcovers like this

Ruffled Chair Cover

A LOOSE COVER FOR A CHAIR WITHOUT ARMS IS EASY TO MAKE AND OFFERS A
SOLUTION TO SEASONAL DECORATING WITHOUT MAJOR COST.

Ruffles and swags make a charming dining setting. See page 168 for how to make the tablecloth

Before you begin

If you are new to making slipcovers, it is best to use a plain fabric or one with a small all-over print that does not need to be pattern matched. Remember, if you are working with floral bouquets or a medallion print, centre the pattern on the front of the chair back and on the seat.

Measuring

Measure the various planes of the chair (such as the width and depth of the back rest and seat, and the height of the seat from the floor) and mark these measurements on a sketch pattern of your chair.

MATERIALS

sufficient fabric (we used approximately 4 m for our chair, allowing for the fullness in the skirt)

paper and pencil

10 cm Velcro tape

pins

scissors

tape measure

tailors chalk

matching sewing machine thread

sewing machine

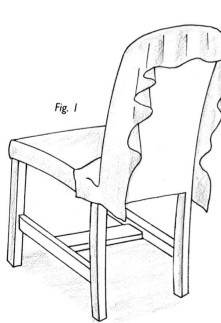

Fig. 1

Method

1 Cut out a rectangle of fabric each for the chair seat, the front of the back rest and the back of the back rest, using the measurements on your sketch pattern and following the grainlines of the fabric. Cut out the skirt to the length required plus 3 cm for the hem and one and a half times the distance around the chair seat. If necessary, join pieces with a flat fell seam to achieve the required length. Add 1.5 cm for each seam allowance. Make sure all the prints match up.

Fig. 2

2 Place the piece for the front of the back rest on the chair with the wrong side facing out (figs 1 and 2). Check the fit. If there is excess fabric bulk, you can pin darts or gather the edge to make the fabric sit more neatly. (See page 120 for how to deal with corners.) Treat the piece for the back of the back rest in the same way as the front.

3 While the pieces are still on the chair, pin the outer and inner back rest pieces together with wrong sides facing out. Check the fit and re-pin the darts if necessary. Mark the seam lines with tailors chalk. Remove the back rest pieces from the chair.

4 Stitch around the top and sides,

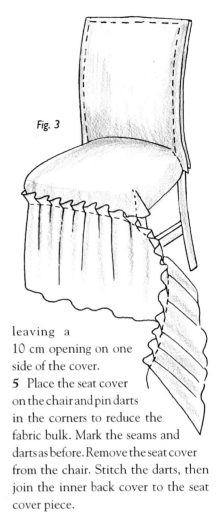

Fig. 3

leaving a 10 cm opening on one side of the cover.

5 Place the seat cover on the chair and pin darts in the corners to reduce the fabric bulk. Mark the seams and darts as before. Remove the seat cover from the chair. Stitch the darts, then join the inner back cover to the seat cover piece.

6 Turn in and press 5 mm on the bottom and the ends of the skirt, then turn in and press another 2.5 cm. Stitch the hems in place. Divide the top edge of the skirt into quarters and mark these points with a pin. Gather the top edge of the skirt.

7 Pin the skirt to the seat cover with the right sides together and the raw edges matching, beginning and ending at one of the back corners (fig. 3). Pull up the gathering to fit, placing a pin mark at each corner. Adjust the gathering, making it a little fuller at the corners. Stitch the skirt into place. Press.

8 Sew Velcro to the back opening to close the cover or make ties from scraps of fabric and sew them to either side of the opening.

9 If you wish to create a very charming effect, make two bows from the same fabric and slipstitch one to each side of the chair back.

Instant Sofa Cover-up

INSTANT LOOSE COVERS REQUIRE LITTLE SEWING, ONLY A SMALL FINANCIAL
INVESTMENT AND NOT A LOT OF TIME.

Before you begin

Practise your skills by draping an old sheet on your chair or sofa. This way you will quickly be able to work out where fabric can be tucked into crevices to anchor it. If the existing sofa has torn covers and you are not likely to use it again in its present state, sew strips of Velcro to the old lounge to marry up with Velcro on the fabric cover. The Velcro will help the fabric to stay neatly in position and it will not crease as much.

Select a fabric, such as a linen or another woven fabric, that is less likely to show creases. Fabric bows on the arms add a further decorative touch and can be attached with Velcro, stitched or pinned into place.

You should use 137 cm wide fabric for a two-seater sofa, as fewer joins will be necessary.

MATERIALS
fabric
pins
tailors chalk
Velcro (if required)
cord, ribbon or sewn ties

Method

1 It may be necessary to join lengths of fabric together to achieve the required width. If this is the case, use flat fell seams for added strength and always carefully match the fabric pattern.

2 Remove the seat cushions. Drape and tuck the fabric piece over the base of the lounge. When you are happy with the draping, mark the hem line with tailors chalk. Remove the cover. Even out any great irregularities in the chalk marks, then trim the excess fabric from the hem. Turn in and press a double hem. Stitch the hem in place.

3 Tie sashes, ribbons or cords around the arms to hold the fabric in place. The ties can be attached with Velcro, pins or by topstitching them into place.

Pleat the fabric at the arms for a neat finish

Wrapped seat cushion

MATERIALS
sufficient fabric
pinking shears
safety pins (optional)
needle and thread (optional)

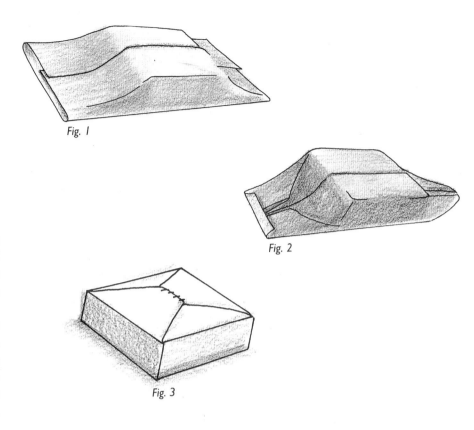

Fig. 1

Fig. 2

Fig. 3

Method

1 Use pinking sheers to cut out a fabric square twice the width and length of your cushion plus 30 cm. Place the cushion in the centre of the fabric, on the wrong side (fig. 4).

2 Wrap the cushion as if it were a present; first fold the fabric to the centre, turning in the raw edges. Secure the fabric on the underside with safety pins or stitches. Place on your chair or sofa to complete the look (figs 1 to 3).

No-sew cushion

MATERIALS
sufficient fabric
pinking shears

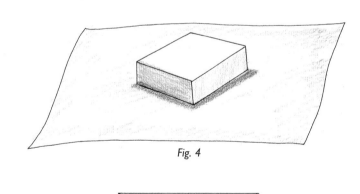

Fig. 4

Method

1 Cut with pinking shears, a rectangle of fabric three times the width of your cushion and twice as wide (fig. 4).

2 Fold the fabric as indicated in the illustration, bringing both ends up to tie in a knot at the top of the cushion (fig. 5). Place the knot to the underside for a tailored look (fig. 6).

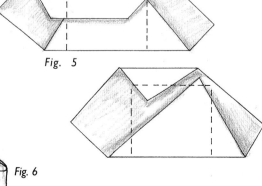

Fig. 5

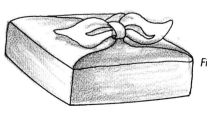

Fig. 6

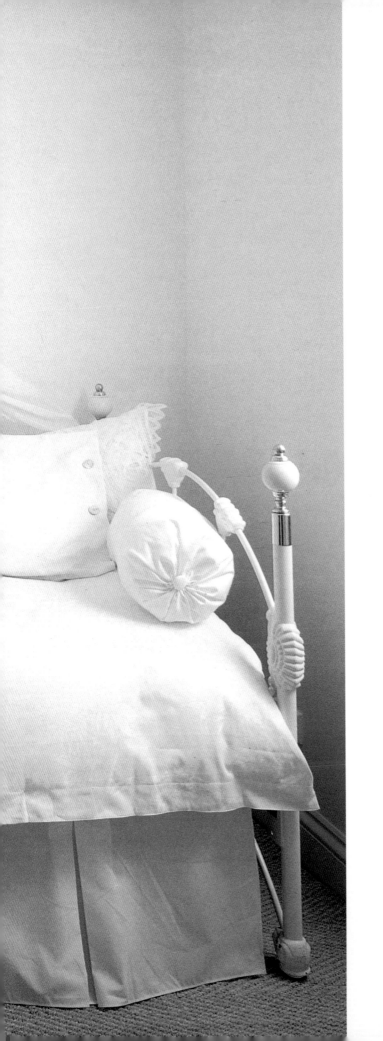

Bed Linen

BED SHEETS
QUILT COVERS
RUFFLED VALANCE
BOX-PLEATED VALANCE
TIERED VALANCE
PILLOWCASES
CONTINENTAL QUILT
QUILTED THROWOVER
TENT CANOPY
SHEER CANOPY
THROWOVER BEDSPREAD
UPHOLSTERED HEADBOARD
NURSERY LINEN

Bed Linen

IN MEDIEVAL TIMES, SERVANTS IN NOBLE HOUSEHOLDS SPUN AND WOVE ELABORATE
SHEETS AND PILLOW SHAMS FROM SILKS AND PURE COTTONS.

Through the ages, bed linen has always been considered a great luxury and was an essential part of a young lady's trousseau. Exquisite bed linen was often traded as part of a dowry or bequeathed in a will. Threads of gold and silver were worked on handmade laces, satins and silks to create sumptuous trims on pillows and linens.

Today's bed linen, in its many colours and styles, was introduced into Europe during the 1960s. Up until this time, bed linen was predominantly white with the bedspread printed in traditional florals. Bed linen has come a long way from those austere times, providing not only warmth and comfort but great decorative possibilities for the bedroom as well.

The colour scheme you select for your bed linen should reflect the total decorative scheme of your room. If you have a number of bed linen components to work with, combine different prints such as checks, stripes and florals, using a common element, such as the colour, to link the patterns together.

If you prefer the clean crisp purity of white linen, consider adding variations in texture to emphasise each of your components. Damask, with its silk and matte combination of weaves, provides wonderful textural qualities whilst the addition of lace edges on pillows and valances adds yet another variation.

Style is another consideration when planning the look of a bedroom. A stately brass or wooden four-poster bed in a formal bedroom, can be shown to advantage with a box-pleated valance, defining the height of the bed, or quilted bed shams in a Jacobean chintz with pillow shams in a coordinating smaller print. Both items can be easily removed to reveal subtle cotton sheets piped in one of the colours detailed in the bed shams. A decorative bolster or neck roll adds shape and proportion to the top of a bed.

Teenagers are often the hardest to select a bed linen scheme for. The great advantage of making your own bed linen is that you can quickly, and without too much expense, change the look as your children grow. For teenagers, it is always pretty safe to work with solid colours as the base of a bed, which can then be combined with plaids, stripes, paisleys, abstracts and florals.

For toddlers and infants, the nursery can be a wonderful place decorated in stimulating bold motifs or pastels. You will need to make all the items to size for your particular child's room; cot and bassinet sizes can vary dramatically.

Openings & closures

You should always leave a generous opening on a quilt cover through which to insert your quilt. The opening is best placed at the bottom of the quilt cover and, when used effectively, opening and closing mechanisms should be virtually invisible and washable. Zippers are not recommended for quilt cover openings, because they will deteriorate in time with the constant laundering. Velcro or press studs are the best type of invisible closure to use; however, decorative closures, such as tailored buttons or a row of tied bows, will give a distinctive effect.

Fabrics

The availability of wide-width sheeting has made it very easy for the home decorator to achieve a totally coordinated look for a bedroom, at relatively low cost. A number of outlets now supply wide-width sheeting which coordinates with their curtain and upholstery ranges. You therefore have the option of covering your window, upholstering the bedroom chair or dressing table stool in a coordinating fabric and then using the wide-width sheeting to make the bed linen or bedspread. A blend of fifty per cent cotton and fifty per cent polyester is recommended because of its easy-care qualities. However, a one hundred per cent cotton fabric, or any other fabric that can be easily laundered, dried and pressed may be used for bed linen.

The advantage of wide-width fabric is that there will be no joins or seams in the middle of your sheets or quilt cover, but you can successfully use fabric of any width for making bed linen.

For the ultimate in luxury, try the fresh feeling of damask or convert a lace tablecloth into a quilt cover. Those crocheted doilies that have never been out of your linen press can now take pride of place as a trim for your new pillowcases or bed cushions. Laces can be bought by the metre. One hundred per cent cotton lace complements damask bed linen beautifully, but remember to preshrink all the fabrics and trims before sewing.

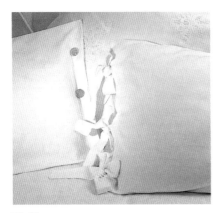

Tied bows

Buttons

Velcro tape

Press stud tape

Measuring

❖

It is always important to measure the bed carefully before you purchase materials – small differences won't matter for flat sheets, but accuracy is important for ruffles or valances. There is little uniformity in bed sizes; the depths of mattresses vary and the addition of castors changes the height from the top of the mattress to the floor. Likewise, pillowcases can vary in size.

Sheeting width varies from 228 cm to 254 cm from selvage to selvage. The quantities given in the instructions in this book are calculated on standard sizes of manufactured sheets and quilt covers. You may need to adjust these for your own use.

Quilt covers should be made to fit individual quilts, so measure your own quilt before purchasing materials. Consider using contrasting or complementary colours or prints for the front and back of your quilt cover.

When measuring for a pillowcase, add 3 cm for the seams to the required finished width and 21 cm to the length for the seam allowance and flap.

To measure a bed, measure the flat surface from the top of the bed to the bottom edge of the bed (A to B) and the flat surface from side edge to side edge (C to D). The depth of the bed is measured from the flat surface at the side edge to the floor (B to E and D to F) (fig. 1).

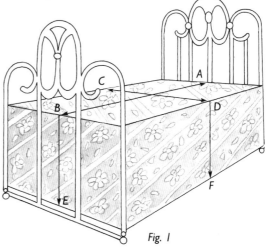

Fig. 1

Fabric requirements

❖

All sheets and quilt covers are cut with selvages forming the top and bottom edges while the sides have raw edges which will be hemmed. The following table may serve as a guide:

	Queen	Double	Single
Flat sheet	2.8 m	2.3 m	1.6 m
Fitted sheet	2.7 m	2.2 m	1.5 m
Quilt cover	4.2 m	3.6 m	2.8 m
	to finish at 2.1 m	to finish at 1.8 m	to finish at 1.4 m

by the width of the sheeting (for all sizes)

Fabric required for pillowcases:

Plain pillowcase	50 cm
Ruffled pillowcase	70 cm
Flanged pillowcase	70 cm

Bed Sheets

Before you begin

For sheets, select a cotton or polycotton blend fabric that will survive the rigours of frequent laundering.

The cutting and sewing methods described apply to all sizes. Use 1.5 cm seams, unless otherwise stated, and neaten all raw edges.

French seams are commonly used for sewing bed linen. To sew a French seam, pin and stitch a 1.5 cm seam with the wrong sides facing. Trim the seam allowance back to 5 mm. Press the seam closed along the seam line with the right sides together. Pin and stitch the seam again with a 1 cm seam allowance, enclosing the raw edges. For more information on how to sew French seams, see page 32.

Cut the fabric according to the dimensions of your bed. If joins are necessary, match the pattern so that the print runs uniformly across the total width of the fabric. To match patterns, cut one piece of fabric at the required length and lay the piece flat on the table. Mark the pattern repeat with two pins or tailors chalk. Fold under the selvages of the fabric piece to be joined then find the beginning of the next pattern repeat and measure your required length up and down from this point, allowing for any necessary seam or hem allowances. Baste the two pieces together before sewing. A more detailed method for matching fabrics can be seen on page 43.

Fitted sheet

MATERIALS
sufficient fabric
1 cm wide elastic
matching sewing machine thread
tape measure
pins
scissors
sewing machine

Method

1 Cut the fabric for the sheet as wide as the mattress plus the depth of the mattress plus 30 cm for the tuck-under on each side and 3 cm for the hem, and as long as the mattress plus the depth of the mattress plus 30 cm for the tuck-under on each side and 3 cm for the hem.

2 Cut squares from each corner of the fabric as illustrated (fig. 1). Note that A to B is the depth of the mattress plus 30 cm for the tuck-under and 1.5 cm for the hem. Pin the sides of the square together, joining the A points. Sew from the outside edge to the inner corner, forming an angle at each corner of the sheet.

3 Turn in and press 5 mm around the outside edge. Then turn in and press another 1 cm. Sew the 1 cm wide elastic to the seam allowance on each corner, starting and finishing 40 cm on either side of the corner seam, using a zigzag stitch and stretching the elastic as you sew (fig. 2).

Above: Brightly coloured cotton is great for a child's fitted sheet

Right: A flat sheet can be trimmed or left plain as you wish

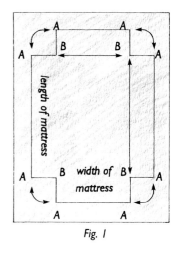

Fig. 1

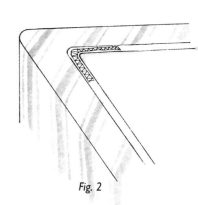

Fig. 2

Flat sheet

MATERIALS
sufficient fabric
matching sewing machine thread
pins
tape measure
scissors
sewing machine

Method

1 Turn in and press 5 mm along the side edges. Turn in and press an additional 1 cm hem on the side and bottom edges. Note that the selvages should be at the top and bottom edges of your sheet. Stitch the hems in place.
2 Turn in and press 5 cm at the top.
3 Trim the top edge with a panel of lace, if desired.

Flat sheet with contrast panel

MATERIALS
sufficient fabric
contrasting fabric, 30 cm x the sheet width
contrasting corded piping, the width of your sheet plus 2.5 cm for turnings
matching sewing machine thread
pins
scissors
tape measure
sewing machine

Method

1 Turn in and press 5 mm along the raw side edges. Turn in and press 1 cm on the bottom edge.
2 Make the length of piping following the instructions on page 21. Pin the piping to one long side of the contrast panel with the right sides facing and the raw edges even. Stitch the piping in place with the zipper foot on your sewing machine, stitching as close to the piping as possible. Press under the raw edges of the piping and the contrasting panel at the piped edge.
3 Pin the plain edge of the contrasting panel to the top edge of the sheet so that the right side of the contrasting panel is facing the wrong side of the sheet. Stitch along the top edge and down the sides. Trim any excess bulk and clip across the corners.
4 Turn the contrasting panel to the right side of the sheet. Press. Pin, then machine-stitch along the piping line.
5 Turn in and press another 1 cm on the sides. Stitch the side and bottom hems. Press.

Contrasting fabrics add interest to a sheet

Quilt Covers

Basic quilt cover

Before you begin Neaten all the seam allowances on the inside of your quilt cover with an overlocker. If this is not possible, consider using French seams. (See page 32 for how to sew French seams.)

MATERIALS
sufficient fabric

approximately 4 m of 1.5 cm wide cotton tape (optional)

Velcro, press fasteners, or press fasteners on a fabric strip

matching sewing machine thread

sewing machine

tape measure

pins

scissors

Method

1 If you are using sheeting, place the selvages at the top and bottom edges. If you are using cotton or polycotton dress fabric, join lengths to achieve the required size, taking care to match any pattern. Cut a top and a bottom for your quilt cover.

2 Place the two pieces together with the right sides facing. Pin and stitch the top two sides and the bottom, leaving a 1 m opening on the bottom edge (fig. 1). Begin sewing at the bottom edge, work along one side to the top and then back down along the remaining side and the bottom edge. Trim the seam allowances and clip the corners.

3 Press in and stitch down the seam allowances at the opening, then sew on the closures of your choice.

4 You may like to sew ties of cotton tape inside the cover at each corner and a corresponding tie on to each corner of the quilt. Tie these together to keep the quilt in place within the cover. Ties sewn to the outside corners of the quilt cover can be used to tie the cover to the bedposts.

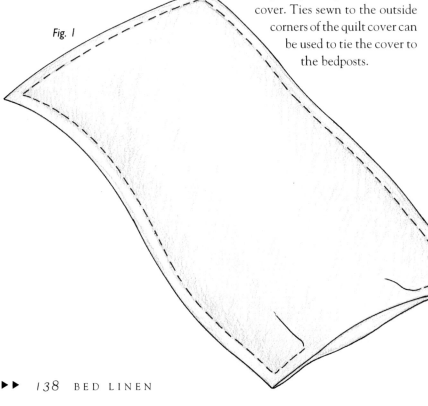

Fig. 1

Buttoned quilt cover

Before you begin Make the buttons a decorative feature of this quilt cover. Choose interesting buttons, perhaps in mother-of-pearl or covered buttons. If you are going to cover buttons, allow at least an additional 5 cm square of fabric for each button.

MATERIALS
sufficient fabric

four buttons for a single and six to eight buttons for a double, queen or king size quilt cover

matching sewing machine thread

sewing machine

scissors

pins

tape measure

sewing machine

Method

1 If you are using sheeting, place the selvages at the top and bottom edges. If you are using cotton or polycotton dress fabric, join lengths to achieve the required size, taking care to match any pattern. Cut a top and a bottom for your cover.

2 Sew a 1.5 cm hem along one short side of each of the two pieces. This will be the bottom end of the cover. With the right sides facing, pin and stitch the three remaining sides together with a flat seam, starting from the bottom, working up one side to the top, then back down along the remaining side. If your fabric looks as though it could fray, it is better to either overlock or zigzag each of the raw edges individually. Trim the seam allowance and clip the corners. Turn the cover to the right side and press.

3 Turn an additional 5 cm along each bottom edge to the wrong side. Pin and machine-stitch the hems into place.

4 Make the required number of buttonholes, evenly spaced, along the bottom edge of the cover and approximately 3 cm up from the turned edge.

5 Sew the same number of buttons in the corresponding positions, 3 cm up from the turned bottom edge. Use buttons with shanks or make thread shanks (fig. 2).

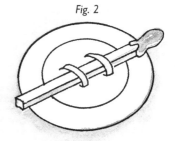

Fig. 2: Stitching over a matchstick which is later removed produces a thread shank for a button

A simple buttoned quilt cover complements a collection of lacy cushions

Reversible piped quilt cover

Before you begin The measurements given here are for a single bed; so adjust the measurements to fit your own bed. Neaten all the seam allowances on the inside of your quilt cover with an overlocker or zigzag stitching.

MATERIALS

1.4 m of each of two different fabrics

2.8 m of 6 cm wide contrasting bias binding (see page 20 for how to make continuous bias binding)

2.8 m piping cord, size 6

2.8 m of 12 cm wide bias binding in a second contrasting colour (see page 20 for how to make continuous bias binding)

2.8 m piping cord, size 12

matching sewing machine thread

tape measure

pins

scissors

sewing machine

Velcro tape, or press fasteners on a fabric strip

Method

1 If you are using sheeting, place the selvages at the top and bottom edges. If you are using cotton or polycotton dress fabric, join lengths to achieve the required size, taking care to match any pattern. Cut the quilt cover top from one fabric and the quilt cover bottom from the other fabric.

2 Pin and baste the smaller piping to the top fabric along two long and one short sides, with the right sides together and the raw edges matching. Piggyback the larger piping over the smaller piping, basting it in place. Stitch both rows of piping to the top of the quilt cover at the same time.

3 Place the top and bottom pieces together with the right sides facing. Pin and stitch the two pieces together, leaving a 1 m opening in the end without piping. Stitch. Trim the seam allowances and clip the corners.

4 Turn in and press 5 mm at the opening, then turn in and press another 1 cm. Stitch. Sew on the Velcro or the fastening tape.

Jumbo piping in bright colours defines the edges of this cheerful quilt cover for a child's bed

Ruffled reversible quilt cover

This is a great way to ring the changes in your bedroom – floral one day, stripes the next; country checks one day and traditional white the next. Teamed with an array of reversible pillowcases you can achieve two totally different looks for the price of one.

Make the quilt cover in exactly the same way as the basic quilt cover but cut the top and the bottom from different fabrics.

Ruffles have also been added to the reversible quilt cover. Ruffles must always be double, so that the ruffle is finished on both sides. For this quilt cover, the ruffle strips were cut 24 cm

Top: Choose a crisp geometric print to team with a floral to give two very different looks

Above: Make certain the pillowcases, valance and sheets match both sides of the quilt

wide in order to finish at 10 cm. Make sure the colour and the fabric you select for the ruffle complement both sides of the quilt cover. (See pages 23 to 24 for how to make and apply ruffles.)

Ruffled Valance

Before you begin To calculate the width of fabric you need for the ruffle, measure the depth of the bed from the top of the bed base to 1 cm above the floor and add 3 cm for the top and bottom hems. The length should be at least twice the length of the two longer sides plus the width of the mattress plus 1.5 cm for any joining seam allowances and side hems needed.

You will also need a rectangle of fabric, the same dimensions as the top of the mattress plus 1.5 cm all around for seam allowances.

MATERIALS

sufficient fabric

matching sewing machine thread

pins

scissors

tape measure

sewing machine

*80 cm of 5 mm wide elastic
(optional – if you have a posted bed)*

*eight 30 cm long fabric ties
(optional – if you have a posted bed)*

A ruffled valance adds charm to a bedroom

Method

1 For beds with no bedposts or board at the foot: Cut out the rectangle of fabric for the base piece. Cut the length of fabric required for the ruffle, joining pieces as necessary to achieve the total length. Hem the bedhead end of the base piece with a double hem, turning in and pressing 5 mm, then turning in and pressing another 1 cm. Hem the short ends and the bottom edge of the ruffle as for the base piece (fig. 1). Gather the remaining raw edge of the ruffle with two rows of gathering stitches. Pull up the gathering so that the ruffle fits around the base piece (fig. 2). Pin the ruffle to the base piece with the raw edges matching and the right sides together. Adjust the gathering, then stitch into place.

2 For beds with bedposts and/or boards, hem the head end of the base piece. Cut the ruffle strip to finish on either side of the posts or board. Hem the short ends and the lower edge of the ruffle by turning in and pressing 5 mm, then turning in and pressing another 1 cm. Gather the upper edges of each ruffle piece separately with two rows of gathering stitches. Pull up the gathering so that each ruffle piece fits the appropriate side of the base piece. Adjust the gathers, then pin and stitch the ruffles to the base piece.

3 You can sew ties to the ruffles on either side of the bedposts or the legs of the bed base, if you wish. Make the ties from scraps of fabric, then sew a 10 cm length of elastic to one end of each tie and the other end of the elastic to the corner of the ruffle. The elastic will take the strain off the ties and prevent the stitching from breaking.

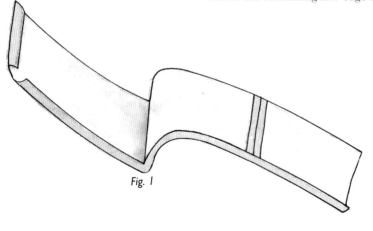

Fig. 1

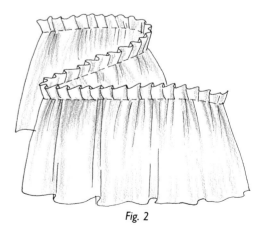

Fig. 2

Box-pleated Valance

Before you begin Box-pleating can be done by hand or with tape. Just as there are tapes to give you different heading styles for your curtains, similar gathering tape can be used to achieve box pleats. In this case we have used folding tape that automatically makes a 20 cm wide box pleat.

Measuring

To calculate the width of fabric you need for the valance, measure the depth of the bed from the top of the bed base to 1 cm above the floor (B to E) and add 3 cm for the top and bottom hems. (The length should be at least two and a half times the length of the two longer sides of the mattress (C to D) plus the width of the mattress plus 1.5 cm for any joining seam allowances and side hems needed (fig. 3).

You will also need a rectangle of fabric, the same dimensions as the top of the mattress plus 1.5 cm all around for seam allowances.

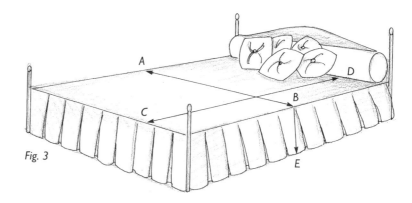

Fig. 3

MATERIALS
sufficient fabric
box-pleating tape, the same length as the sum of the two long sides of the mattress plus the width
matching sewing machine thread
pins
scissors
tape measure
sewing machine
80 cm of 5 mm wide elastic
(optional – if you have a posted bed)
eight 30 cm long fabric ties
(optional – if you have a posted bed)

Method

1 For beds with no bedposts or board at the foot: cut out the rectangle for the base piece. Cut the length of fabric for the valance, joining pieces as necessary to achieve the total length. Finish the valance bottom and the two short sides with a rolled edge or a double hem.

2 Pin the tape to the top edge of the wrong side of the valance and sew into position. Pull up the tape from one end to form the box pleats. Press the pleats into position. Stitch over the pleats at the top edge of the tape. Some tapes can be removed once the pleats are set and can be used again later.

3 With the right sides facing, pin and sew the box-pleated valance to the base piece. Double hem the top edge of the base piece. Press.

4 For beds with posts make a separate valance for each side and the bottom of the bed.

A plain cotton box-pleated valance is very suitable for a child's bed

Tiered Valance

YOU CAN ADD A TOUCH OF EXTRAVAGANT GLAMOUR WITH TWO, OR EVEN THREE, LAYERS OF RUFFLES OF VARYING LENGTHS, MIXING DIFFERENT TEXTURES, COLOURS AND PRINTS.

Before you begin Calculate the width of the first base ruffle in the same way as for the standard bed ruffle or valance. For each additional ruffle, subtract 10 to 20 cm from the depth, depending on the height of your bed. Make sure you have enough of each contrasting ruffle showing. All other measurements remain the same.

MATERIALS
sufficient fabric for each contrasting ruffle

matching sewing machine thread

pins

scissors

tape measure

sewing machine

*80 cm of 5 mm wide elastic
(optional – if you have a posted bed)*

*eight 30 cm long fabric ties
(optional – if you have a posted bed)*

Method

1 For beds with no bedposts or board at the foot: Cut out the rectangle of fabric for the base piece. Cut the required length of fabric for each ruffle, joining pieces as necessary to achieve the total length required. Hem the headboard end of the base piece with a double hem, turning in and pressing 5 mm, then turning and pressing in another 1 cm.

2 Hem the short ends and the bottom edge of each ruffle as for the base piece.

3 Lay the ruffles on top of one another with the deepest ruffle on the bottom, so that all the top raw edges are even and all the right sides of all the ruffles

Choose a combination of plain and patterned fabrics

are facing upwards. Gather all the top raw edges together through all thicknesses. Pull up the gathering so that the ruffle fits around the base piece. Pin the ruffle to the base piece with the raw edges matching and the right sides facing. Adjust the gathering evenly. Stitch the ruffles into place.

4 For beds with posts, make a separate tiered valance for each side and the bottom of the bed.

Pillowcases

THERE ARE MANY STYLES OF PILLOWCASES THAT YOU CAN ACHIEVE
WITH JUST A LITTLE TIME AND SOME INSPIRATION.

Basic pillowcase 1

Before you begin This pillowcase is made out of one continuous piece of fabric with a turned flap which covers the pillow. Fabric for the pillowcase is cut to the dimensions of your pillow: the width of the pillow plus 1.5 cm for each seam allowance and twice the length of the pillow plus 1.5 cm for each turning and hem plus 15 cm for the flap.

MATERIALS
sufficient fabric
matching sewing machine thread
pins
scissors
tape measure
sewing machine

Method

1 Cut the fabric to the required size. Turn in and press 5 mm on both raw short ends. Turn in and press another 1 cm. Machine-stitch the hems into place.
2 With the right sides together, fold back one end of the fabric to measure approximately the length of the pillow. Press with a warm iron to form a crease.
3 Place the fabric with the shorter part on the bottom. On the top section, fold back the 15 cm flap as shown in fig. 1. Stitch along both long sides through all thicknesses. Trim and neaten the raw edges if necessary. You can use French seams if you prefer. (See page 32 for how to sew French seams.)
4 Turn to the right side and press.

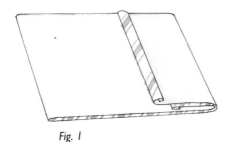

Fig. 1

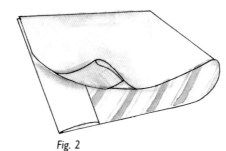

Fig. 2

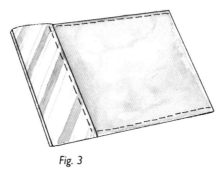

Fig. 3

Basic pillowcase 2

Before you begin This pillowcase resembles a bag without a flap and is ideal if you want to use buttons or ties. You will need a piece of fabric cut to the dimensions of your pillow: the width of the pillow plus 1.5 cm for each seam allowance and twice the length of your pillow plus 1.5 cm for all turnings and hems, plus 20 cm for the cuff turnings at the opening.

MATERIALS
sufficient fabric
matching sewing machine thread
pins
scissors
tape measure
sewing machine

Method

1 Cut the fabric to the desired size. Turn in and press 5 mm on the raw short ends. Fold the fabric over double widthways so that the right sides are facing. Sew the sides with a 1.5 cm seam allowance. Overlock or zigzag the raw edges.
2 Turn in and press 10 cm all the way around on the open end for the cuff (fig. 2). Stitch the cuff in place, close to the inner edge with one continuous line of stitching (fig. 3).
3 Turn the pillowcase through to the right side. Press. Add the closure of your choice.

Use either method for making this basic pillowcase

Pillowcase with bows

Before you begin Braids and ribbons are both suitable for the bows, but you will need to sew a double hem on the ends to stop them from fraying. Preshrink ribbons or braids and test for colour fastness.

Measuring

You will need a piece of fabric cut to the dimensions of your pillow: the width of the pillow plus 1.5 cm for each seam allowance and twice the length of your pillow plus 1.5 cm for all turnings and hems plus 20 cm for the cuff turnings at the opening.

MATERIALS

sufficient fabric

six strips, each 8 cm x 30 cm, for the bows

matching sewing machine thread

pins

tape measure

scissors

sewing machine

tailors chalk

turning hook or knitting needle

Method

1 Make the basic pillowcase, using method 2.

2 Fold the ribbon for the ties over double. Sew one short end and one long end with a 1.5 cm seam allowance. Trim the seam and turn through to the right side with the turning hook or knitting needle. Slipstitch the remaining end closed. Press each tie flat.

3 Mark three evenly spaced positions on the right side of the front cuff.

4 For three ties, sew the end with the slipstitches to the inside edge of the front cuff at the markings. Sew another tie to correspond on the inside edge of the back cuff.

Pristine white is lovely for a bedroom

Buttoned pillowcase

MATERIALS

two pieces of fabric, one 50 cm x 1.52 m and one 14 cm x 50 cm

five buttons (if you are going to use covered buttons, allow an additional 5 cm square of fabric for each button)

matching sewing machine thread

contrasting piping

pins

tape measure

scissors

sewing machine

tailors chalk

turning hook or knitting needle

Method

1 Place the two pieces of fabric together along a 50 cm end with the right side of the small piece facing the wrong side of the larger piece and the raw edges matching. Stitch along the 50 cm end. Press the small piece to the right side of the larger piece.

2 Turn in and press 1 cm on the other 50 cm raw edge of the small piece. Tuck the contrasting piping under this pressed edge and stitch the edge down, through all thicknesses.

3 Turn in and press 1 cm on the other 50 cm raw edge of the larger piece, then turn in and press another 5 cm. Stitch.

4 Fold the pillowcase with the right sides together and the short ends matching. Stitch the sides, securing the stitching firmly at the opening edge. Turn the pillowcase to the right side and press.

5 With tailors chalk, mark the positions of five evenly spaced buttonholes across the front edge of the opening, 4 cm down from the opening. Stitch the buttonholes then sew the buttons on the other side of the opening to correspond.

6 Bind the opening edges if you wish.

Flanged pillowcase

MATERIALS

one piece of fabric, 70 cm x 86 cm, for the pillowcase front

two pieces of fabric, one 65 cm x 70 cm and one 35 cm x 70 cm, for the pillowcase back

sewing machine thread in a contrasting colour and a matching colour

pins

scissors

tape measure

tailors chalk

sewing machine

Method

1 Narrow hem one 70 cm end of each back piece. Place the back pieces on the front piece with the right sides facing, the hemmed edges of the back pieces overlapping and all the raw edges matching. Stitch around the outside edge. Trim the seams and turn the pillowcase to the right side. Press.

2 With tailors chalk, mark a guideline 8 cm from the outside edge all around the pillowcase. Stitch along this line to form the flange.

Ruffled pillowcase

MATERIALS

one piece of fabric, 50 cm x 78 cm, for the pillowcase front

two pieces of fabric, one 50 cm x 70 cm and one 22 cm x 50 cm, for the pillowcase back

2.5 m of 20 cm wide fabric, for the ruffle strip

matching sewing machine thread

pins

scissors

tape measure

sewing machine

tailors chalk

The checked flanged pillowcase and the floral ruffled pillowcase work well together

Method

1 Join the short ends of the ruffle strip to form a circle. Fold the ruffle strip over double with the wrong sides together and raw edges matching. Gather the raw edges with two rows of gathering stitches along the raw edges. Pull up the gathering to fit around the front piece.

2 Pin the ruffle around the front piece, with right sides facing and raw edges matching. Adjust the gathering. Baste (fig. 1).

3 Narrow hem one 50 cm edge of each back piece. Place both back pieces on the right side of the front piece (over the ruffle) with the right sides facing, overlapping the hemmed edges and having all the outside edges matching. Stitch around the outside edge through all thicknesses. Turn to the right side and press.

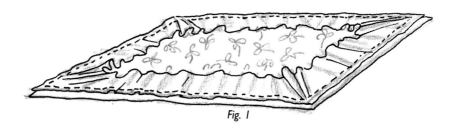

Fig. 1

European pillowcase

Before you begin These instructions are for a flanged European pillowcase but a European pillowcase can be trimmed with ruffles, lace inserts or piping detail.

MATERIALS

*70 cm square of fabric,
for the pillowcase front*

*two pieces of fabric, one 46 cm x 70 cm
and one 39 cm x 70 cm, for the
pillowcase back*

matching sewing machine thread

65 cm square insert

tailors chalk

tape measure

pins

scissors

sewing machine

Method

1 Turn in and press a 5 mm hem along the 70 cm edges of both back pieces. Turn in and press an additional 1 cm hem. Stitch.

2 Place the two back pieces with the right side of the larger piece facing the right side of the smaller piece and with the larger piece overlapping the smaller piece for 12 cm. Baste the overlapped edges together.

3 Place the front piece and the back pieces together with the right sides together and the outside edges even. Pin. Stitch along three sides through all thicknesses excluding the flap edge for the opening. Trim the seams and corners. Remove the basting. Turn the pillowcase to the right side and press.

4 Using tailors chalk, mark a line 5 cm from the edge on all four sides of the pillowcase. Stitch along this line to form the flange.

Above: A collection of plump European pillows

Below: Make this child's charming pillow by attaching cotton lace to the ruffle strip before gathering. The pillowcase is then made in exactly the same way as the one on page 147.

A tray doily slipstitched on to the front of a pillowcase makes a pretty feature

Scalloped pillowcase

MATERIALS

piece of fabric, 72 cm x 82 cm, for the pillowcase front

two pieces of fabric, one 67 cm x 72 cm and one 12 cm x 67 cm, for the pillowcase back

matching sewing machine thread

polyester fibre fill or a 65 cm square insert

Battenburg lace

cardboard, 5 cm x 72 cm, for the template

water-soluble marking pen

small plate to use for the template

pencil

sewing machine

tailors chalk

needle

thread

Method

1 Cut out the lace pattern to be embroidered. Look for strong solid lines. Pin the lace pattern to the pillowcase front. Using a small zigzag stitch, embroider the lace design on to the pillowcase front.

2 Make a template for the scalloped pattern, by drawing around the outline of the small plate on to the piece of cardboard. Our scallops are approximately 6.5 cm wide and 1.5 cm deep. Using the template and the water-soluble pen, draw a row of scallops down each side of the pillowcase front.

3 Stitch along the pattern with a satin stitch. When the stitching is complete, use sharp scissors to snip into the scallops and cut away the excess fabric along the raw edge.

4 Stitch a double hem on the smaller back piece, turning in and pressing 5 mm, then turning in and pressing another 1 cm. Stitch the hem in place. Repeat this process on one short edge of the larger back piece.

5 Turn in and press 5 mm on the raw edges on the remaining three sides of the smaller back piece. Place this piece (right side up) on to the wrong side of the embroidered front piece. Topstitch it in place, stitching 5 cm in from the scalloped edge.

6 Turn in and press 5 mm on the three remaining sides of the larger back piece. Pin the hemmed edge of the back piece to match the topstitched edge of the smaller back piece. This will form the side opening. Stitch the three sides into place, 5 cm in from the scalloped edges. The larger back piece should completely cover the smaller back piece which now forms the pillowcase flap.

Continental Quilt

THESE FEATHER- OR DOWN-FILLED QUILTS, ALSO CALLED DUVETS OR DOONAS, ARE THE IDEAL SOLUTION FOR COLD WINTER NIGHTS. THEY PROVIDE THE WARMTH OF SEVERAL BLANKETS WITHOUT THE WEIGHT.

Continental quilts make bedmaking a breeze

Before you begin The size of your quilt is entirely up to you. Generally a double bed quilt should be approximately 2 m x 2 m and a single bed quilt 2 m x 1.6 m.

Use a very closely woven fabric like japara (not always easy to find), down-proof cambric or a very closely woven furnishing chintz or cotton. Don't use sheets – feathers can work their way through the weave and escape.

If you are joining lengths of fabric use flat fell or French seams.

The choice of filling is up to you. Down is more expensive than feathers, but is warmer, lighter and bulkier. A combination of feathers and down is a good compromise. Polyester fibre is suitable for anyone allergic to feathers.

Generally, filling is sold in packs, by weight. Approximately 1.5 kg of a feather-and-down-combination filling was needed for this double bed quilt. Polyester fibre weighs slightly more than feathers. Experiment until you are happy with the weight and feel of your own quilt.

Tape is used to create channels for the filling. Choose firm cotton twill tape, not bias binding. The quantity of tape will depend on how many channels you make. For this double bed quilt, 20 cm wide channels suited the fabric pattern. This gave us nine rows of tape (giving us ten channels), so we used 18 m of twill tape. The length of tape required is equal to the number of rows of tape multiplied by the length of the quilt cover. Decide on the width of channels best for your fabric.

A feather quilt is, theoretically,

washable – but the bulk is daunting when hanging it out to dry. Drycleaning is effective. Hanging your quilt out regularly to air in the sun will keep it smelling clean and fresh.

The experienced say that one should only work with feathers and down in the bathroom with the door shut! When filling your quilt, place the opened bag of feathers in the bath. This helps to confine the flyaway feathers to a relatively draught-free area with little for them to stick to. (Remember to remove the towels!)

Ties at the corners allow you to bundle up the quilt neatly for storage

MATERIALS

sufficient fabric to cut a front and back of the required size plus 10 cm all around for turnings

fabric strip, 30 cm wide, for the ties

filling of your choice
(see Before you begin)

5 cm wide cotton twill tape
(see Before you begin)

pins

tape measure

matching sewing machine thread

scissors

sewing machine

Method

1 Press in 10 cm all around each quilt piece to mark the final fold line for the hem. Fold the quilt along the tape lines at predetermined distances for the channel widths. Press along each line to make a guide for sewing. This step is not necessary if you have striped fabric as the stripes provide a guide for the channel widths.

2 Stitch one edge of the tape along one stripe/crease on the wrong side of one quilt piece (fig. 1). Then stitch the other side of the tape to the same stripe/crease on the wrong side of the other quilt piece. Be sure to stitch very close to the edges of the tape. Do this for all the channels.

3 Turn in and press 3 cm on the sides and lower edge. Turn in and press another 3 cm. Topstitch the hems in

place through all thicknesses, closing the quilt at the same time. Fill the channels evenly, smoothing the filling right down the channels. When you are satisfied with the quantity of filling, fold over the top edge and sew it in the same way as the sides (fig. 2).

4 You can attach ties to the bottom end of your quilt for attaching it to your bed or for tying the quilt into a bundle for storage when it's not in use.

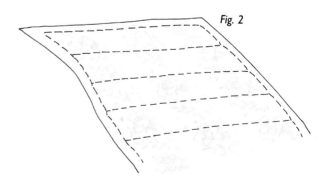

Fig. 1

Fig. 2

Quilted Throwover

A QUILTED THROWOVER IS ANOTHER ATTRACTIVE DECORATIVE TOUCH YOU CAN MAKE FOR YOUR BED.

Before you begin

Providing only minimal warmth but very high in the fashion stakes, a decorative throwover is thinner than a continental quilt and is filled with polyester wadding rather than the bulkier down and feathers. A decorative throwover made in the same fabric as a quilt, or in a fabric that coordinates with it, could make an ideal summer/ winter combination in any bedroom. A throwover can also be reversible, giving a pleasant look if the throwover is rolled down over a bedspread because the contrasting fabric peeps through.

Use the same dimensions as those given for the continental quilt cover.

The quilting can be done by machine or by hand and there are many different quilting patterns you can use. Remember, busy or ornate fabrics work best with simple quilting patterns, but with plain fabrics a more intricate quilting design can be used. If you are unsure about quilting, manufacturers of custom-made bedspreads will quilt fabric by the metre for a set price. Investigate if this is a possibility and if the costs involved are warranted.

MATERIALS

fabric cut to the required dimensions plus 1 cm around all the edges to allow for the quilting taking up some slack

quilting thread

6 cm wide bias-cut fabric for binding the edge

matching sewing machine thread

pins

scissors

tape measure

tailors chalk

quilting pattern

sewing machine

Method

1 Make sufficient bias binding to go around the edges. See pages 20 to 21 for how to make and join bias binding and piping.

2 Prepare the quilt fabric by sandwiching the polyester wadding between the two pieces of fabric. The wadding should run vertically down the fabric. Pin with safety pins or baste all three layers together, basting rows 30 cm apart from the top to the bottom of the fabric and all the way across.

3 Mark your quilting pattern on the top fabric with tailors chalk. Machine- or handquilt the pattern (fig. 1). Press well.

4 Finish the raw edges with a rolled hem or bias binding.

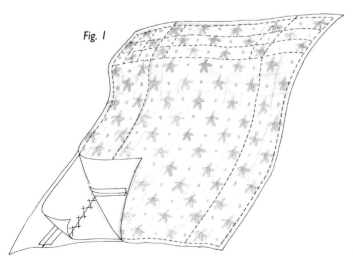

Fig. 1

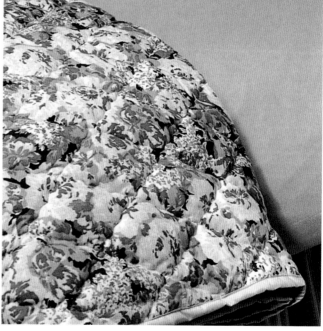

Tent Canopy

PURELY DECORATIVE, THIS STYLE OF CANOPY CAN BE SUSPENDED FROM THE CEILING ON POLES, REPLACING A HEADBOARD AND CREATING A STUNNING VISUAL EFFECT.

Before you begin To calculate how much fabric you will need, measure from the floor over the pole and back to the floor plus 30 cm for extra draping. The fabric should be approximately 70 cm wide by this measurement long. If you need to join lengths allow 1.5 cm for each seam allowance and 5 cm for the finished hem.

MATERIALS
decorative pole, approximately 75 cm long

two contrasting pieces of fabric of the required size

sufficient 6 cm wide contrasting bias-cut fabric to bind all the long edges of the canopy

matching sewing machine thread

curtain mounting bracket

ceiling hook for attaching the cord

decorative cord and tassel

tape measure

pins

scissors

sewing machine

Method

1 Place the two fabrics together with the wrong sides facing and the raw edges even. Baste them together along all sides.

2 Make continuous bias binding as instructed on page 20. Pin and baste the bias binding along two long sides, enclosing the raw edges and turning under the ends of the bias binding at the bottom. Stitch.

3 Fold the fabric in half, lengthways. Stitch across the width of the canopy at this point and then stitch again a few centimetres away, forming a casing.

The casing should be the diameter of the pole plus 1 cm.

4 Fit the canopy on to the pole and mark the hem position. Trim any excess length before turning in and pressing 5 mm then turning in and pressing another 4.5 cm. Stitch the hem.

5 Fit the canopy on the pole. Tie the decorative cord and tassel to the front end of the pole and attach the other end of the cord to a hook in the ceiling. Make coordinating tiebacks for an added look of luxury.

Far left: A close-up of the quilted throwover
Above: Coordinate colour and fabric for a pleasing effect

Sheer Canopy

CANOPIES WERE ORIGINALLY USED IN THE TROPICS TO ALLOW PEOPLE TO ENJOY THE
COOL NIGHT AIR PROTECTED FROM THE BITING INSECTS.

Before you begin You will need a round hoop on which to hang your canopy, as well as a strong hook that can be mounted into a beam in the ceiling to support the canopy.

Fabric and trims will vary depending on the effect you are trying to create. Our canopy is made from a printed voile, trimmed with one hundred per cent cotton lace trim. Sheer netting and any suitable preshrunk lace will give a similar whimsical effect.

Measuring

Measure around the base of the bed to determine the diameter that the fabric must cover. Divide this number by the width of your fabric to determine how many drops of fabric you will need. Add one additional drop to ensure that there is still some gather in the canopy when it is closed around the bed.

MATERIALS
hook
cane, wood or plastic hoop,
30 to 40 cm in diameter
fabric
lace for trimming
fishing line or suitable twine for suspending
the canopy from the ceiling
50 cm narrow cotton tape
cord for attaching the canopy to the ceiling
matching sewing machine thread
pins
scissors
tape measure
sewing machine

Today, canopies are largely decorative

Method

1 Fix the hook to the ceiling. With the twine or fishing line, suspend the hoop from the hook. Experiment to find the hanging length that suits the proportions of the bed and the room. Measure the drop from 30 cm above the hoop to the floor, adding 50 cm for proper coverage of the bed.

2 Stitch the drops of fabric together, using French seams for a neat finish.

3 Fold the fabric in half, in the direction of the seams, with the wrong sides together. Pin the two edges together for 20 cm from the top and stitch a French seam.

4 Pin and attach lace to the front opening edges if you wish. Again use French seams or overlock for a neat finish. Stitch a narrow hem all the way around the base of the canopy.

5 Mark the position where the canopy should fall over the hoop, approximately 30 cm down from the top edge. From this point taper the fabric up to make a circle measuring 15 to 20 cm in diameter. Make a hem at the top edge of the canopy to form a casing and thread the cord through the casing, then pull up the fullness of the fabric. Stitch a loop of tape at the casing. Thread the cord through the loop and attach it to the hook in the ceiling. Slipstitch lace to the outside edge of the hoop, if you wish.

Throwover Bedspread

Before you begin For the length of the throwover, measure from the floor to the top of the bed, including the height of your pillows and add an additional 60 cm for the tuck under the pillows. The finished width of your bedspread will be the width of the top of the bed plus the drop to the floor. You may wish to add a little extra to allow the finished bedspread to 'puddle' or hang loosely on the floor. If you are using a lightweight fabric that requires lining, allow for a 1.5 cm seam allowance all around. If the bedspread is to be unlined, allow 2.5 cm on each side for a double hem.

For our throwover bedspread, we were lucky enough to find some antique damask to which we added a 10 cm deep bullion fringe. To show off the fringe to its best advantage, this bedspread finished 8.5 cm above the floor before the fringe was attached.

MATERIALS
sufficient fabric, approximately 4.2 m for a double bed
5.5 m of bullion fringe
matching sewing machine thread
pins
scissors
tape measure
sewing machine

Method

1 Cut out the fabric, allowing a 5 cm seam allowance at the top end.

2 Turn in and press 2.5 cm, then turn in and press an additional 2.5 cm on the top end. Stitch. On the remaining three sides, turn in and press 5 mm, then turn in and press another 1 cm. Stitch.

3 Pin the bullion fringe 1 cm above the hem of the bedspread, with the right side facing out. Stitch the fringe into place along the woven band.

Dress a simple rectangle of fabric with a luxurious fringe to make a stylish throwover bedspread

Upholstered Headboard

INEXPENSIVE CRAFT WOOD CAN BE USED FOR THIS STYLISH HEADBOARD.

Before you begin The headboard can sit behind the bed, be attached to the wall or affixed to the mattress base with corner brackets. The bottom can be left flush so that it sits evenly on the floor or you can make some sturdy legs.

The height of the headboard should be 25-60 cm above the bed. It can be shaped to any style.

The quantities given here are for a single headboard.

MATERIALS
craft wood

spray adhesive suitable for fabric

woodworking glue

staple gun and staples

thumb tacks

tailors chalk

main fabric, enough to cover the headboard back and front plus an allowance for overlaps and turnings

contrasting fabric 30 cm wide x three times the perimeter of the headboard for the shirred strip

6 m of 60 cm wide thick polyester wadding

needle and quilting thread or sewing machine and matching sewing machine thread

tape measure

scissors

Method

1 Cut out the wood to the desired shape. Glue the thick polyester wadding to the entire board, using the spray adhesive. Trim away any excess even with the edge of the board.

2 Using the board as a pattern, cut out the front fabric with the grain of the fabric running down the board and allowing extra to go over the edge and on to the back. Cut another piece of fabric with the grain of the fabric running down the board for the back that is the same size and shape as the headboard. Spray the adhesive on the back of the front fabric piece then glue it over the wadding on the headboard. Hold the fabric in place with occasional thumb tacks, then staple or tack the fabric into position on the back of the headboard. Turn under the bottom raw edge on the back piece, then glue it on to the back of the headboard over the raw edges. Staple the edges in place on top of the front piece.

3 With tailors chalk, mark the fabric on the front of the headboard at 10 cm intervals and 15 cm in from the edge. Join up the marks to form an arc.

4 Join the pieces for the shirred strip with flat fell seams, if necessary, to achieve the required length. Gather both long sides of the strip and pull up the gathering so the strip is the length required to go around

the headboard. Final adjustments can be made when the shirred strip is tacked in place.

5 Place the middle of the shirred strip in the middle of the top edge of the headboard with the right side of the strip facing the right side of the front of the headboard and the bottom gathering line on the chalk line. Staple the bottom edge of the shirred strip to the chalk line, placing the staples end to end. Continue stapling down one side, turning under the raw edge at the end and stapling it in place.

6 Cut the remaining wadding into 3 cm wide strips. Working from the back, begin stuffing the area behind the shirred fabric with the strips of wadding, puffing out the shirring. At the same time, bring the edge of the shirred panel over the stuffing on to the back of the headboard, stapling it in place.

7 Repeat steps 5 and 6 for the other side of the headboard.

Nursery Linen

MAKING YOUR OWN NURSERY LINEN OFFERS A GREAT OPPORTURNITY
TO DECORATE WITH FABRIC.

Nursery quilt

Before you begin You will need 50 cm of 120 cm wide fabric in each of two contrasting fabrics for the front of your quilt and 2.5 m of a third contrasting fabric for the additional squares on the front, the quilt back, the ruffles and the bows.

As the finished quilt will need to be washable, preshrink all fabrics before sewing the quilt.

MATERIALS
sufficient fabric
polyester wadding
matching sewing machine thread
pins
scissors
tape measure
sewing machine

Method

1 Cut out eleven 20 cm squares in two of the fabrics and ten 20 cm squares in the third fabric.

2 Arrange the squares on a flat surface in eight rows of four squares each. To form the diagonal pattern, make sure you begin each row with the same fabric as you used on the end of the previous row. Sew each row together with 1 cm seams. Sew the eight rows together to form the quilt top. Press well.

3 From the third fabric, cut a strip 20 cm wide and one and a half times the circumference of the quilt top for the ruffle. Join strips if necessary to achieve the total length. Sew the short ends of the ruffle strip together to form a circle. Press the ruffle strip over double with the wrong sides together. Gather the raw edges.

4 Pin the ruffle to the quilt top with the right sides together and the raw edges match. Adjust the gathering to fit around the quilt top, then stitch the ruffle in place.

5 Cut the wadding to size with a 1 cm allowance all around. Baste the wadding to the wrong side of the quilt top.

6 Cut the quilt back to size with a 1 cm seam allowance all around. Place the quilt top and the quilt back together with the right sides facing and the raw edges even. Stitch around the outside edge, leaving a 30 cm opening in one side for turning. Turn the quilt to the right side. Press, then slipstitch the opening closed.

7 Make 25 cm lengths of rouleau, knot the ends, then stitch them to the meeting points of the squares.

Choose a combination of pastel plains and prints in easy-care cottons for a totally coordinated nursery. Make the ruffled pillowcase as instructed on page 147

Fitted cot sheet

Before you begin As cot mattresses vary a great deal in size, it is often difficult to buy one that fits your cot. Sometimes, it is easier to make your own fitted cot sheet to ensure the best fit possible. Stretch towelling, polycotton or cotton are suitable fabrics. Remember to preshrink the fabric before you sew.

Measuring

Measure the width, length and depth of the mattress and add 25 cm for the tuck-under. Cut a piece of fabric to this measurement.

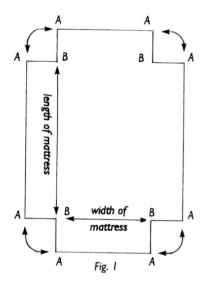

Fig. 1

MATERIALS
sufficient fabric
40 cm of 6 mm wide elastic,
cut into four pieces
pins
tape measure
matching sewing machine thread
scissors
sewing machine

This cot quilt can be enlarged by adding extra squares

Method

1 Cut the fabric for the sheet, as wide as the mattress plus the depth of the mattress plus 25 cm for the tuck-under on each side and 3 cm for the hem, and as long as the mattress plus the depth of the mattress plus 25 cm for the tuck-under on each side and 3 cm for the hem.

2 Cut squares from each corner of the fabric as illustrated (fig. 1). Note that A-B is the depth of the mattress plus 25 cm for the tuck-under and 1.5 cm for the hem. Pin the sides of the squares together, joining the A points. Sew from the outside edge to the inner corner, forming an angle at each corner of the sheet.

3 Turn in and press 5 mm around the outside edge. Then turn in and press another 1 cm. Sew the 6 mm wide elastic to the seam allowance on each corner, starting and finishing 20 cm on

either side of the corner seam, using a zigzag stitch and stretching the elastic as you sew (fig. 2).

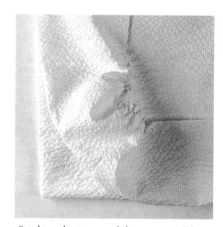

Stitching elastic around the corners will keep the sheet in place

Fig. 2

Moses basket

MATERIALS

paper for making the templates

pencil

scissors

fabric tape – to measure the circumference of the basket

one piece of fabric, the size of the base template plus 1.5 cm for seam allowances all around

piece of wadding, the depth of the basket x the circumference

two pieces of fabric, the depth of the basket x the circumference plus 10 cm for seams

fabric for the ruffle, twice the circumference of the basket x 20 cm wide

2 m of 2.5 cm wide ribbon if your basket has handles

sufficient elastic to go around the basket, stretched quite tightly

quilters thread

quilters chalk

matching sewing machine thread

pins

scissors

tape measure

ruler

sewing machine

Method

1 Make a paper template of the base of your basket. Cut out the template and place it inside the basket to check the fit. Trim if necessary.

2 Using the template, cut two base pieces from the fabric, allowing a 1 cm seam allowance all around. Cut a piece of the wadding to the same size.

3 Sandwich the wadding between the wrong sides of the two layers of fabric. Baste across the width and length of the base, forming a cross. Decide how you wish to quilt the base piece and mark the quilting pattern on the fabric with the chalk. Checks or diamonds work very well. Machine-quilt the design. Remove the basting.

4 Make a paper template for the sides of the basket. Using the template, cut out two pieces of fabric, allowing 6 cm extra allowance around the top edge for turnings and 1 cm around the bottom edge. Cut the wadding to the same shape as the template without any extra allowances.

5 Sandwich the wadding between the wrong sides of the fabrics, as before, and baste through all the thicknesses around the top and bottom edges with the quilting thread. Mark your quilting pattern on the fabric with the chalk – vertical lines are easy and look effective if spaced approximately 8 cm apart. Stitch, using a narrow zigzag stitch, starting from the bottom edge and stitching up to 3 cm from the top edge. Note that the wadding does not go all the way up to the top.

6 Turn in and press 5 mm on the short sides of the ruffle strip, turn in and press another 5 mm. Stitch.

7 Make a double ruffle by folding the ruffle strip over double with the wrong sides together. Gather the raw edges together. Adjust the gathering to fit the top edge of the quilted side piece. Pin the ruffle to the top edge of the side piece with the right sides together and the raw edges even. Stitch.

8 Insert the elastic into the ruffle through the open ends.

9 If your basket has handles, slit the fabric where the handles are joined to the basket and narrow hem the edges. Attach ribbon to the edges.

10 Pin the base to the side piece at the raw edges. Stitch then overlock or zigzag to neaten the raw edge. Place the liner into the basket, bringing the elasticised ruffle over the side of the basket and passing the handles through the slits.

This pretty liner for a basket is easily removed for washing

Table Linen

Table Linen

A grand table set with flowers, china, crystal and silverware can be quite breathtaking. Crisp white linen tablecloths and napkins provide the perfect backdrop against which all the other elements are placed. Linen napkins provide an additional touch of elegance as well as serving a more practical purpose at the dinner table.

All tablecloths and table linen are functional in that they protect your furniture and your clothes from soiling. They can be as decorative as you wish

and, depending on the time and place of their use, they can be either casual or formal in style. Their plain, no-fuss construction often means they can also be reversible.

Everyday table linen should be made from easy-care washable fabrics, so that it can survive the stresses of frequent use and the resultant wear and tear. Cotton, polyester and cotton, cotton sateen, gingham and cotton linens are all suitable for casual table linen. Damask and silks add a touch of formality

and luxury to a dining table, while a vivid combination of textured fabrics provide a touch of drama.

Contrast and textures create exotic effects even with the most simple of fabrics. Try mixing fabrics, such as linen and satin, to create truly elegant table napkins. Incorporate appliqué or embroidery stitches for an individual look. You can stencil calico napkins with a variety of prints to take you from breakfast to an afternoon tea with a homely country feel.

Instructions for making this elegant linen are on page 178

The finish you choose will add touches of interest to your table. Layers of mitred corners in a variety of coloured fabrics and textures create a look and style that will leave your guests wondering where you bought the extravagant display.

In a more formal dining room, try to match the table linen to the overall room scheme. For example, use the background colour of your curtains as the base colour for a cloth on a side table to create an interesting harmony of colour and shape in your room. On the other hand, if you want the table to blend into the room, so that a prized vase or collection of china is the focus, select a fabric in a similar colour to your walls, then create an accent with a tandem cloth in a similar texture.

Measuring for tablecloths

❖

When making tablecloths always try to get a fabric that is wide enough to cover the width of the table without seams. You will also need to decide how deep you wish the overhang to be – just to your lap or near to the floor or somewhere in between.

Square tablecloth
Measure across the width of the table. To this measurement, add twice the desired overhang measurement and the hem allowance.

Rectangular tablecloth
Measure across the table. To this measurement, add twice the overhang to find the width of the tablecloth. Measure the length of the table and add twice the overhang to find the length, then add the hem allowance (fig. 1).

Round tablecloth
Measure the diameter of the table through the middle. To this measurement, add twice the desired overhang and the hem allowance.

Oval tablecloth
Measure across the table. To this measurement, add twice the overhang to find the width of the tablecloth. Measure the length of the table and add twice the overhang to find the length. Add hem allowances in each case.

If the width of the table is greater than the fabric width and fabric widths need to be joined, it is important that these joining seams be placed along the table edges and not in the middle.

Joining fabric

❖

You may need to join fabric to achieve the required length and width for a tablecloth. It is important to place these joining seams where they will be as unobtrusive as possible. Usually this means placing them along the table edge (fig. 2). For an oval or a round table place the seams as shown in figs. 3 and 4 below. Always use a flat fell seam when joining fabric so as to avoid thick seams.

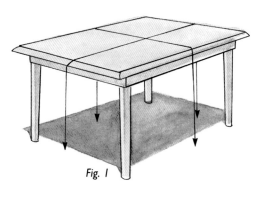

Fig. 1

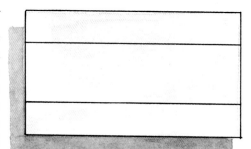

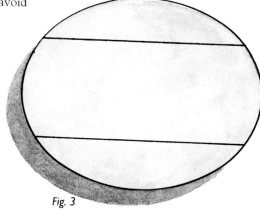

Fig. 2

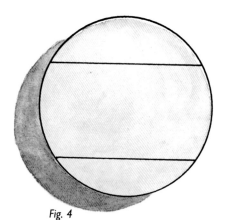

Fig. 3

Fig. 4

Stencilled Napery

Before you begin Sometimes fabric can be so wide that you do not have to join pieces to achieve the required size. If this is not the case, join three pieces together with seams that run close to the table edges, not two pieces joined with a seam down the middle of the table.

It is best to choose a one hundred per cent cotton fabric with a smooth finish for a tablecloth and napkins. Cotton launders well and is pleasant to handle. If you prefer the wearing qualities of man-made fibres, try using a polyester/cotton mixture.

There are many ways to locate the stencil design on your tablecloth, depending on the size of the cloth, the particular design you have chosen and your own preference. You could place the design at each place setting, as a continuous border around the edge of the cloth or positioned to sit in from the edge of the table. Bear in mind when planning your design and the layout, that the edge of the tablecloth is not likely to be visible when you are seated at the table so much of the effect of any stencilling along the edges could be lost.

Measuring

Measure your table, following the steps given in measuring for tablecloths on page 163. Calculate your fabric requirements using these measurements.

MATERIALS
sufficient fabric for the tablecloth
60 cm square of fabric for each napkin
matching sewing machine thread
pins
scissors
sewing machine
tape measure
purchased stencil or firm plastic for making a stencil
pencil
fineline marker pen
sharp craft knife for cutting a stencil
cutting board for cutting a stencil
suitable fabric paints
stencilling brushes
masking tape

Method

1 Mitre the corners of the tablecloth as shown in the diagrams (figs 1 to 3) and on page 22.

2 Turn in and press 5 mm on all the raw edges. Turn in and press another 1.5 cm. Stitch the hems in place.

3 If you are making your own stencil from the bow design given on page 165, trace the stencil design on to the plastic and then cut out the stencil with the sharp craft knife.

4 Position the stencil on the fabric. Paint in the first colour, using a dabbing action, then apply any other colours one by one. Cover with masking tape any area that you wish to paint a different colour.

5 To set the colours, press on the wrong side of the fabric with a dry iron on a setting suitable for the fabric.

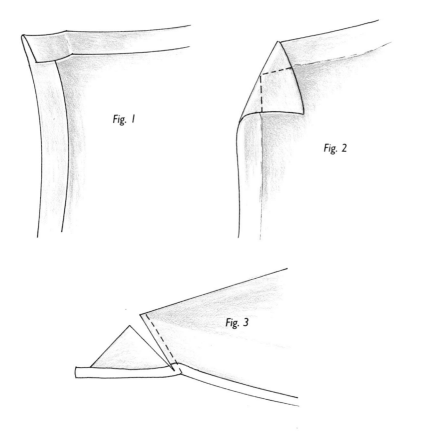

Fig. 1

Fig. 2

Fig. 3

Stencil the same bow design around the edge of the tablecloth

Circular Tablecloths

CIRCULAR TABLES ARE A PRETTY WAY TO FILL AN EMPTY CORNER. THERE IS NO GREAT MYSTERY TO MAKING CIRCULAR TABLECLOTHS. THE SECRET LIES IN MEASURING AND CUTTING ACCURATELY, THEN THE SEWING IS JUST A STRAIGHT LINE.

Round tablecloth

Before you begin Measure from the centre of the table to the floor. Add extra for a hem if you plan to turn the edge under rather than add a ruffle or lace. Take the edge trimmings into consideration and add or subtract accordingly. This will be your basic measurement. Purchase four times this basic measurement in fabric plus 10 cm. Omit the extra 10 cm if your fabric is as wide as twice the basic measurement or your table is small. Wide sheeting (254 cm wide) is ideal for a tablecloth on a small bedside table because no seams are necessary.

MATERIALS
sufficient fabric
matching sewing machine thread
pins
scissors
tape measure
tailors chalk
sewing machine
trims and ruffles as desired

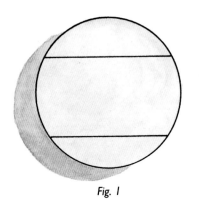

Fig. 1

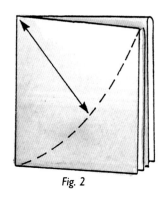

Fig. 2

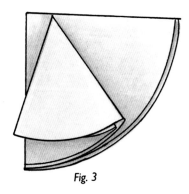

Fig. 3

Method

1 Join your fabric to make one piece large enough for the circle. To do this, cut two pieces, each twice the basic length plus 10 cm. Leave one piece aside. Cut the other piece down through the middle, parallel with both selvages. Using a flat seam, join the selvages of these cut pieces to the selvages of the large uncut piece (fig. 1).

2 To cut out the tablecloth, fold the prepared fabric in half. Fold in half again, so that your original fabric is now folded into quarters. Place one end of the tape measure at the folded point and mark the basic measurement point at one edge of the fabric. Swing the tape measure around, marking out the arc of the circle with the chalk, following the basic measurement point on the tape measure (fig. 2). Cut through all the thicknesses of fabric along this chalk line (fig 3).

3 If you are adding lace, measure around the circumference of the cloth to determine the quantity of ungathered lace or bias binding required. If you are gathering lace or making a fabric ruffle, use at least one and a half times this measurement. For a simple hem, turn in and press 1.5 cm on the edge and stitch. You can stitch narrow piping cord into the hem using the zipper foot on your sewing machine.

Jumbo-edged round cloth

Before you begin

Measure your table as for the round tablecloth on page 166. Subtract 4.5 cm from this measurement for the width of the jumbo binding. This is the length of fabric you will require. If necessary, join lengths to achieve the width, using flat fell seams along the edges of the table.

MATERIALS
sufficient fabric
6.5 m of extra-thick piping cord
*6.5 m of 10 cm wide bias-cut fabric plus
1.5 cm for each seam allowance*
*matching or contrasting sewing machine
thread*
sewing machine
scissors
tape measure

Method

1 Cut out the fabric as for the standard tablecloth. The raw edges can be overlocked or zigzagged to prevent fraying.

2 Make a continuous bias strip as instructed on page 20. Join the ends of the bias strip to form a circle.

3 Fold the bias-cut fabric over double with the right sides out, enclosing the piping. Using the zipper foot on your sewing machine, sew a row of stitching as close to the piping as possible. Interweave the cord ends where they meet (figs. 4 to 6).

4 With the right sides together and the raw edges matching, pin the jumbo piping around the outer edge of the tablecloth, then stitch it in place, following the first stitching line. Trim away any excess seam allowance if necessary. Neaten the raw edge with overlocking or zigzag stitching.

Silk taffeta is the perfect choice for this elegant round cloth

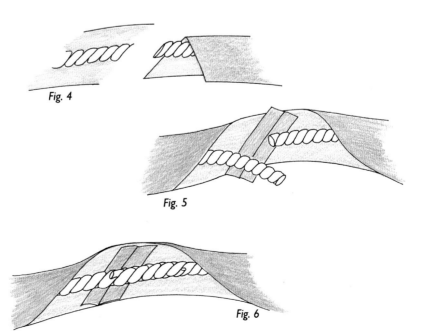

Fig. 4

Fig. 5

Fig. 6

Overcloths

Square overcloth

Before you begin

Plan how large you want the overcloth. Make sure the proportion is right for the circular cloth that will be underneath it.

Measuring

To calculate the quantity of fabric you will require, measure the diameter of your table top and add 30 cm for the overhang. For the bias trim, you will need a bias strip of fabric in contrast colour, 4 cm wide and the same length as the sides of the square.

MATERIALS
sufficient fabric
contrasting fabric for bias trim
matching sewing machine thread
scissors
pins
sewing machine
tape measure

Method

1 Make and join the continuous bias strip as shown on page 20. Press in 5 mm on both sides of the bias strip.

2 Cut a perfect square from the fabric to your required measurements. Turn in and press 5 mm, then turn in and press another 5 mm. Stitch the hem in place. Make sure the corners are stitched into neat points. (See page 22 for stitching corners.)

3 Pin a length of bias strip to two opposite edges of the tablecloth with both the right side of the bias and the right side of the tablecloth facing upwards. Turn in 1 cm on each end of each of the bias strips and secure the ends under the cloth with a pin. Stitch down each side of the bias strip, 2 mm in from each edge. Repeat the process on the other two sides. Press.

For a simple country look, checked cotton can be bias-trimmed following the instructions given here

---

Swagged overcloth

Before you begin

You can attach fabric bows to the cloth with Velcro for added effect. Measure the diameter of the table and add to this measurement the overhang and hem allowance you require. You may need to join the fabric as instructed on page 166.

MATERIALS
sufficient fabric
28 cm of 1 cm wide bias binding
40 cm of 75 mm wide elastic
matching sewing machine thread
pins
scissors
tape measure
sewing machine

Method

1 Make the overcloth, following the same method as for making the round tablecloth on page 166. Turn in and press 5 mm around the outer edge, then turn in and press 1 cm. Stitch the hem.

2 Mark the quarter points on the circumference. On the wrong side of the fabric at each of the quarter points and beginning at the edge of the cloth, sew a 7 cm length of bias binding to form a casing. Thread 10 cm of elastic through each casing, stitching the end of the elastic to the outer end of the casing at the cloth edge. Leave the inner end of the casing open. Stitch another length of elastic to the wrong side of the tablecloth, just above the top of the casing. Draw up the elastic in the casing and tie the ends of the two pieces of elastic together, gathering up the casing. Release the elastic for washing and pressing the tablecloth.

Appliquéd linen napkins

MATERIALS

*piece of fabric, 40 cm x 60 cm,
for the basic placemat*

*60 cm square of fabric, for
the basic napkin*

fabric motifs for the appliqué

matching sewing machine thread

pins

scissors

tailors chalk

tape measure

sewing machine

Method

1 Cut out the motifs, allowing a 6 mm excess around them.

2 Position the motifs on the placemat and napkin. Baste them in place. Machine-stitch around the edge of each motif, 6 mm from the edge, using a small zigzag stitch. Cut away the excess fabric close to the stitching.

3 Adjust your sewing machine stitch to a wider satin stitch. Stitch again over the previous stitching, enclosing the raw edge as you stitch.

4 Make a narrow double hem around all sides of the napkin. Press.

Satin-stitched napery

Before you begin Measure the size of your table and determine the drop you require, then add 2.5 cm for the hem allowance. Refer to page 163 for further instructions on measuring your table and determining the size of your tablecloth.

MATERIALS

*piece of fabric, 32.5 cm x 42.5 cm,
for each placemat*

32.5 cm square of fabric for each napkin

*sufficient fabric for the
tablecloth, cut to size*

*matching or contrasting sewing
machine thread*

sewing machine

scissors

tape measure

Method

The method is the same for all items.

1 Turn in and press 2.5 cm on all the raw edges, mitring the corners (figs 2 to 4).

2 Machine-stitch a satin stitch border around all sides over the raw edge. Remember to pivot at the corners.

Primary brights in crisp cottons are the perfect choice for these satin stitched napkins and tablecloth

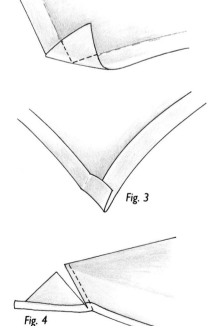

Fig. 2

Fig. 3

Fig. 4

Napkin with contrast border

MATERIALS
47 cm square of fabric

four strips of contrasting border fabric, each 8 cm x 47 cm (you can vary the width to suit the fabric pattern)

1.8 m of purchased bias binding or 1.8 m of 3 cm wide bias-cut fabric strips

matching sewing machine thread

pins

scissors

tape measure

sewing machine

Method

1 Turn in and press 1 cm along the long inner edge of each border strip. Cut the ends to perfect diagonals, then join them with mitred corners.

2 Place the border strip and the fabric square together so that the right side of the border faces the wrong side of the square. Stitch around the outside edge. Trim the corners, then turn the napkin to the right side and press.

3 Press the bias binding over double with the wrong sides together. Tuck the bias binding under the inner pressed edge of the border, leaving 5 mm of the bias binding protruding. Stitch the inner pressed edge down into place, stitching through all thicknesses.

4 If you are using ribbon or braid which has finished edges, there is a very simple method you can use to achieve the same result. Turn in and press 1 cm on the edges of the napkin, then turn in and press another 1 cm. Stitch. Pin the ribbon or braid around the edge of the napkin, folding the corners as shown (figs 1 to 3). Stitch down close to both edges of the ribbon or braid.

The red and green checked placemat has been made in the same way, omitting the bias binding trim. It has no wadding and is not quilted.

Tartan is terrific for this placemat and napkin

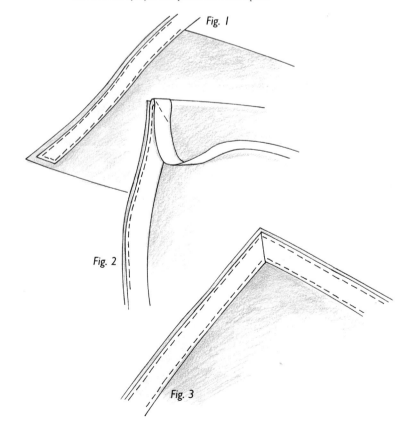

Fig. 1

Fig. 2

Fig. 3

Pleated placemat

MATERIALS

piece of fabric, 30 cm x 137 cm,
for the pleated body

piece of fabric, 10 cm x 160 cm,
for the border strip

fusible interfacing, 30 cm x 90 cm

matching sewing machine thread

sewing machine

pins

thread

tailors chalk or water-soluble marking pen

ruler

Method

1 cm seams are allowed.

1 With the chalk or the pen, mark every 1.5 cm along the length of each long side of the main fabric piece. Begin to fold in the pleats with your fingers and secure the pleats with pins as you go. Pressing with a warm iron will also help to hold the pleats in place while you work. Baste along both edges. The pleated panel should be approximately 25 cm x 40 cm when it is complete.

2 Cut the border into two strips, 10 cm x 30 cm, and two strips, 10 cm x 50 cm. Cut fusible interfacing to the same size and fuse it to the wrong side of the border pieces.

3 Turn in and press 5 mm along the long edges of each border piece. Fold each border piece in half lengthways with wrong sides together and press. Sandwich the pleated centre piece between the folded edges of the border pieces. On the wrong side, overlap the border pieces at the ends so the short and long border pieces meet in an L-shape at the corners (fig. 4). Pin the edges to hold them in place.

4 On the right side, fold the corners to form mitres. Baste through all thicknesses, then machine-stitch in the following way: Begin at the outer edge of one mitred corner, stitch towards the centre down the angle of the mitre then back to the outside edge of the next mitred corner. Repeat the process on the opposite side and then stitch the two remaining inside border edges individually.

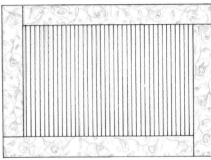

Fig. 4

This unusual pleated effect is very easy to achieve

Quilted Napery

SIMPLE QUILTING IS A FEATURE OF THIS NAPERY.

Before you begin

You can quilt your own fabric, using a quilters guide to plan the squares and spaces. The guide looks like an arm that extends from behind the sewing machine's presser foot into the centre of the machine. The first row of stitching is made, then the guide is adjusted to sit along this stitching. Further rows of stitching are made, each the same distance from the previous one, as measured by the guide.

Placemat

MATERIALS

piece of main fabric, 34 cm x 50 cm

piece of wadding, 34 cm x 50 cm

piece of the main fabric or a contrasting one, 34 cm x 50 cm, for the backing

1.8 m of corded piping

matching sewing machine thread

pins

scissors

tape measure

sewing machine

Method

1 Place the main fabric and the wadding together. Pin or baste the layers together and quilt through all thicknesses.
2 Using the rim of a cup as a guide, round off the corners of the main and backing fabric pieces.
3 With the right sides facing and the raw edges matching, pin the piping around the quilted main piece, clipping the seam allowance at the curves for ease. Overlap the ends of the piping where they meet. Draw out a little cord from the piping and cut it off to eliminate bulk. Stitch the piping in place.
4 Place the main and the backing pieces together, with the right sides facing and the raw edges matching. Stitch around the edge, following the previous stitching line and leaving an opening for turning. Turn the placemat to the right side and press. Handsew the opening closed with small stitches.

Napkin

MATERIALS

50 cm square of the main cotton fabric

50 cm square of the contrasting cotton fabric

2.1 m corded piping

matching sewing machine thread

50 cm bias binding in the same colour as the corded piping

pins

scissors

tape measure

sewing machine

Method

1 Using the rim of a cup as a guide, round off the corners of the main and contrast fabric pieces.
2 Make the napkin in the same way as the placemat, omitting the quilting.
3 Fold the bias binding over double, lengthways, with the wrong sides facing and the folded edges matching. Stitch along the folded edges. Knot the ends of the bias binding then stitch the centre 12.5 cm down from one corner of the napkin.
4 Fold the side with the tie attached in half, with wrong sides facing. Roll the opposite side of the napkin towards the end with the tie. Wrap the tie around the rolled napkin and tie it into a bow.

Damper napkin

MATERIALS

piece of fabric, 41 cm x 51 cm

matching sewing machine thread

pins

scissors

tape measure

sewing machine

Method

Overlock or zigzag the fabric edges or turn the hem and then zigzag it in place. Knot the napkin around the damper.

Tea cosy

Before you begin

Measure the height and width of your teapot. On a piece of paper, mark the dimensions, allowing an additional 10 cm for seams and turn-under. You will need contrasting bias binding, 6 cm wide by the circumference of the tea cosy plus the length of the arc (see step 1).

MATERIALS

paper

pencil

sufficient quilted fabric

contrasting piping and bias binding

matching sewing machine thread

pins

scissors

tape measure

sewing machine

Method

1 With the dimensions you have calculated, draw your teapot pattern. Draw an arched shape from the centre point to each side point. Cut a front and a back for the tea cosy following this pattern.

2 Pin and baste the piping around the front piece with right sides together and raw edges matching. Pin the front and back together with the right sides facing and the raw edges matching, leaving a 1 cm seam allowance on all the bottom edges. Stitch, catching the piping in the seam.

3 Turn in and press 5 mm on the bottom edges, then turn in and press another 2 cm. Stitch.

4 Bind the bottom edges with the bias binding.

Clockwise from left: Tea cosy, Placemat, Napkin, Damper napkin

Festive Setting

SMART AND CHIC, THESE SLIPCOVERS AND TABLECLOTHS MAKE A
FESTIVE TABLE FOR A SPECIAL OCCASION.

Make the meal a real celebration with this tablecloth and matching chair covers

Tablecloth

Before you begin

Cloths and slipcovers like these can also be used where the furniture is worn or the chairs are mismatched. Napkins and placemats can be added to complete the setting.

Measuring

Measure your table and on a sheet of paper draw the pattern pieces A to G, marking in the following measurements:

A and B (short side overlay swags) = table width x 58 cm for the scallops + 4 cm for the hems.

C and D (long side overlay swags) = table length x 58 cm for scallops + 4 cm for the hems.

E and F (long side tablecloth panels) = length = as for piece G, width = drop to floor + 4 cm for hem and seam. Cut 14 cm into the panel on one side where the marks fall on panel G.

G (table top plus floor drops) = length = table top length + 5 cm for seams + twice the drop. Mark where the floor drop meets the table top on each side.

MATERIALS
paper and pencil
sufficient fabric (we used approximately 9 m of 137 cm wide fabric for a table 90 cm x 150 cm)
matching sewing machine thread
pins
scissors
tape measure
tailors chalk
sewing machine

Method

1 Using your drawings as a guide, cut out all the pieces from the fabric. Place the main piece G on the table and mark a line with tailors chalk where the drop begins at each end of the table so you will know where to attach the side overlays later (fig. 1). Place pieces E and F on the table and mark them in the same way.

2 Turn in and press a narrow double hem on one long and both short edges of each of the side overlay pieces A, B, C and D. Stitch the hems. Sew a row of gathering stitches along the short sides of all the overlay pieces but do not pull up the gathering.

3 Stitch overlay pieces A and B to the main table top piece G along the marked line, leaving 2 cm free at each end so the ends can be pulled up to form the scalloped corner at a later stage.

4 Join the long side overlay piece C to the side panel F and the long side overlay piece D to the side panel E between the marked lines.

5 Gather up the ends of all the side overlay pieces, so that they pull up to approximately 16 cm at the corners to form the swags. Slipstitch the gathered sections to the side panel pieces.

6 Join the side panels E and F (with the overlays attached) to each side of G (fig. 2).

7 Place the cloth on the table, arranging the corners attractively over the gathering.

Chair cover

Before you begin

The chair cover shown here is made in exactly the same way as the one on page 128 with the addition of a huge fabric bow. To make the bow, follow the instructions below.

MATERIALS
approximately 2.3 m of 137 cm wide fabric
matching sewing machine thread
pins
scissors
tape measure
sewing machine

Method

1 Cut a piece of fabric for the bow, 1.2 m x 60 cm plus 1.5 cm seam allowance. Fold the strip in half with the right sides together and the raw edges matching. Sew around all the sides, leaving a 5 cm opening for turning. Trim the seams and corners, turn through to the right side and press.

2 Cut the tie, 30 cm x 60 cm plus 1.5 cm for seam allowances. Make the ties the same way as the bows, cutting the ends at an angle before stitching.

3 Cut a third rectangle for the loop, 5 cm x 10 cm plus 1.5 cm seam allowances. Make the loop in the same way as the bow and the tie.

Fig. 2

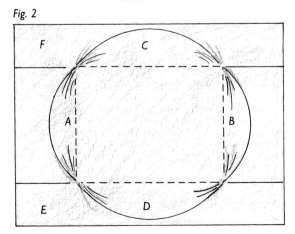

Fig. 1

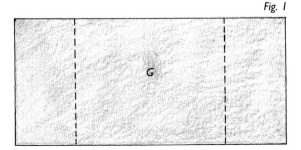

Scalloped Napery

THIS SIMPLE BUT ELEGANT TABLECLOTH IS VERY EASY TO ACHIEVE.

MATERIALS
*140 cm of 140 cm wide fabric
for the tablecloth*

*40 cm square of main fabric
for each napkin*

matching sewing machine thread

cardboard

marking pen

cup

20 cent piece

water-soluble pen

sharp-pointed scissors

pins

scissors

tape measure

sewing machine

Method

1 To make a template of the scallops on the cardboard, use the twenty cent piece to draw continuous half circles across the edge of the cardboard. Make another template the same way using the edge of the cup. Cut out the templates.

2 For the tablecloth, place the larger template on the edge of the fabric and mark the pattern all along the edge with the water-soluble pen.

3 Using a long close zigzag or satin stitch, work along the scalloped pattern, turning the fabric between each scallop.

4 Using the sharp scissors, cut close to the edge of the stitching, snipping into the scallops as you go. It may also be necessary to run a second row of zigzag stitches over the first, if you want a more dramatic effect.

5 Make the napkins in the same way using the smaller template.

The scalloped edge creates a very elegant appearance

Fringed Napery

UNEVEN WEAVE FABRICS, INCLUDING LINENS AND LOOSELY WOVEN
COTTONS, PROVIDE THE BASE TO CREATE INTERESTING YET VERY SIMPLE
TABLE NAPKINS AND CLOTHS WITH FRINGED EDGES.

This technique works best on a patterned fabric

Before you begin

Measure the size of your table. Determine the drop you require for the tablecloth and add 3 cm for the fringing allowance. Fringing works best on a rectangular or square tablecloth.

MATERIALS

*piece of fabric, 32 cm x 42 cm
for each placemat*

27 cm square of fabric for each napkin

*sufficient fabric for the tablecloth,
cut to size*

scissors

pin or needle

Method

1 Ensure that all the fabric edges are as straight as possible.
2 Using a pin or needle, pull out the threads down each long side and then each short side of each piece so that you make approximately 2 cm of fringing on each side. For the tablecloth, make the fringing 3 cm wide.

An Added Touch

Lined Basket

FABRIC LINED BASKETS HAVE MANY USES AROUND THE HOME.

Before you begin If you want the basket to hold books or magazines, ensure that it is wide enough so that books can be laid flat without buckling. If you don't wish to display the contents of your basket, make sure it has high sides or, better still, a lid.

MATERIALS

fabric strip for the side panel, equal to the inside depth of the basket plus 6 cm x twice the inside basket circumference

cardboard and polyester wadding, the same size as the base of the basket

fineline permanent marker pen

piece of fabric, 2.5 cm larger than the inside base of the basket

matching sewing machine thread

ribbon or cord, the same length as the inside circumference of the basket plus 5 cm

fabric strip, 8 cm x 50 cm, for the bow

turning hook or knitting needle

sewing machine, or needle for handsewing

scissors

tape measure

pins

spray adhesive

PVA adhesive

Method

1 Turn the basket over so that the base is facing up. Using the cardboard and marker pen, draw, then cut out a template of the base. Place it inside the basket to check the fit. Remove the template.

2 Using the base template, cut out the wadding. Glue the wadding to the cardboard with a light spray of the adhesive. Using the same template, cut out the fabric for the base, allowing an additional 2.5 cm all around. Lightly spray the wadding with adhesive and fix the fabric to the wadding.

3 When the base cover is dry, turn it over to the reverse side. Snip into the 2.5 cm allowance around the edge of the fabric, then glue the edge of the fabric to the cardboard with the PVA adhesive.

4 Stitch the short ends of the side panel with right sides together to form a circle. Turn in and press 5 mm along the top edge of the side panel, then turn in and press another 4.5 cm. Stitch the hem in place.

5 At the bottom raw edge of the side panel, stitch two rows of gathering stitches 5 mm apart and 1 cm from the edge. Pull up the gathering to fit around the base of the basket. Glue the gathered area of the strip around the base piece, placing the finished edge of the base piece over the gathering.

6 Unpick the seam for 3 cm in the top casing. Thread the length of ribbon or cord through the casing. Place the fabric inside the basket, then using the ribbon or cord, gather in the casing and adjust the gathers evenly around the top edge of the basket. Slipstitch the casing seam closed.

7 Fold the fabric strip for the bow over double with the right sides together and the raw edges matching. Stitch one short edge and one long end. Trim the seams and clip the corners. Turn it through to the right side. Press. Slipstitch the remaining edge closed. Tie the bow around the handle of the basket.

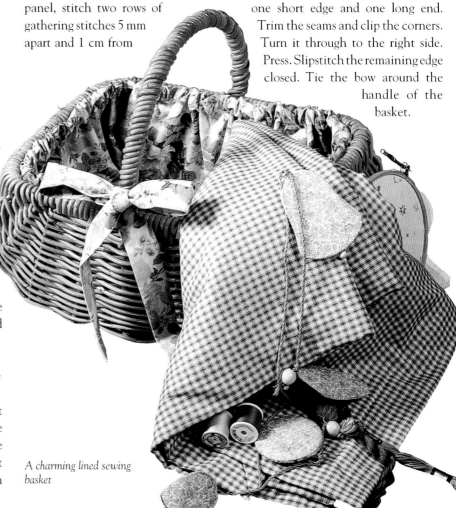

A charming lined sewing basket

Wastepaper Basket

ADD TRIMS AND BRAIDS IF YOU ARE FOLLOWING A THEME FOR YOUR
ROOM OR AS AN ADDED DASH OF INTEREST.

MATERIALS

wastepaper basket

*fabric strip, equal to the inside depth
plus 15 cm x twice the inside basket
circumference, for the side panel*

*cardboard and polyester wadding, the same
size as the base of the basket*

*piece of fabric, 2.5 cm larger than the
inside base of the basket*

fineline permanent marker pen

matching sewing machine thread

2.5 cm wide ribbon for the bow

*elastic, 1 cm wide x the circumference of
the basket top*

sewing machine, or needle for handsewing

scissors

tape measure

pins

spray adhesive

PVA adhesive

pegs (optional)

Method

1 Turn the basket over so that the base is facing up. Using the cardboard and marker pen, make a template of the base. Cut out the template and place it inside the basket to check the fit; trim it if necessary. Remove the template.
2 Using the base template, cut out the wadding. Glue the wadding to the cardboard with a light spray of the adhesive. Using the same template, cut out the fabric for the base, allowing an additional 2.5 cm all around. Lightly spray the wadding with adhesive and fix the fabric to the wadding.
3 When the base cover is dry, turn the base cover over to the reverse side. Snip into the 2.5 cm allowance around the edge of the fabric, then glue the edge of the fabric to the cardboard with the PVA adhesive. Hold the fabric in place with pegs if necessary, until all the adhesive is dry.
4 Join the short ends of the side panel with the right sides together to form a circle.
5 Turn in and press 5 mm along the top edge of the side panel, then turn in and press another 2.5 cm. Stitch the hem in place, forming a casing.
6 At the bottom raw edge, stitch two rows of gathering stitches 5 mm apart and 1 cm from the edge. Pull up the gathering to fit around the base piece. Glue the gathered area of the strip around the base piece, placing the finished edge of the base over the gathered edge.
7 Unpick 1.5 cm in the seam of the top casing. Thread the elastic through the casing, securing the ends with a knot or with slipstitches. Slipstitch the opening closed. Place the fabric liner in the basket. Tie the ribbon into a bow and slipstitch it into place.

A fabric-lined wastepaper basket finds a place in many rooms of the house

Hat Boxes

HAT BOXES PROVIDE EXCELLENT STORAGE FOR A VARIETY OF BITS AND PIECES.

Before you begin How much fabric and wadding you need will depend on the size of your box and whether you are covering it or just lining it. For our fabric-covered box, we used approximately 1.3 m of 115 cm wide fabric and 50 cm of wadding for the lid. Allow an extra 1.5 cm for turn-unders and overlaps around the edges of all the fabric and wadding, unless instructed otherwise.

MATERIALS
sturdy box with a lid

one strip of cardboard, the width of the outer lip of the lid and the same length as the circumference of the outer lip

PVA adhesive

spray adhesive

small paintbrush to apply the adhesive

sufficient fabric

medium thickness polyester wadding

strip of a complementary fabric, 20 cm x 90 cm, for the bow (optional)

braid, ribbon, masking tape or fabric to cover the joins (optional)

Method

1 Cut one lid from the fabric, 2.5 cm larger than the top of the lid all around. Cut one lid from the wadding without any additional allowance. Cut one strip of fabric the circumference of the base by the depth of the box plus 5 cm. Cut one strip of fabric the circumference of the lid by the depth of the lid plus 1 cm. Cut one strip of cardboard the circumference of the lid by the depth. Cut a circle of fabric for the base, 2.5 cm larger all around than the base. Cut one base from the cardboard, without any additional allowance.

2 Glue the wadding on to the lid and centre the fabric piece on top. Clip into the 2.5 cm allowance of the fabric. Glue the clipped allowance down on to the sides of the lid, pulling the fabric quite taut. Trim away any excess fabric.

3 Glue the strip of fabric for the side of the lid to the corresponding strip of cardboard with the 1 cm allowance left free all around. Clip into the allowance, then glue the fabric on one long side and both short ends to the wrong side of the cardboard. Glue the fabric-covered cardboard strip to the outside lip of the lid.

4 Turn in and press one short end of the fabric for the side of the box. Place the fabric around the outside of the box with the turned end covering the raw end and a 2.5 cm allowance at the top and the bottom. Glue into place. Clip into the allowance all around the top and the bottom.

5 Turn the allowance at the bottom of the box over on to the base. Glue into place. At the top of the box, turn the allowance to the inside of the box and glue the allowance into place on the inside.

6 Place the fabric circle for the base face down on a protected surface. Clip into the allowance for 2.5 cm all around the fabric piece. Spray the wrong side of the fabric with adhesive. Place the corresponding cardboard circle on the adhesive and press down. Turn the clipped allowance on to the cardboard and stick it into place.

7 Spray the base of the box with adhesive and glue the fabric-covered cardboard circle on to the base, covering all the raw edges.

8 Cover the joins on the inside of the box with braid, ribbon, masking tape or fabric. Make a bow in the complementary fabric, if desired, and glue it to the lid of the box.

Lampshades

LAMPSHADES ARE AN ESSENTIAL ELEMENT OF MANY DESIGN SCHEMES. AVAILABLE IN AN ARRAY OF SHAPES AND SIZES, THEY WILL BRIGHTEN A DULL CORNER.

Before you begin

The three styles of lampshades shown here are variations on a basic shade, but with individual finishing treatments.

Lampshade frames can be bought from any good craft shop or, if you have existing shades that could do with an update, it's simple to remove the old shade and re-cover the frame yourself. Measure the existing frame to work out quantities of fabric needed.

Always buy a plastic-coated wire lampshade frame to prevent it from rusting over time.

All frames that are to be covered in fabric must be bound with a white or cream cotton tape so that the shade fabric can be stitched to the frame.

Binding the frame

To determine how much binding tape you will need, measure the circumference of the two circles to be covered and all the vertical supporting spokes that connect the two circles. Do not measure the wire or supporting wires where the bulb is to be inserted as these wires will not be covered. Multiply your total length by three to obtain the total length required

To bind the frame: First cover the vertical spokes, tucking the tape under and around the frame (fig. 1). Tuck one end of the tape under the last loop to secure it. Repeat the process for the top and bottom circles so that all the external parts of the frame are covered. In some instances it is easier to secure the tape ends with pins until the binding is complete and then stitch or glue the ends in place.

Stiffened shade

MATERIALS

metal lampshade frame, stripped bare
approximately 1 m of 120 cm wide fabric
approximately 1 m of 120 cm wide buckram iron-on stiffened interfacing
bias strip, 4 cm wide and as long as the combined circumferences of the top and bottom circles plus 2 cm for turnings
PVA adhesive
pegs (optional)
pins
cotton binding tape to cover the frame (see Before you begin)
strong handsewing needle and thread
large piece of paper for the pattern
scissors
fineline marker pen
tape measure

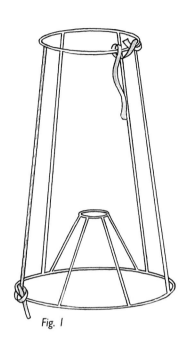

Fig. 1

This elegant shade needs no ornamentation

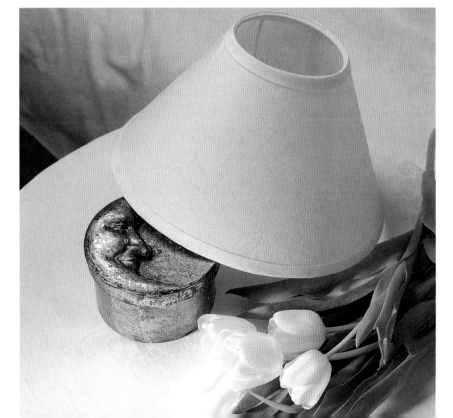

Method

1 Bind the frame as shown.

2 Place the frame at one end of the sheet of paper, then roll the frame across the paper, marking the line with the marker pen to show the outline of the pattern. Cut out the pattern (fig. 1). Check that it fits your frame before cutting out the fabric.

3 Cut out the fabric, allowing 5 mm seam allowances on either end and 5 mm at the top and bottom edges for turnings. Cut the buckram to size.

4 With a warm iron, fuse the buckram to the wrong side of the fabric, leaving all the side turnings free.

5 On both long sides of the bias strip, turn in and press 5 mm.

6 Stitch the bias binding to the top and bottom raw edges of the fabric, with the right sides together, leaving a 1 cm seam allowance on the fabric and stitching in the fold line of the bias binding. If you prefer, you can bind the edges by hand after the fabric has been attached to the frame (fig. 2).

7 Press the raw edges of the fabric over the buckram and fit the shade to the frame. Use pegs or pins to keep the shade in place until all the stitching is complete. Fold under 5 mm on one short end and overlap this end over the raw edge where the two ends meet. Glue the overlap. Slipstitch the fabric to the binding on both top and bottom circles.

8 Fold the free side of the bias binding over the frame and slipstitch or glue it into place on the wrong side.

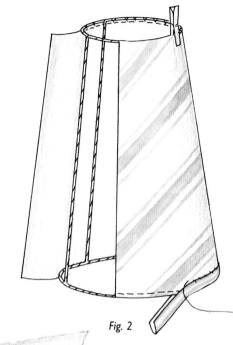

Fig. 2

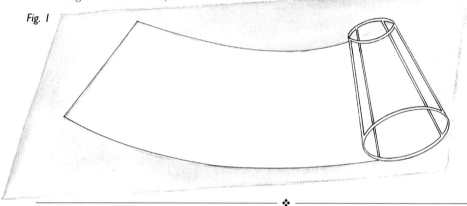

Fig. 1

❖

Pleated shade

Before you begin Measure the circumference of the frame and multiply that measurement by one and a half to give the length of fabric required. Cut bias strips 4 cm wide x the circumference of both circles plus 2 cm for turnings.

MATERIALS
sufficient fabric
metal lampshade frame, stripped bare
approximately 40 cm of fabric for bias strips or purchased bias binding
PVA adhesive
pegs
pins
scissors
cotton binding tape to cover your frame
strong handsewing needle and thread

Method

1 Bind the frame with cotton tape. (See page 185 for more information.)

2 Using your measurements, cut a rectangle of fabric, adding 2 cm to each side for turns. Fold the fabric with the right sides facing and stitch the short ends together in a 2 cm seam. Press the seam open and turn the circle of fabric to the right side.

3 With needle and thread, gather along

the top and bottom edges but do not pull up the gathering.

4 Divide the fabric into four equal sections and mark these points at the top and bottom edges with pins. Place the fabric over the frame, drawing in the gathering threads so that the four pairs of pins are equally spaced around the frame. Use pegs to hold the fabric in position. Arrange the gathered fabric into pleats, evenly spaced around the frame. With your fingers, press the pleats all in one direction and secure them with pins before stitching the pleats into place. Trim any excess fabric.

5 Remove the shade from the frame. Stitch the bias binding to the top and bottom raw edges of the fabric, with the right sides together, leaving a 1 cm seam allowance on the fabric and stitching in the fold line of the bias binding.

6 Place the shade on the frame. Turn the free edge of the bias binding over the frame and slipstitch it in place.

❖

This is a very pretty lampshade for a formal sitting room

We have created this very formal lampshade, following our basic lampshade pattern. Use matching bias binding for the top and bottom trim and a subtly contrasting colour for the centre trim. Apply the two smaller rows of piping so that their seam allowances are touching. Make a third length of 5 cm wide bias binding, turning in and pressing 5 mm on each side. This wider bias strip covers a length of foam cording available from your craft store. Glue the bias to the flat back of the cording and then centre and glue it directly over the top of the bias binding already attached at the base of the shade. Neatly fold under all the ends of the bias to disguise any joins.

Lined shade with ruffle

MATERIALS

metal lampshade frame, stripped bare

approximately 1 m of 115 cm wide fabric for the cover

approximately 1 m of 115 cm wide lining fabric

contrasting fabric for bias binding and ruffles can be cut from scraps, but if in doubt allow another 40 cm of fabric for ruffles

large sheet of paper for the pattern

fineline marker pen

PVA adhesive

approximately 6 m narrow cotton tape

handsewing needle and strong sewing thread

masking tape

scissors

tape measure

Method

1 Bind the frame as instructed on page 185.

2 Place the frame at one end of the sheet of paper, then roll the frame across the paper, marking dots with the marker pen to show the outline of the pattern. Join all the dots and cut out the pattern (see fig. 1 on page 186). Check that it fits your frame before cutting out the fabric.

3 Using the pattern, cut out the lining and main fabric, leaving a 5 cm allowance all around.

4 Fit the lining around the frame, pinning it to the tape. Pin the ends closed as a seam. Remove the lining from the frame and sew the seam as it is pinned. Trim the seam allowance back to 1 cm. Repeat this process for the main fabric.

5 Place the lining inside the frame with the seam following the line of one upright strut. Pin the lining to the binding tape.

6 Cut sufficient 6 cm wide bias strip to go around the top and bottom rings. Turn in and press 1 cm on both long sides of the bias strip, then fold it in half with the wrong sides together. Stitch the binding to the main shade fabric, 1 cm from the edge and stitching in the fold line of the bias binding. Replace shade on the frame. Turn the free edge of the bias binding to the inside and slipstitch it in place.

7 Cut sufficient 10 cm wide ruffle strips which when joined measure at least one and a half or twice the total circumference of the top and bottom rings, depending on the thickness of your fabric. Make each ruffle in the following way: Join the ends of the strip to form a circle. Fold the strip over double with the wrong sides together and the raw edges matching. Overlock or zigzag the raw edges. Gather the raw edges. Draw up the gathering to fit inside the bias-trimmed top and bottom rings. Glue the ruffle into place. Glue the bias binding over the gathered edge, tucking under the short ends at the overlap.

8 Cover the raw edges inside the shade with the masking tape.

A ruffled shade like this needs very little sewing

Decorative Screen

FABRIC-COVERED SCREENS CAN BE MADE FROM ANY TYPE OF WOOD
THAT IS STURDY ENOUGH TO SUPPORT ITS OWN WEIGHT.

Before you begin

If you wish to shape the top of the screen, you will need a jigsaw and a paper pattern to follow when cutting.

MATERIALS
large sheet of paper
pencil
3 panels of craft wood, each 16 mm x 50 cm x 1.6 m
jigsaw
5 m of 120 cm wide fabric
1.3 m of 1 to 1.5 cm wide braid
10 m of 60 cm wide polyester wadding or 5 mm thick foam
6 brass hinge brackets and screws
screwdriver
scissors
wood glue
PVA adhesive
spray adhesive
staples and staple gun, or upholstery tacks

Method

1 Make a paper pattern for the curved top of the screen panels. Using the pattern, mark the curve in pencil on top of each panel of craft wood, then cut it out with the jigsaw.

2 Cut two pieces of fabric, each 55 cm x 1.6 m for each panel. Cut two pieces of wadding or foam, each 50 cm x 1.6 m. Using the spray adhesive, glue the wadding or foam to the front and back of each panel.

3 Lightly spray the adhesive on to the wadding, then lay the fabric on top, trimming the top edge in the curved shape of the wood panels with a 2.5 cm allowance.

4 Staple or tack the fabric edges in place. Trim away the excess fabric.

5 Starting at the bottom, turn in the end of the braid, staple or tack it over the fabric edge, then proceed to glue the braid all around each panel, covering the raw edge of the fabric. At the other end, turn under the raw edge of the braid and staple or tack it in place.

6 Attach the hinges. The first hinge should be approximately 20 cm from the bottom and the other hinge should be approximately 20 cm from the top of the screen.

Use a screen to divide a room, provide a private space or hide what you don't want to be seen

Towels with Flair

A SIMPLE BUT VERY EFFECTIVE DECORATION IN THE BATHROOM IS A STACK
OF PRETTY TRIMMED TOWELS ON AN OPEN SHELF OR DRESSER.

A lace trim turns a plain towel into a very special one

Trimmed towels

Before you begin Across the ends of most towels is a flat, woven band. This is the ideal place to stitch rows of ribbon or braid. You can also stitch lace or scalloped trims under the edge of a length of ribbon or fabric.

Always wash laces before stitching them on so that the trims do not pucker after washing. Remember to trim your face cloths, bath mats and hand towels to match, for a truly coordinated look in your bathroom.

Prewash dark-coloured towels in cold water with cooking salt added to allow for any dye loss. This is especially important if you are working with light-coloured contrasting trims. Prewash the trims to allow for any shrinkage.

To determine how much trim is required for each towel, measure the width of the towel plus 5 cm for turnings.

MATERIALS
towel or item to be covered
trim
matching handsewing thread
needle
pins
scissors

Method

1 If you are using a trim with one finished edge, such as lace, pin the trim on the woven band with the wrong side of the trim facing upwards. Tuck in both raw ends, then stitch along the straight side of the trim, 5 mm from the edge (or at the distance that best suits the design of the trim).

2 Turn the trim to the right side and press. Topstitch along the folded edge, leaving the lacy edge free.

3 If you are using a fabric strip as a trim, turn in and press all the raw edges, then topstitch the trim in place by stitching around all the pressed edges.

Elegant lace-trimmed towels are a feature of this traditional bathroom

---

Appliquéd hand towel

Before you begin

For an ensuite bathroom, try this quick and easy appliqué method to coordinate your towels with your bedroom decor, using your bedspread or curtain fabric for the appliqué.

Fusible webbing is a quick and easy method of fusing two layers of fabric together without sewing and is available from fabric and craft shops.

MATERIALS
towel, hand towel, washcloth
fabric with a suitable motif
fusible webbing
scissors

Method

1 Roughly cut out any flower heads or interesting motifs from the fabric.

2 Lay the rough side of the webbing on the wrong side of the motifs. Press for five seconds with a hot dry iron, then let the fabric cool.

3 Carefully cut around the motif. Peel off the backing paper and position the motif on the towel.

Cover it with a damp cloth and press for a further ten seconds with the iron on the wool/steam setting.

4 It is not essential to machine-stitch, but to make it look like a true appliqué you can outline the motif with a tight zigzag stitch around the outer edge.

Any simple motif can be appliquéd on to a towel

Picture Bows

THESE LOVELY ACCESSORIES ARE THE PERFECT FINISHING TOUCH,
BUT DON'T FORGET THEY ARE PURELY DECORATIVE
AND NOT INTENDED TO SUPPORT A WEIGHT.

Bow 1

Before you begin This picture bow has been bagged out in such a way that the lining fabric is visible around the edges of the main fabric.

Determine the length you wish your bow to be, measuring between the point where you would like the bow to sit and 5 cm down behind the picture frame.

Allow an extra 5 cm at the top end for the turned casing that will become the centre of the bow. Determine the width of your bow relative to the frame.

MATERIALS
25 cm of main fabric
30 cm of contrasting fabric
matching sewing machine thread
fabric glue
small hook or ring
sewing machine
pins
scissors
tape measure

Method

1 Cut one main strip to the required width plus 2 cm for seam allowances. Cut the contrasting fabric 2 cm wider.

2 Pin the main fabric and the contrasting fabric together with the right sides facing and the raw edges matching. Stitch the two long sides (fig. 1). Stitch one short side. Trim the seams. Turn the piece through to the right

side and press. There should be a narrow border of the contrasting fabric showing on the right side. Slipstitch the open end closed. This is the tail section.

3 To make the centre of the bow, fold the top end of the tail piece over to the front, forming a loop. Topstitch the loop in place; the tighter the loop, the fuller the finished bow will be.

4 Cut a piece of the main fabric, 25 cm x 50 cm, and of the contrasting fabric, 27 cm x 50 cm, for the bow centre. Join the pieces in the same way as for the tail section. At the back of the bow centre, pin and stitch the closed end over the slipstitched end. Slide the bow centre through the loop on the tail section, centring it with the seam under the loop at the back. Secure the bow with a couple of stitches at the back. Sew the hook or ring to the back of the loop.

5 Glue the bottom edge of the tail section to the back of the picture frame. Hang the picture, then attach the bow to a hook on the wall.

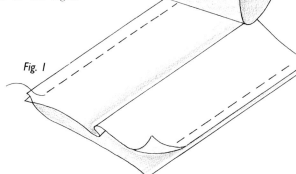

Fig. 1

Method

1 Cut a strip for the bow loop to the required length and width, adding 2 cm for seam allowances. Cut another strip for the bow tails, the same width and the length you have calculated, allowing for the turned casing that wraps around the bow loop.

2 Fold both strips over double with right sides together and raw edges even. Sew the long sides. Turn the strips to the right side through the open ends. Press.

3 Fold the ends of the bow loop so that they meet at the centre back. Slipstitch them together.

4 Fold the tail section in half. Fold 6 to 8 cm at the top over to the front to form the casing. Slipstitch the casing into place. The smaller the casing, the tighter the bow centre will be. Experiment until you are pleased with the effect. Pass the bow loop into the casing so that the slipstitching on the back of the loop falls inside the casing. Slipstitch the loop into place. Sew the ring or hook to the back of the bow.

5 Glue the ends of the tails to the back of the picture. Hang the picture first, then position the bow and attach it to the wall above the picture.

Method

1 Make the tail section in the same way as for bow 1 on page 192.

2 Cut the additional pieces of the main and contrast fabric for the bow centre as for bow 1, but this time cut four pieces instead of two. Make two bow centres as for bow 1.

3 Place the second bow centre over the first and at right angles to it. Stitch them together through the centre. Gather in the bow centres to form a series of tiny gathers in the middle.

4 Gather the square of contrasting fabric and cover the button with it. Stitch the button over the gathers. Secure the bow with a few stitches from the back. Sew the hook or ring to the back of the double bow.

5 Complete as for bow 1.

Bow 2

Before you begin Determine the length you wish your picture bow to be, measuring between the point where you would like the bow to sit and 5 cm down behind the picture frame. Allow an extra 5 cm at the top end for the turned casing that will become the centre of the bow. Determine the width of your picture bow relative to the width of the frame.

MATERIALS
50 cm of fabric
matching sewing machine thread
small hook or ring
sewing machine
pins
scissors
tape measure

Bow 3

MATERIALS
approximately 25 cm of main fabric
30 cm of contrasting fabric
matching sewing machine thread
fabric glue
small hook or ring
sewing machine
one button to cover
5 cm square of contrasting fabric to cover the button

Picture Frames

WE ALL HAVE PHOTOGRAPH COLLECTIONS OR A FAVOURITE CROSS STITCH
OR EMBROIDERY PROJECT THAT WE WOULD LIKE TO FRAME.

Before you begin Use your decorative talents to make a special frame by covering the mounting board with fabric, or you can cover the frame in a suitable fabric to make its own statement. This can be especially effective in children's rooms where a favourite nursery print can be placed inside a frame which is covered in gingham or brightly coloured fabric.

Fabric-covered mounts

Before you begin The mount fits inside a photograph or picture frame, so select a fabric that is suitable for the frame as well as for the picture it contains. A natural- or ivory-

Choose a small print fabric to cover the mounts so as not to overwhelm the photograph

coloured silk will add a subtle textured look to a silver frame, whilst a mount covered with a small cottage print will add interest to a floral cross stitch. Select a pattern that is in proportion to your frame. A large print or one that is too sparse will lose its detail if used on a small mount.

MATERIALS
stiff craft board
metal ruler
sharp craft knife
pencil
fabric
spray adhesive
fabric glue
PVA adhesive
scissors
pegs or large paper clips

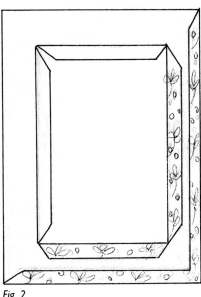

Fig. 1   Fig. 2

Method

1 Draw the desired shape and size of the mount on the craft board and then cut it out, using the metal ruler and sharp craft knife.

2 Cut out the fabric, using the mount as the pattern, allowing at least 1.5 cm all around for the overlap. Spray the adhesive on to the surface of the board and then place the fabric over the top so that it will remain in position. Make sure that there are no wrinkles in the fabric.

3 With the craft knife or the scissors, trim the fabric from the inside of the frame to 1.5 cm from the board edge. Do the same for the outside edge, if necessary. On the inside edge, snip into the fabric at each corner at an angle of 45 degrees (fig. 1). Turn the fabric to the back and glue down all the sides and edges with the PVA adhesive (fig. 2). On the outside clip across the corners, level with the frame. Hold the fabric in place with pegs or paper clips until all the glue is dry.

This is a clever way to smarten up an old picture frame. Glue some smart ribbon inside the frame, mitring the corners

Drawstring Bag

A DRAWSTRING BAG CAN BE USED FOR MANY DECORATIVE
YET PRACTICAL APPLICATIONS.

Choose a fabric that suits the purpose of your bag

Before you begin Choose a fabric appropriate for the proposed use of the bag; PVC fabric could be used for toiletries, and a light sheer fabric could be used for lingerie. A brightly coloured children's print could be used to take toys to grandma's, or used as a library or book bag, or even for carrying a sleeping sheet to kindergarten. You can make the bag any size you like; the measurements given here are for a toiletry bag.

MATERIALS
60 cm fabric
1.6 m drawstring cord or ribbon
matching sewing machine thread
tailors chalk
sewing machine

Method

1 Fold the fabric over double, lengthways, with the right sides together. Stitch the sides together in a 1.5 cm seam. Neaten the raw edges with overlocking or zigzag stitching.

2 Turn the bag through to the right side. Turn in and press 5 mm at the top edge then turn in and press another 5 cm. Stitch through all thicknesses along the fold and again 1.5 cm away, forming a casing.

3 Open the stitching at the side seams for approximately 1.5 cm. Thread an 80 cm length of cord or ribbon in one opening through the whole casing and out the same opening. Repeat for the other 80 cm of cord or ribbon, threading it through the other opening. Knot the ends of the cord or ribbon together.

Fabric-covered Box

THIS PADDED, CHINTZ-COVERED BOX STARTED LIFE AS A TOY BOX
THAT HAD BECOME RATHER BATTERED.

Before you begin Decide on your fabric. Stripes are attractive, but you will have to match them carefully from the front to the back and over the lid. The easiest fabric is one with a small print or an all-over pattern that does not require matching.

Measuring

Measure your own box carefully. You may find it easier to measure each panel of the box and draw these outlines and measurements on paper. Using these drawings, you can calculate the fabric quantities you will require, adding extra for turning under and overlapping.

Provided your box is solid and has suitable timber for holding the fabric, looks don't matter.

For our box we needed 4.5 m of main fabric and 4 m of lining fabric. We also used 4.5 m of furnishing braid.

MATERIALS

sufficient main fabric and lining fabric

*the same quantity of medium-thickness
polyester wadding*

narrow, ornate furnishing braid

*approximately 1.5 m strong cord
or fine chain*

four screw-in eye hooks

staples and staple gun

craft glue

handsewing needle and thread

decorative upholstery tacks

pliers

decorative handles

*three hairline hinges (these are less visible
than conventional hinges)*

strong dressmakers pins

small tack hammer

Method

1 Cover the box completely with wadding, using staples to secure the edges. Cover the top of the box with extra wadding if you want it to be more softly padded. Make sure the edges are neat and that you use enough staples to keep the wadding edges flat.

2 Line the box with the lining fabric, covering each panel of the box with fabric pieces cut to size plus a turn-under allowance. Glue these carefully into place. Take the lining all the way up to the lip of the box.

3 Cover the outside of the box with cut-to-size (plus turn-under allowance) pieces of the main fabric, as for the lining, allowing sufficient fabric to come over the top of the box down into the inside of the box to overlap the lining and down on to the outside base of the box. Hold the fabric in place with pins, until you have secured the side edges with decorative tacks. Space these tacks at about 2 cm intervals. When you have folded the main fabric into the inside of the box, secure the edges with staples placed in a row about 3 cm down from the lip of the box. Fold the fabric neatly into the corners. If necessary, sew the edges together by hand to hold

Cover any joins with decorative braid

the pieces together. Glue braid over the line where the fabrics meet, securing it with a few tacks.

4 Take the main fabric on to the inside base of the box, folding the corners as necessary. Cover the base with lining fabric and braid, if desired.

5 Cover the outside of the lid, bringing the fabric inside the lid as for the box. Cover the inside of the lid with a panel of lining fabric and cover the line where the fabrics meet with braid. Tack the corners.

6 Screw the hinges to the box and the lid, to hold the lid evenly in place. Screw eye hooks inside the lid and the sides of the box. Establish a suitable angle at which the lid remains open and cut two lengths of the cord or chain to hold the lid at this point. Tie a length of cord between the eye hooks on each side of the lid and the box. Knot and glue the ends of the cord neatly, perhaps binding over the raw

edges of the cord with a band of thread. If you are using chain, open a link at each end with pliers and then reclamp them around the eye hooks on the box and the lid.

7 Attach decorative handles to the sides and the centre front of the box.

8 Any overlap of fabric inside the box that does not sit well can also be tacked.

Index

Acknowledgements

LOCATIONS: Brian and Marie Livingstone, Kedron homestead; John and Michele Dounan, Topiary Farm; Brian and Helen Dounan; Judy and Jim Poulos

ADDITIONAL PHOTOGRAPHS: Maurice Kain Textiles, Sanderson Fabrics, Ashley Wallpaper, P. Rowe Fabrics, Wilson Fabrics, Design Plus

MAKERS: Judy Timmins, Shelagh Dounan, Ivy Skrabanich, Christine Aggar, Adele Horsfall

SET DESIGN: Phillip Skrabanich

PROPS: Victoria Amos, Paul White, Louise Grimes

The publishers would also like to thank the following companies and organisations who helped with the preparation of this book: Maurice Kain Textiles Limited; Design Plus; Curtain Industry Association of Australia and New Zealand; Ashley Wallpapers; Instyle; Sekers/Jawatex; Fieldcrest Cannon; Sanderson Fabrics; Waverly Fabrics; P. Rowe Fabrics, Sheridan Textiles; Marco Fabrics; David Whitehead and Sons; World of Curtains (workroom); Mathvena Imports (accessories); Domestications Decore (accessories); Pan Pacific Distributing Co. (trims and braids); The Sleep Doctor, Sans Souci (beds); A. and G. McKinnon (cane furniture)